Essays on Performance Theory

1970-1976

Essays on Performance Theory

1970-1976

Richard Schechner

Drama Book Specialists (Publishers) New York

Library of Congress Cataloging in Publication Data

Schechner, Richard, 1934-
    Essays on performance theory, 1970-1976.

    Bibliography:
    1. Theater—Addresses, essays, lectures. I. Title.
PN 2039.S37   792   77-23197
ISBN 0-910482-81-0
ISBN 0-910482-88-8 pbk.

Printed in the United States of America

To & For Joan MacIntosh

Acknowledgments

"Actuals: A Look Into Performance Theory" first appeared in *The Rarer Action: Essays in Honor of Francis Fergusson,* Rutgers University Press, 1970. "Drama, Script, Theatre and Performance" appeared in TDR, T-59 (1973). It was revised for this book. "From Ritual to Theatre and Back" was delivered as a paper at the Rassegna Internazionale de Teatri Stabili in Florence in April, 1974; it was printed, in a revised version, in the *Educational Theatre Journal* vol. 26, no. 4, (1974); it is further revised for this volume. "Kinesics and Performance" appeared in TDR, T-59 (1973). I thank Cynthia Mintz, with whom the essay was written, for permission to reprint it here. "Towards a Poetics of Performance" was delivered as a paper at the Ethnopoetics Symposium sponsored by the Center for Twentieth Century Studies of the University of Wisconsin-Milwaukee in April 1975; it was revised for this book. "Selective Inattention" appeared in *Performing Arts Journal* vol. 1, no. 1 (1976) but was written for this book. "Ethology and Theatre" was also written for this book. I would especially like to express my thanks to the Solomon R. Guggenheim Foundation.

Contents

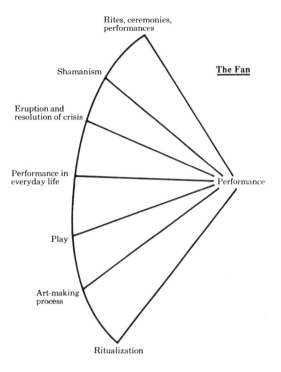

Rites, ceremonies,
performances

Shamanism

The Fan

Eruption and
resolution of crisis

Performance in
everyday life

Performance

Play

Art-making
process

Ritualization

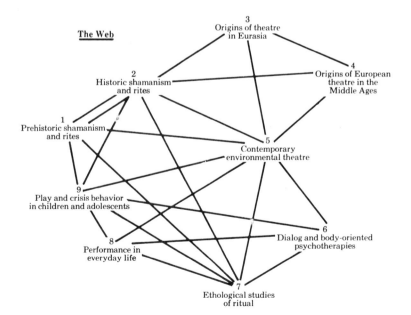

The Web

3
Origins of theatre
in Eurasia

2
Historic shamanism
and rites

4
Origins of European
theatre in the
Middle Ages

1
Prehistoric shamanism
and rites

5
Contemporary
environmental theatre

9
Play and crisis behavior
in children and adolescents

6
Dialog and body-oriented
psychotherapies

8
Performance in
everyday life

7
Ethological studies
of ritual

Introduction

This isn't a pot-luck book of essays. The themes are organized around a system which can be pictured as both a fan and a web. This system has occupied me both in my theorizing and in my practical work, in my home work in New York and my away work in Asia. Performance is a very inclusive notion of action; theatre is only one node on a continuum that reaches from ritualization in animal behavior (including humans) through performances in everyday life—greetings, displays of emotion, family scenes and so on—to rites, ceremonies and performances: large-scale theatrical events.

The web is the same system seen in a more active, totally interconnected aspect. It's no accident that I put my own work—environmental theatre—in the center: this position is totally arbitrary. An ethologist would put himself at the center of another web that includes items that don't figure in my scheme—genetics and evolutionary theory, for example. Also I mix historical, speculative and artistic "events" as if they all exist on the same plane. My method is like that of the Aborigines who credit dreamed events with the same authenticity as events experienced while awake.

The web isn't uniform. Connections among items 1 through 4 can be demonstrated historically, and may be linked to performances around the world from paleolithic times on. Connections among items 6 through 9 reveal the "deep structures" of theatre—so that these items actually underlie the first five. These deep structures include preparations for performance both on the part of the performers (training, rehearsal, preparations immediately before going on) and spectators (deciding to attend, dressing, going, settling in, waiting) and what happens after a performance. These cooling off procedures are less

1

studied but very important. They include spreading the news of the performance, evaluating it (getting it "into" the system of ordinary life), putting the space to rest, returning the performers to ordinary life. Also the patterns of drama deal everywhere and at all times with crisis, schism, conflict and the resolutions of these disruptions. The themes of drama focus on rebellion, sexuality, conflict between generations and rites of passage (changing status). Theatrical techniques center on transformation: how people can turn into other people, either temporarily as in a play or permanently as in a rite; or how beings of one order can inhabit beings of another order; or how unwanted inhabitants (demons) can be exorcised. But the systems of transformations also include transformations of time and space: doing "there and then" in this particular "here and now."

Performance is doing something "make believe," "in a play," "for fun." Or, as Victor Turner said: in the subjunctive mood—the famous "as if." Performance not only plays out a mode but it plays with modes not necessarily followed through; the theatrical event is fundamentally experimental. Any semiotics of theatre must start from these bases. Because the theatre is subjunctive, liminal, dangerous, duplicitous it must be hedged in with conventions: means of making the place and the event safe. In safe precincts at safe times actions can be carried to extremes, even for fun.

NEW YORK, 1977

Actuals:
A Look Into Performance Theory

Tiwi society is established on what we would consider an absurdity. These north Australians make no connection between intercourse and pregnancy. The mother is the sole biological source of the child. The mother's husband controls his wives and his children and of these he particularly values his daughters. Women, like money with us, are the main means of exchange. It is not necessary to detail the system. The result is that old men have young wives and young men, if they are lucky, marry crones.

Where there are old men with young wives and young men without sex mates there will be adultery. A Tiwi elder accuses a young man of adultery by coming to the center of the village, preferably on a feast day so he can be sure of a large crowd, and calling the offender out. The old man is painted from head to toe in white. In one hand he carries some ceremonial spears and in the other hunting spears. A crowd arranges itself in an ellipse with the old man at one elongated end and the young man at the other. Everyone in the village, and often outgroupers too, are present—men, women, children, dogs. They sit, stand, move about, according to their excitement. The young man is naked, except for a few strokes of white. The more white he wears the more defiant he declares himself to be. Perhaps he carries a spear or two or only a throwing stick. The old man begins a harangue of about 20 minutes duration. He details the young man's worthlessness and ingratitude—talking not only of the offence at hand but the whole life of the young man. The old man stamps his feet and chews his beard: he puts on a good show. The young man takes in this verbal assault in silence. When the harangue is over the old man throws a hunting spear at the young man. The young man dodges—which is not hard to do because the old man is throwing from 40 to 50 feet away. If the young man moves too far from the end of the ellipse the crowd jeers him. If the old man is wild in his throws, he is jeered. The trial/duel continues until the young man has dodged enough spears to prove his prowess, but not too many to appear insolent. Allowing himself to be hit takes great skill and the crowd enjoys a young man who takes a spear in the fleshy part of the thigh or the upper arm. There is much blood and no permanent harm. The young man is wounded; the crowd happily applauds both parties to the dispute. The old man's authority and dignity have been repaired and the young man's bravery and humility have been demonstrated.

Such is the Tiwi ritual combat according to the rules. But sometimes a young man is extremely defiant. He dodges too many of the old man's spears, or he answers the harangue, or he returns the old man's fire. In such cases the old man is joined by other old men, while still others restrain the relatives of the young man. Spears are thrown in volleys and the young man is driven from the village permanently, seriously wounded, or killed.

The Tiwi trial does not determine "right" or "wrong." It doesn't matter whether in fact the young man is guilty of adultery, or if there are extenuating circumstances. The trial is a test of the young man's willingness to confirm the authority of the old man. Whenever that authority offers itself for confirmation, Tiwi custom demands submission. Tiwi society rests on the authority of the old, and the only capital offence is defiance of that authority. The crowd enjoys the spectacle which makes the law tangible. If the ceremony were a true trial with a doubtful outcome, Tiwi society would collapse.

In 1967, Allan Kaprow composed *Fluids,* "a single event done in many places over a three-day period. It consists simply in building huge, blank, rectangular ice structures 30 feet long, 10 feet wide, and 8 feet high. The structures are built by people who decide to meet a truck carrying 650 ice blocks per structure. They set this thing up using rock salt as a binder—which hastens melting and fuses the block together. The structures are to be built (and were) in about 20 places throughout Los Angeles. If you were crossing the city you might suddenly be confronted by these mute and meaningless blank structures which have been left to melt. Obviously, what's taking place is a mystery of sorts."[1]

I could multiply examples of similar "mysteries." The tradition of Happenings, from the Italian Futurists through the Dadaists, surrealists, and on to practitioners of earth art[2] and other kinds of avant-gardes, introduces us to the idea that art is not a way of imitating reality or expressing states of mind. At the heart of what Kaprow calls mystery is the simple but altogether upsetting idea of art as an event—an "actual."

Plato in Book X of *The Republic* attacks the arts. "The tragic poet, too, is an artist who represents things; so this will apply to him: he and all other artists are, as it were, third in succession from the throne of truth." Art is an imitation of life and life merely a shadow of the ideal forms. Thus "the work of the artist is at third remove from the essential nature of things." Cornford comments that "the view that a work of art is an image or likeness *(eikon)* of some original, or holds up a mirror to nature, became prominent towards the end of the fifth century together with the realistic drama of Euripides and the illusionistic painting of Zeuxis. Plato's attack adopts this theory."[3]

Plato's student Aristotle agrees that art is mimetic but asks precisely what does art imitate and how? Art does not imitate things or even experience, but "action." Action is a problematical idea and, at best, I can only sketch an interpretation of what Aristotle might have meant. Art imitates patterns, rhythms, and developments. In art, as in nature, things are born, they grow, they flourish, they decline, they die. Form, which is crystalline in Plato, is fluid in Aristotle. Each organism (animate, natural, artistic[4]) conceals a determining pattern-factor that governs its development. This DNA-like factor determines the growth rate, shape, rhythm and life-span of every organism. Everything has its own life plan, its own "indwelling form." It is this form which art imitates.

Aristotle's idea is sublime. It imparts to everything—from thought to the slow unwinding of a galaxy to the lives of men to the grain of sand—a living, intrinsic and dynamic participation in creating, being, becoming and ceasing. From the Aristotelian perspective "individuality" is seen in its original meaning: not divisible. Things are integral both inherently and in their relationships to their environments. Destiny is the interplay between what is inborn and what is met. Every acorn is an oak-in-process. But between acorn and oak is sun, rain, wind, lightning and men with axes. "Count no man happy until the day of his death," intones the chorus of *Oedipus*. That tragedy is fulfilled, and ended, but not so Oedipus who goes on to other adventures. "Tragedy, then, is the imitation of an action that is serious, complete and of a certain magnitude." Of an action, not of a man's life. Oedipus offered to Sophocles two complete actions—*Oedipus* and *Colonus*.

From a naive biographical vantage, tragedies are about broken lives, early death, unfulfilled promises, remorse, maimed ambitions and tricks of fate. What has a "beginning, middle and end" is the artwork. At the deepest level a play is about itself. Aristotle suggests that the playwright takes from life an impulse—a story, an idea, an image, a sense of person. This impulse is the kernel of the artwork whose process is a twisting and transformation of the impulse until, at a decisive moment, the artwork breaks off and becomes itself. From then on, the artwork makes its own demands in accord with its indwelling form or action. These, as artists know, may be stubbornly unlike those of the original impulse or conscious plan.

Thus an Aristotelian artwork lives a double life. It is mimetic in the Platonic sense, but it is also itself. As Fergusson points out, the relationship between artwork and experience is one of "analogy." The root idea of *mimesis* is sophisticated by Aristotle, but not transmuted. Art always "comes after" experience; the separation between art and life is built into the idea of *mimesis*. It is this coming after and separation that has been so decisive in the development of Western theatre.

An analogy will make clear exactly what I mean by "coming after." Cooked food "comes after" raw food. Cooking is something that is done to raw food to change it and to (apparently) make it more pure. All cooked food was once raw; all raw food is cookable. There is no way for raw food to "come after" cooked food. So it is with art and life. Art is cooked and life is raw. Art is the process of transforming raw experience into palatable forms. This transformation is a mimetic one, a representation. Such, at any rate, is the heart of the mimetic theory.

The hot interest in anthropology over the past generation or so has not been all good. Artists and critics alike have turned to "primitive" man with embarrassing yearning. Leslie (1960) said "There is . . . a fashionable modern conception of 'primitive man' as inhabiting a 'mystical' world of 'timeless,' 'cosmological,' 'metaphorical' and 'magical' presences. Costumed in the 'archetypal' masks of tribal art, and possessed of a special 'primitive mentality,' this phantasmagoria is said to perform 'ritual dramas' of 'mythic reality.' This particular conception of primitive man enjoys greatest currency in artistic and literary circles [where] primitive cultures are to modern thought what classical antiquity was to the Renaissance."[5] But it is no better to think of the Tiwi as the guys next door. Leslie thinks this counter-current attributing an urban pragmatism to primitive men an apologia for that kind of rationality which many anthropologists feel is in jeopardy. What makes *The Savage Mind* so satisfying is Levi-Strauss's ability to uphold the claim of what is special in primitive peoples while not denying what is common to all men. The logic of Aristotle is not universal, but an appetite for classification is. Peoples think differently, but every people thinks systematically in its own terms. Levi-Strauss does not resurrect the noble savage or blur differences with an archetypal smear.

We live under terrible stress. Politically, intellectually, artistically, personally and epistemologically we are at breaking points. It is a cliché to say that a society is in crisis. But ours, particularly here on this North American continent, seems to be gripped by total crisis and faced with either disintegration or brutal, sanctioned repression. The yearnings of the young may be a combination of infantile wishes for the wholeness of mama's breast and a thrashing towards an impossible Utopian socialism. Or these yearnings may indicate a genuine alternative to our horrific destiny. I cannot distinguish between the true and the false. But I can identify yearnings which have triggered not only an interest in primitive peoples but artistic movements that concretize that interest and start to satisfy those yearnings.

Wholeness. Participatory democracy, self-determination on the local, national, and international levels. Therapies which start from the oneness of mind/body/feelings. "Getting it together." Total theatre, intermedia, integrated electronic systems, McLuhanism. An end to the dichotomies:

a whole person	not mind/body
families	not fragmented individuals
communities	not government vs. governed
jobs like play	not alienated work
art where we are	not in museums far away
one world in peace	not wars and international rivalries
man one with nature	not ecological warfare

Process and organic growth. An end to the assembly line, for the production of goods and the conformism of people. Animosity to the police, the military-industrial complex. "Process, not product." "Do your own thing." "Turn people into artists, not on to art." Turbulence and discontinuity, not artificial smoothness. Organic foods. Kicking out your feelings. Ritual art, all-night dances.

Concreteness. Down with theories, abstractions, generalizations, the "biggies" of art, industry, education, government, etc. Make your demands known, act them out and get an answer now. Radicalize the students. Street and guerrilla theatre, Provo action, marches on Washington, demonstrations on campus. Arm the blacks, urban warfare in the ghettoes. Dig the physicality of experience. Sensory awareness, involvement, and expression. Happenings, earth art, concrete poetry and music, pornography.

Religious transcendental experience. Mysticism, shamanism, messianism, psychedelics, epiphanies. Zen, yoga, and other ways to truth through participation or formulation, as in macrobiotics and yoga exercises. Eschatological yearnings: what is the meaning of life? Make all experience meaningful. Sacralize everyday living. Sung poetry, encounter theatre, marathons, T-groups, theatre made in and by communities, tribalism, rock festivals, drugs, trips, freak-outs, ecstasies.

Wholeness, process and organic growth, concreteness and religious transcendental experience are fundamental to primitive cultures. The terms differ from culture to culture, and differ radically from any primitive culture to our own. But we have uncovered links between us and them. These links, or metaphors, are strongest and clearest between what we call art, particularly new theatre, and what they call by names ranging from play to dancing to doing.

The four categories are inseparable. They overlap, interpenetrate, feed from each other, exchange, transform into one another. Any separation is artificial. In many cultures the very separations that make this essay possible would be impossible.

A try at explaining actuals involves a survey of anthropological, sociological, psychological and historical material. But these are not organized to promote the search. And the scope of this essay prohibits me from taking anything but a quick glance at the sources. There I find an incipient theory for a special kind of behaving, thinking, relating and doing. This special way of handling experience and jumping the gaps between past and present, individual and group, inner and outer, I call "actualizing" (perhaps no better than Eliade's "reactualizing," but at least shorter). Actualizing is plain among rural, primitive peoples and it is becoming plainer among our own young and in their avant-garde art. The question is not polemical, but structural: not whether the new theatre (and life style) is good, but how is it built and what, precisely, are its bases. Then, what are its functions and how do these relate to the life we live individually and collectively. I think we will find that the new theatre is very old, and that our localized urban avant-garde belongs next to a worldwide, rural tradition.

What might we make of the possible etymological link between the word "drama"—from the Greek *dran*: to do, to act, to make—and the word "dream"—from the Old English and the Old Frisian *dram*: a dream, a shout of joy? Somewhere in that pretty connection is the feel of actualizing. "According to the [Australian] aborigines," says Lommel, "in the dream state man has a share in the creativity of nature, and if he were to be creatively active in this state he would really, as the painter Baumester expressed it, 'not create after nature, but like nature.'"[6]

Understanding actualizing means understanding both the creative condition and the artwork, the actual. Among primitive peoples the creative condition is identical with trances, dances, ecstasies; in short, shamanism.[7] Shamanism is "a method, a psychic technique"[8] of which the "fundamental characteristic . . . is ecstasy, interpreted as the soul forsaking the body."[9] This technique is very ancient, with roots among Central Asian peoples during the Alpine Paleolithic period, some 30,000 to 50,000 years ago. "No one has yet shown that the

ecstatic experience is the creation of a particular historical civilization or a particular culture cycle. In all probability the ecstatic experience, in its many aspects, is coexistent with the human condition."[10] What is an ecstatic experience? Eliade and Lommel quote
examples. And Rothenberg cites Isaac Tens' own account of how he
became a *shaman*.

> Then my heart started to beat fast, and I began to tremble,
> just as had happened before. . . . My flesh seemed to be
> boiling. . . . My body was quivering. While I remained in
> this state, I began to sing. A chant was coming out of me
> without my being able to do anything to stop it. Many
> things appeared to me presently: huge birds and other
> animals. . . . These were visible only to me, not to the
> others in my house. Such visions happen when a man is
> about to become a *shaman*; they occur of their own accord.
> The songs force themselves out complete without any
> attempt to compose them. But I learned and memorized
> those songs by repeating them.[11]

Rothenberg thinks that Tens' experience is "typical of 1) the
psychology of shamanism, 2) the *shaman's* 'initiation' through dream
and vision, 3) transformation of vision into song."[12] Eliade and Lommel cite similar examples. Eliade says there are three ways of becoming a *shaman*: as Tens did through the "call"; by inheritance; and by
personal ambition or the will of the tribe. A *shaman* is authenticated
only after having received two kinds of instruction. The first is ecstatic (for example, dreams, visions, trances); the second is traditional (for example, shamanic techniques, names and functions of the
spirits, mythology and genealogy of the clan, secret language).[13] The
instruction of the fledgling *shaman* first by older *shamans* and then by
the spirits is a universal aspect of shamanism. Its structure is much
like Dante's travels with Virgil through the Christian other worlds.
Lommel describes an Australian shamanic instruction.

> At sunset the *shaman's* soul meets somewhere the shadow
> of a dead ancestor. The shadow asks the soul whether it
> shall go with it. The *shaman's* soul answers yes. . . . Then
> they go on together, either at once into the kingdom of the
> dead or to a place in this world at which the spirits of the
> dead have gathered. . . . The spirits begin to sing and
> dance. . . . When the dance is over the spirits release the
> *shaman's* soul and his helping spirit brings it back to his
> body. When the *shaman* wakes, his experiences with the
> spirits seem to him like a dream. From now on he thinks of
> nothing but the dances which he has seen and his soul
> keeps on going back to the spirits to learn more and more
> about the dances. . . . Then he will first explain the dances
> to his wife and sing them to her, and after that he will
> teach them to everyone else.[14]

The *shaman's* journeys are neither gratuitous nor for private use. He goes to get something and he must deliver what he gets back to his people—he must teach them what he learns. His work is social work.

The *shaman* is prized by his people. He is "the exemplar and model for all those who seek to acquire power; [he] is the man who *knows* and remembers."[15] But sometimes his powers fail him, his link with the other world breaks. This is a crisis for the entire community. (I am reminded forcefully of the plague which starts the search for Laius's murderer. King Oedipus is a *shaman.* His sacrifice cures Thebes, and his search, assisted by the townsfolk, is a paradigm of shamanic quest. The story is overlaid with other things, but its roots go deep into pre-Aristotelian patterns of feeling and doing.) Lommel says that in Australia when a *shaman* loses touch with the other world "his poetic gift for creating songs and dances vanishes." All the men of the community sit in a circle around the *shaman.* They sing for hours a "regularly rising and falling note" and rub his body. The *shaman* goes into trance. He seeks a spirit of a dead ancestor whom he tells that he "cannot 'find' any more songs." The spirit promises help and the *shaman* comes out of trance. Several days later the *shaman* "hears a distant call. It is his helping spirit calling him. He goes off by himself and converses for a while with the spirit." A few days later his soul leaves his body. "Many spirits now come up from the underworld [and] tear the [shaman's] soul to pieces and each spirit carries a piece into the underworld. There, deep under the earth, they put the *shaman's* soul together again. They show him the dances again and sing songs to him."[16] The *shaman* is whole; his link is repaired. Everyone helped him get it together.

What are we to make of these experiences? It has been customary to "interpret" reports like these—to find in our way of thinking analogues making such experiences rationally acceptable. Thus Lommel says that the quest for the missing ceremonial link is "an authentic account of the nature of artistic creativity [which shows vividly] the connection of an artist's creative potency with tradition—with the ancestors."[17] Eliade never tires of showing that shamanic experiences are prototypes of our own religious beliefs. Psychoanalysts interpret in the direction of instinctual needs and unconscious processes. I accept these interpretations. But they are not complete. Shamanic experiences are real and whole. Our interpretations diminish and fragment them—we want to make the experiences "other worldly," "transcendental," or "fantasies." But these experiences are the result of something which Cassirer notes about primitive thought. "By a sudden metamorphosis everything may be turned into everthing. [There is] the deep conviction of a fundamental and indelible *solidarity of life* that bridges over the multiplicity and variety of its single forms."[18] Everywhere there are overlaps, exchanges, and transformations. For example:

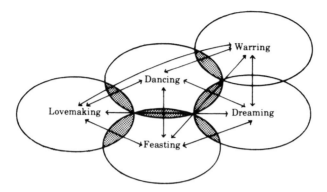

Experience is not segregated onto hierarchical planes. It is not that everything is the same, but that all things are part of one wholeness, and that among things unlimited exchanges and transformations are possible.

Artists among us experience the way the Australians do. Artists treat experience as something indivisible but exchangeable; as endlessly varied but on the same plane; as here and now but other worldly. It is this hard-to-talk-about-in-our-language thing that Levi-Strauss means when he says that "there are still zones in which savage thought, like savage species, is relatively protected. This is the case of art. . . . Savage thought is definable both by a consuming symbolic ambition such as humanity has never again seen rivaled, and by scrupulous attention directed entirely towards the concrete, and finally by the implicit conviction that these two attitudes are but one."[19] From here it is just a short step to understanding actualizing.

Eliade does not define reactualization. Instead he gives examples of it. An initiation is a ceremony in which "a new generation is instructed, is made fit to be integrated into the community of adults. And on this occasion, through the repetition, the *reactualization,* of the traditional rites, the entire community is regenerated."[20] The actualization is the making present of a past time or event. Eliade describes a puberty initiation of Eastern Australia called a *Bora.* The initiates are surprised at home and "kidnapped" to the place of initiation. There they are secluded and instructed in the lore, dances and songs of their tribe. This schooling lasts for months. During it, the initiates are kept under strict discipline. The ceremonial area is a "sacred space" within which ordinary time has been abolished and Dream Time is. Dream Time is the time of the first initiation rite performed by Baiamai, the supreme being. Finally, amid dancing and singing, the initiates are circumcised: their bodies irrevocably marked with a sign of their belonging to the tribe. The *bora* ground is Baiamai's first camp had the initiators are those who were with Baiamai when he inaugurated these ceremonies. This reintegration of time and place is not peculiar to the Australians. It is true "for the entire primitive world. For what is involved here is a fundamental concept in archaic religions—the repetition of a ritual founded by Divine Beings implies the reactualization of the original Time when the rite was first performed. This is why a rite has efficacy—it participates in the completeness of the sacred primordial Time. The rite makes the myth present. Everything that the myth tells of the Time of beginning, the *bugari* times [Dream Time], the rite reactualizes, shows it as happening, *here and now*."[21]

This is true not only of compact rites but of those which are narrative and of long duration. The Elema of New Guinea celebrate a cycle called the *Hevehe,* after the majestic 30-foot high mask-spirits whose appearance and dances climax a process that takes from six to 20 years or more to complete. The masks are built in the men's ceremonial house, the *eravo,* which is lengthened and heightened to accommodate the painstaking work. A number of ceremonies mark the *Hevehe* over the years—there is a close knitting of the *eravo,* the masks being built in it, the political and economic life of the people, the life cycle of individuals in the community and the *Hevehe* which gives to both individual and social life meaning and continuity. Some cycles which Williams observed were started in 1914 but not finished by 1937 when he gathered his data. Others, begun at about the same time, were completed in 1920, 1932 and 1934. "It may be thought that this dragging out of the cycle is the result of modern influences, as if the *Hevehe* were drawing a series of long, dying gasps. [But] there is ample evidence to show that formerly, as well as now, the *Hevehe* cycles occupied very long periods."[22] A man with a full life might participate in three, possibly four, *Hevehe.*

In a cycle that takes as long to complete as the *Hevehe* things are not so strict moment to moment as they are in the *Bora.* The cycle develops in bursts, with intensive activities surrounding particular ceremonies, and long periods of inactivity between. The ceremonies all take place in and around the village, and many involve the women and children. In one, people from neighboring villages wearing small dancing masks, *eharo,* invade the host village. Bunched around the *eharo* are enthusiastic women and children and resisting the invaders are hundreds of people who shower the invaders with coconut flakes. A mock battle is fought on the beach and then the invaders sweep into the village. Erotic pantomimes vie with more staid dancing and children run about the village armed with toy bows and arrows which they shoot at bunches of banana or sago. Throughout all this some of the village elders lounge on the veranda of the *eravo,* seemingly disinterested and certainly unperturbed. This carnival mock-war dance seems altogether different from the *Bora.* There the ceremony was formal, far from the village in total seclusion and no women or children were permitted to watch or even know of the rituals. The elders

were the most important participants. Here, everything is the opposite; but the differences are not of an essential kind.

The climax of the cycle is the month-long dancing of the *Hevehe*
masks. Months of hard preparation have laid away stores of food, and
inside the *eravo* the last touches have been completed on the masks.
The night before the emergence drumming begins from the upper
level of the *eravo*. Before dawn a large crowd of women and children
gather before the *eravo*'s 30-foot double doors. The drumming suddenly stops and the pushing and shoving of the crowd reaches a "perfect fury of joy and excitement."

> There are many dramatic situations in the cycle, but none
> can compare with this supreme moment which the *hevehe*,
> after wellnigh twenty years of confinement, issue forth to
> commence the brief fulfillment of their existence. In the
> grey light of early morning the first of them, "Koraia,"
> stood framed against the blackness of the open door—a
> tall, fantastic figure, silvery white, its colored patterns in
> the atmosphere of dawn appearing pale and very
> delicate. . . . For a brief moment "Koraia" stood there, the
> great crowd of spectators gazing in silence. Then, with a
> thump of the drum and a prodigious rattling of *harau*, it
> started down the gangway. Immediately behind it came
> "Pekeaupe"; and after that, in crowded succession, 120
> others.[23]

As each mask starts dancing, groups of women and children detach
themselves from the large crowd and dance around masks worn by
fathers, husbands, brothers and sons. The women carry green twigs
and they flick the legs of the mask-dancers.

> In the center are the portentous figures of the *hevehe*, with
> their staring eyes and their fierce jaws abristle with teeth
> their mantles rising and falling and their human arms
> vigorously belaboring the drums and kicking up the dust.
> Though they are 20 feet high and more they dance, not
> lightly (that would be a sheer impossibility) but with
> amazing animation.[24]

The *hevehe* dance throughout the village and on the beach. They
dance all day and part of the night for a month. It is hot, and a man
dances his mask for from 15 minutes to an hour. Then he returns to
the *eravo* and attaches his mask to its hook.

> Streaming with perspiration, the last wearer sits down to
> cool off; but presently he will be seen fitting some other
> mask over his head, shuffling a little to get it balanced to
> his satisfaction and then making his way towards the door,
> fully prepared for a further tour. Any man, in fact, may
> wear any mask with its owner's permission; nor is the
> owner likely to refuse it, since he is flattered to see his
> *hevehe* in frequent use.[25]

The dancing is a performance, but of a special kind. It is thought that when a man wears a mask he is "animated by the spirits which are derived from the myths." Each *hevehe* has a name because each is a spirit. The spirit moves only when a man is in the mask. Conversely, a man dances well only when he is moved by the spirit. Two autonomous, symbiotic existences support each other. The women and children know who is in the masks—they accompany their close relatives and tease them into more vigorous dancing. Men freely exchange masks, animating and being animated by many spirits in one day. Here is a clear example of the exchange between two realities which the Elema put on one plane: 1) the masks which are living things; 2) the men who wear the masks. The masks do not represent the spirits or contain the spirits; the masks are the spirits.

At the end of the month of dancing the *hevehe* make their way to the beach for the last time. The women "rush to the giant masks and embrace their projecting jaws and kiss their faces, while not a few were shedding tears."[26] Some beat their breasts and others try to stop the *hevehe* from reaching the beach. But the masks get there and dance. Then one by one, in no set order, each gives up its drum and slowly they form into two lines. These lines start a solemn procession back from the beach to the *eravo.* Soon all but eight of the 122 *hevehe* have gone into the *eravo.* The last eight masks are intercepted by some young women and a ritual combat begins. The men have arranged that the last eight masks should be small and light and the men in them strong.

> Next moment they were circled about by a score of robust
> females clasping one another's hands. Almost immediately
> the circle broke up into two, one for either *eravo*-side and
> each imprisoning four *hevehe.* . . .
> . . . The *hevehe* try again and again to burst through the
> circle. They turn side on and hurl themselves on the
> out-stretched arms of the women. But the women are
> strong, and they are reinforced by others, standing outside
> the ring, who clamp their hands together. They easily hold
> their own and send the *hevehe* staggering back into the
> center; but after repeated charges the wall begins to break
> and one after another the prisoners escape.[27]

When the last *hevehe* enters the *eravo* the 200 women turn towards the *eravo,* raise their arms over their heads and chant. Some hours later, after a feast, four of the masks re-emerge. A *shaman* arms his bow and says, "I, Aku-akore, stand here and am about to kill you. I am taking all you possess." He shoots through the face of a mask. "Very realistically, as if mortally wounded, the *hevehe* staggered and fell."[28] The women cry out in grief and flee from the village. The other three masks are shot.

> With the fall of the four *hevehe* and the exodus of the

women there began a scene of deliberate destruction.
Masks, no longer worn but carried, came pouring out of the
door to be propped against the house-walls or thrown
carelessly on the ground. Without the slightest trace of
reverence or regret their owners proceeded to strip them of
their *mae* mantles and their feathers.[29]

Parts of the masks are kept for the next cycle; parts are loaned to
neighboring villages. The dead hulks are taken to the stream and
thrown into three piles. "It seemed as if the masks were to be disposed
of without any touch of ceremony whatever, so keen was everyone on
the practical side of the business." But, before the masks are burned,
the *shaman* says, "Now I am going to burn you. Look kindly on the
men of my *eravo*. When they hunt let not the arrow stick in the
ground, but in the eye of the pig. I do no harm to you. Constantly, from
long ago I have fed and fostered you. Do not be angry with us." Or, "I
have called you up because of my pigs and sago. I have fed you constantly. In the future some other strong men will call you. Do not be
angry." Or, "The man of pigs, the man of dogs, calls you. But now I
burn you. Ivo and Leravae, our women, girls and little boys—let no
centipede sting them, no thorns pierce them, no snakes or sharks bite
them. Guard them well."[30] There is personal variation and style in the
invocations. The masks have life and must be killed. When they are
burnt, the *hevehe* spirits go back to the bush. "Why the *hevehe* should
be killed at all is a question which no native was ever able to answer."[31] The spirits are immortal and they will be recreated in the
next cycle. The *eravo* is empty.

Gradually the great grey building falls into decay; the
floor-boards rot; thatching, ripped off by the wind, goes
unrepaired; and rain falls miserably upon deserted
hearthsides. One by one the members seek other sleeping
quarters, and at last the *eravo* is a ruin. Then, when it
threatens to collapse, . . . the community will make a
strenuous effort and demolish it. For some years, perhaps,
they will content themselves with humbler lodgings; but at
last, if spirit is willing and flesh is strong, they will set to
and build themselves another *eravo,* and with that the long
Hevehe cycle will start all over again.[32]

The cycle is majestic. Its duration, the harmony among its many parts
and the close-fitting almost symbiotic ties between it and other aspects of the life of the Elema make it one of mankind's great creations.
But along with its solemnity and grandeur is a joviality and irrever-
ence that at first glance jars.

The women are not supposed to see parts of the cycle, or the masks
hanging dead inside the *eravo.* Eliade says that when men swinging
bullroarers enter the village "they have the right to kill any woman or
non-initiate who tries to discover their identity."[23] But Williams tells

of many times when concealment is treated casually. The doors of the *eravo* are often left open and the women see "quite enough to dispel their curiosity."[34] If a woman dances with the *hevehe* of a son rather than a husband, the offended man may get very angry. During the "cutting off" combat the women are strong enough to keep the eight masks trapped indefinitely. But Williams heard one young man brag how he told his sister, "Isn't it time you let me go?" and at the next charge he was free.[35]

The *Hevehe* cycle mixes the ceremonial and the personal without diluting or blending either. A mask dances because it is alive. A man dances because he is animated by the mask. A mask dies when its face is shot through by an arrow. Parts of its hulk can be used again. The spirits may suffer as they are killed. Yet they do not die but go to the bush and wait to be recalled. After the audience of weeping women leave the village, the masks are killed simply by being thrown down. Both the dancing and the dying are performances—and all performances are vis-à-vis someone. There is an absolute separation between the performance and the performer. A separation that encourages exchange and transformation. Bravado, joking, rehearsing and special backstage behavior are possible because the Elema know when they are onstage and when they are off. Their performances are not impersonations, but possessions and exchanges; the spirit and the man interpenetrate each other without either losing his identity. The dancing of the *hevehe* lifts the whole community to a month of exaltation. When the *hevehe* are killed and the spirits gone, the *eravo* falls to shambles.

What is the relationship between the mask and the masker? At every moment during each ceremony during the long *Hevehe* cycle the people know two independent but reciprocating realities.

a) The reality of the *hevehe* masks and the autonomously unfolding cycle. These spirits are not abstract or generalized. They move in space, can be touched and seen, and are known *personally* by the men building them. Slowly they are built in the *eravo*, and each phase of building is marked by celebration. The masks are never half-alive, but like embryos they are not ready for independent dancing life outside the *eravo* until they are complete and whole. When they emerge they dance among all the people for a month. The spirits can be heard in the roar of the bullroarers and the clamor of the gongs. They do not die, but they must be killed anyway, and not mysteriously but by bow and arrow, and then burnt by fire.

b) The reality of the villagers' everyday lives—of hunting and farming, feasting, sharing, exchanging, marrying, child-rearing, politicking, fighting, ageing, sickening, dying. In theatrical terms neither the performed (masks) nor the performers (villagers) is absorbed into each other; one does not "play the role" of the other. They stand whole and yet autonomous. Their relationship is what Grotowski calls "confrontation." It is not that one reality reflects, represents or distills the other. Both move freely through the same time/space. The realities confront, overlap, interpenetrate each other in a relationship that is extraordinarily dynamic and fluid.

The burning of the *hevehe* masks and the circumcizing of the initiates at the *Bora* are culminating irrevocable acts proclaiming that there can be no turning back. The Australians mark off a special place where the men bring the boys into the whole community. The initiation is relatively swift and certainly intense, convulsive and isolated. Contrarily, the Elema cycle unfolds among the villagers' homes, meeting places and playgrounds. After the masks are burned, the village is only half alive until the start of the next cycle. But the apparently opposite actuals of Australia and New Guinea are founded on the same belief in multiple, valid, equivalent and reciprocating realities. The actuals are here and now, efficacious and irrevocable.

Joan MacIntosh, playing Dionysus in *Dionysus in 69*, had to start her performance each night by emerging naked amid an audience of 200 and saying, "Good evening, my name is Joan MacIntosh, and I am a god." Only by finding, releasing and showing her deepest impulses of fear, hilarity, fraud and humiliation could she begin to cope with the actuality of her preposterous situation. Her claim to divinity is thinkable only in the terms of the trapped *hevehe* who said to his sister, "Isn't it time you let me go?"

When a performer does not "play a character" what does he do? Stand-up comics play aspects of themselves. Essential are injoking and a straightman who leads the comic into traps or kids him about that aspect of himself that is the core of his act. Disclosure is the heart of the comic's art. He carefully keeps to the edge—just a little too much and his act is embarrassing and painful. The audience teeters between knowing it is being put on and glimpsing brief, but deep, looks into the "real man." Like a Malibu Beach muscleman, the comic overdevelops parts of his personality and displays these shamelessly.

The movie star wears a different story and costume in each film. But he is groomed for one limited set of traits and these vivify all his roles. The cynical, easy violence of Bogart; the austere integrity of Cooper; the slurred, rough goodness of Wayne; the virgin-who-will-fuck of Doris Day; the slut-who-is-good of Marilyn Monroe. The star has his own thing that organizes the filmic "vehicle" around it. One is never sure how much of the "star personality" is genuine, and how much put on. The star is usually not sure either. A stereotyped mask thickens and freezes—this mask is worn publicly and privately throughout life.

Circus performers are like performers of actuals—except that at the circus everything is made to look more glamorous and dangerous than it is. The motive of the circus is "I dare you" and this is blatantly stimulated in the audience by the performers and ringmaster. The great circus performers are those who go to the utmost limit, seem about to fail, recover and succeed brilliantly. Hokum and skill—coming out of a near fall with a perfect landing capped by a superbly graceful bow to the cheering house: that's the essential circus.

Athletes, like circus performers, display their skills. The rules of games are designed to show prowess, quick judgment, speed, endurance, strength and teamwork. Also the rules encourage spectators to measure performance against some objective standard. Athletics are embellished by the ballyhoo and excitement natural to large crowds and focused by the intense competitiveness of our way of sporting. But competition is dispensable. Among Mexico's Tarahumaras racing is participatory—men, women, and children, old and young race together. It doesn't matter who finishes first—to arrive last is as honorable as to arrive first. The whole race is of interest to all spectators who measure performance against ability. What counts is that everyone who participates does his best. To be a laggard brings shame on you and your family. The idea of danger is exploited by the circus; that of excellence is the kernel of athletics. This combination of risk and mastery is asked of the performer of actuals. He is not a *shaman* or an acrobat or an athlete—but he shares the qualities of these.

An actual has five basic qualities, and each is found both in our own actuals and those of primitive peoples: 1) *process,* something happens *here and now;* 2) *consequential, irremediable* and *irrevocable* acts, exchanges, or situations; 3) *contest,* something is *at stake* for the performers and often for the spectators; 4) *initiation,* a *change in status* for participants; 5) space is used *concretely* and *organically.* Each of these basic qualities deserves extensive explication. I shall only be able to skim what is available.

Process, something happens here and now. This is largely a matter of emphasis. Even the most conventional actor affirms that something goes on inside him during a performance. But most training and rehearsals are designed to hide this process or to bring it entirely in line with the playwright's intentions as envisioned by the director so that the performance reveals not the actor but the character he is playing. The goal of conventional acting and the basis of Stanislavsky's great work is to enable the actor to "really live" his character. Nature ought to be so skillfully imitated that it seems to be re-presented on stage. The tendency of an actual is the opposite. Instead of the smooth "professionalism" of the "good actor," there are rough and unexpected turbulences, troubled interruptions. These are not stylistic, but the genuine meeting between performer and problem.

Two processes unfold simultaneously. The first is the one shaped by author and director, the "play and the *mise-en-scène*." But just as important is the more evanescent process of the performer. The play and *mise-en-scène* have a quality of having-been-lived, while the performance has the quality of living-now. The play will be completed only if the performer is able to carry through the process he starts afresh each night. That process cannot be rehearsed.

Perhaps this will be clearer if I relate an analogy told to me by Ryszard Cieslak of the Polish Teatr Laboratorium. I did not understand what Cieslak meant by "score" and I asked him to explain.

> We work in rehearsals to find an objective set of actions and relationships that, understood apart from anything we the performers might feel, communicate to the audience the images, actions and meanings we want to communicate. This process takes months and it is a *via negativa*—that is, we reject more than we accept and we search so that we can remove obstacles to our creativity. We play out the actions at hand, the associations that offer themselves to us. Grotowski watches. He helps us remove blocks, things that prevent us from fully confronting and experiencing the actions at hand.
>
> Finally we construct a coherent score. This score, which grows minutely day by day, includes all the objective things a spectator sees from night to night. For example, in *Akropolis* my score includes how my body lies in the wheelbarrow, what tone my voice has, how I breathe, how my fingers move. The score even includes the associations I have, what I think about from moment to moment. These associations I change from time to time, as they get stale. And as it is for me, so it is for everyone else. Ideally the score is whole and does not need completion or revision. In practice, it is never that way. Only a percentage of each production is scored when we begin performing it for audiences. After four years of performing *Akropolis* about 80% of it is scored for me.
>
> The score is like the glass inside which a candle is burning. The glass is solid, it is there, you can depend on it. It contains and guides the flame. But it is not the flame. The flame is my inner process each night. The flame is what illuminates the score, what the spectators see through the score. The flame is alive. Just as the flame in the candle-glass moves, flutters, rises, falls, almost goes out, suddenly glows brightly, responds to each breath of wind—so my inner life varies from night to night, from moment to moment. The way I feel an association, the interior sense of my voice or a movement of my finger, I begin each night without anticipations. This is the hardest thing to learn. I do not prepare myself to feel anything. I do not say, 'Last night, this scene was extraordinary, I will try to do that again.' I want only to be receptive to what will

> happen. And I am ready to take what happens if I am
> secure in my score, knowing that, even if I feel a minimum,
> the glass will not break, the objective structure worked out
> over the months will help me through. But when a night
> comes that I can glow, shine, live, reveal—I am ready for it
> by not anticipating it. The score remains the same, but
> everything is different because I am different.

Grotowski describes the score as the "two banks of a river" and the performer's process as the "water flowing between those banks."[36]

We conventionally think of "process" as the sequence of events in the script—if these were "really happening" the story would be "inevitable." Thus the "death" of Hamlet or the "blinding" of Oedipus. When I think of process, I think of something that occurs in fact here and now: the melting of the ice-liths in *Fluids,* the dodging and ultimate taking of spears in the Tiwi trial, the dancing of the *hevehe.* These processes are not gimmicks, but fundamental elements of the performance structure.

The whole of the Living Theatre's *Paradise Now* is a process. The audience is given a program which is a chart of the event in phases. The performance passes through eight phases from "The Rite of Guerrilla Theatre" to "The Street." There is no time limit, and many performances take six hours or more. To my knowledge, all eight steps have never been genuinely accomplished—that is, the permanent revolution has not happened. (It is, of course, an error to think that one could. The Australians are more modest and successful with their ceremonies. And insofar as *Paradise Now* is a "demonstration," it is mimetic.) *Paradise Now* is built so that the performance incorporates disruptions the spectators act out. *Paradise Now* is pushed and pulled this way and that, seemingly in total disarray, until you realize that the performers are like tour guides—they want to move the thing along, but only after most of the audience is ready to move on. If anyone wants to stop off here or there, to examine a detail, to "put on a show," to shout, protest or in any way detour the performance, that is fine. *Paradise Now* develops through random movement towards goals and through phases. It distends and collapses, intensifies and slackens, coheres and fragments. But still it does move as the performers decide when one phase has been sufficiently explored and then initiate another. Many spectators cannot adapt themselves to a structure that appears so disorderly. But *Paradise Now* is very well organized if one recognizes diversion, disruption and side-tripping as part of that organization. It is much briefer than most primitive ceremonies—many of which also include sidetrips in the guise of new dances and stories, and disruptions when the community runs out of wealth or is threatened by hostile outgroups. Our sense of smooth time is jolted by *Paradise Now* which treats time as lumpy, malleable and turbulent.

The performers in *Paradise Now* have two tasks. They act things and they nudge the audience along. Like *shamans* they are the principle performers and the masters of ceremony. Throughout the performance spectators wisecrack and taunt the performers. This is not irrelevant—each phase must pass through ordeals to achieve the next stop. Taunts and mockery are also part of many primitive ceremonies. Even the not-paying-attention is part of some solemn occasions—like the Yom Kippur service of Hassidic Jews, from which the Living Theatre took elements of *Paradise Now*. Eventually *Paradise Now* is at the eighth phase and the performers, accompanied by many spectators, confront the police outside the theatre. I am reminded of Irma's little speech at the end of *The Balcony*. "You must now go home, where everything—you can be quite sure—will be even falser than here." The Living Theatre turns Genet on his head.

Consequential, irremediable and irrevocable acts. There are almost none of these in our theatre. Irrevocability is finely expressed in the circumcision of initiates. But it could also be taken from the exchanges of goods and people that vivify primitive life. Mauss calls these each "a total social fact." Levi-Strauss interprets them as events which have "significance that is at once social and religious, magic and economic, utilitarian and sentimental, jural and moral."[37] Even at Christmas and on birthdays or anniversaries we are not likely to involve ourselves in such whole exchanges. To demonstrate this I devised a classroom exercise. I asked everyone to choose a partner and to exchange something for fun. Men gave their wallets, shoes, pens; women their rings, cosmetics, handbags. Then I said, "Now exchange something for real." People gave each other empty cigarette packages, blank paper, matches.

Ralph Ortiz's *The Sky Is Falling* includes elements that are irrevocable. In it mice and chickens are killed, a piano axed to bits and participants doused with blood. Participants are divided into a small number of Initiators and a large number of Initiates. The scenario is written in the terminology of primitive ceremony, freely using words like "ritual" and "shaman." Initiates are interrogated by the Initiators and verbally abused when they refuse to participate in any detail of the piece. Violence is combined with sexuality and scatology. The violence increases through a series of overlapping and simultaneous "rituals" culminating in the "Piano Destruction Rite" and the "Birth of Henny Penny Rite." Preparatory events include breaking eggs, killing mice, cutting paper screens on which images of human dissections are projected, burning clothes, burning food, ripping and kicking apart overstuffed furniture, dismembering dead chickens, tearing clothes off participants and throwing blood at each other. The piano destruction is carefully orchestrated and precisely performed by Ortiz. He is exact about how the demolition should be done. "One hundred live mice in a wire screen and two gallons of blood in plastic bags are to be placed inside the piano behind the panel above the keys." The axe must be "brand new," the piano "pushed on its back to the floor—the keyboard and hammer sections smashed away so that the harp is completely exposed," and so on. The "Birth of Henny Penny" has two "men Initiators wearing maternity full-length dresses ... under spotlights ten feet apart. Each has a live chicken tied between his legs under the dress. There is also fifteen feet of tubing connected to a balloon tied low on their waists under the dresses which extends to an upright tire pump." Initiates are "harangued into pumping the pumps." The dresses inflate, all participants "join in the sighing moaning groaning and sexual motions" which continue until the balloons explode and the chickens are "delivered." Two initiators (now called Shamans) raise the birds "victoriously ... , then waving the chickens like flags they race through the Ritual Room shouting irrational violent sounds" which convert into a "Henny Penny" chant. The other Initiators pick up the chant and then attack the Shamans, grabbing the chickens and bring them to the demolished piano. The chickens are spread-eagled over the piano harp. The Initiators form a tight circle. The Shamans, outside the circle, start chanting "The sky is falling." They take the axe, the circle admits them, and each Shaman decapitates the other's chicken. As this happens, everyone cries like children "Mommy!" The decapitated heads are worn in plastic baggies "taped inside the fly" of each Shaman's pants. The cry changes to "Mousie" as the tight circle opens and the Initiators go to "zones" where the Initiates have watched the sacrifice. The Initiators shout at the Initiates, "You're just a bunch of fucking voyeurs!" Then the Shamans give each Initiator a live mouse. The Initiators surround the mouse trap area and throw the live mice in. Led by one of the Shamans, the Initiators begin to leave the room, "seeking out Initiates and seductively and lovingly telling them 'You love me, you love me.' "[38] The room after the performance was strewn with guts, living, dead and half-dead mice. The floor was about an inch deep in blood. Bits of furniture, tatters of clothes, mashed food, a student vomiting—and on a platform to one side and 15 feet high were 10 observers, some with cameras. The room stank of guts and blood. The effect was hideous.

Eliade comments that modern "so-called initiation rites frequently betoken a deplorable spiritual poverty. ... But the success of these enterprises likewise proves man's profound need for initiation, that is, for regeneration, for participation in the life of the spirit.[39] *The Sky Is Falling* is a moralizing piece founded on a belief in Artaud's dictum that violence will purge violent feelings. This, in turn, is Aristotelian catharsis escalated towards the Roman reality games of gladiators and armies in deadly combat for fun. There is, however, another frame for Ortiz's piece. Those who did not choose to participate or watch from the platform saw everything on closed-circuit TV. During a discussion which followed the performance a woman berated Ortiz for "promoting such things. How can you kill animals?" she asked. Ortiz answered, "You were watching on TV, you knew where it was happening, why didn't you stop it?" This converted *The Sky Is Falling* into a political parable: the room was Vietnam, the TV viewers were American citizens, the Initiates were draftees, the Initiators were the regular army, the Shamans were the brass and top government officials. But I don't think we can leave it at that. *The Sky Is Falling* raises the question of what kind of irrevocable acts?

Roman reality games and mimes are the ultimate mimetic spectacle. Ortiz's work shares that mimetic ambition. His mirror is distorted and the stakes are not so high—animals, not people. Unlike the Maori of New Zealand who press earth on an initiate's chest to make him understand death, Ortiz takes animal blood and chops the heads off chickens. The "symbolic ambition" Levi-Strauss detects as the motor of savage thinking is converted into reductive imitation. Irrevocability is understood as something which happens to the objects of the drama—the chicken and mice, the pianos and furniture—not to the subjects of the piece, the Initiates and spectators. At best these are put through a harrowing hour and left with scalding memories. Or, perhaps, like soldiers they finally weary and are blunted to bloodshed. When violence, cruelty, sacrifice, even ritual murder and combat (as among the Dani of New Guinea[40]) are incorporated into authentic ceremonies, they are always part of a *known system*. Violence without the system is meaningless and destructive. Ortiz tries to invent a system through mini-violent homeopathic demonstration. His scenario is rich with the terminology of primitive religion, but without a link to a system. Irrevocable acts are rare in our theatre. They can't be made by magic. When they happen they usually manifest themselves as metaphors. And they act on the people, not the props.

Contest, something is at stake for the performers and often for the spectators. In *Dionysus in 69* there is a scene about halfway through that starts when Dionysus offers Pentheus "any woman in this room." Pentheus says he can have his pick without Dionysus's help. "Okay," says Dionysus, "try it yourself." Pentheus is left alone in the center of the room. Almost every night some woman comes to him and offers help. The scene plays privately between them, and ends with the woman going back to her place. The performance resumes and Pentheus, defeated, is sacrificed. Once it did not happen that way. In the words of William Shephard who played Pentheus.

> The one time the sequence was completed was when
> Katherine Turner came out into the room. . . . The
> confrontation between us was irrational. Her concern for
> me was not based on the play, my playing a role, whether
> or not I was going to die, or any of that. What happened
> was that I recognized in one moment that the emotional

> energy Katherine was spending on me literally lifted me
> out of the play, as though someone had grabbed me by the
> hair and pulled me up to the ceiling. I looked around and I
> saw the garage and the other actors and I said, 'It finally
> happened.' The play fell away, like shackles being struck
> from my hands. The way the play is set up Pentheus is
> trapped inside its structure. But on that night it all seemed
> to fall away and I walked out of the door.[41]

Joan MacIntosh was playing Dionysus that night. Her reactions were
different.

> Bill got up and left the theatre with the woman. I
> announced that the play was over. 'Ladies and gentlemen,
> tonight for the first time since the play has been running,
> Pentheus, a man, has won over Dionysus, the god. The play
> is over.' Cheers and cries and celebrations. . . . I felt
> betrayed. I was hurt and angry at Shephard. . . . I learned
> something corny but true: that if you invest all of yourself
> in the work, the risks are very great.[41]

On only one other occasion was the performance similarly torn from
its rehearsed path. But many times people came into the play challenging performers, participating in the "death ritual" (where Pentheus is "killed"). Some of this participation was naïve, but much of it
came from people who had seen *Dionysus in 69* more than once. In
June 1969, Shephard was "kidnapped" by five students from Queens'
College who planned to stop the "killing" of Pentheus and spent an
afternoon working out their strategy. Many of the performers felt that
the play should not stop because Pentheus was not "genuinely" res-
cued. I agreed and asked for a substitute Pentheus from the audience. A young man of 17 volunteered—he did very well: he had seen
the play five times and knew what was expected of him.

It is hard to build into a performance both narrative power and the
tensions of a sporting match. The two ambitions cross each other.
Suspense does not describe the tensions of sports which come not from
the spectators being in doubt about the outcome but from the doubt
and resulting struggle among the players. There is some doubt like
this in all performances because actors seek the unknown in their
partners. In conventional theatre an actor's creativity is most powerfully engaged in the narrow band between the details of the *mise-en-
scène* and the obligation not to throw your partner by doing something
wholly unexpected.

The band is much wider in *Dionysus in 69* and theatre like it. Those
in the audience who know the performance can enter it at any of
several places and change the flow of the action. In the scene cited the
play can end abruptly. Mostly, however, the changes are modular—in
tone, speed, intensity. Even those who are at the performance for the
first time can participate if they stick to the rules. These are implicit:

you can do anything that will not prevent the performers from performing. What varies wildly from night to night is not the text or the story but the quality of the action. If we expand Cieslak's analogy, the gestures and text are the candle-glass and the action is the flame.

Grotowski thinks that Artaud's proclamation that "actors should be like martyrs burnt alive, still signaling through the flames" contains the "whole problem of spontaneity and discipline, this conjunction of opposites which gives birth to the total act (which is) the very crux of the actor's art."[42] Both spontaneity and discipline are *risks* for the performer. His entire effort is in making his body-voice-mind-spirit whole. Then he risks this wholeness here and now in front of others. Like the tightrope walker on the high wire, each move is absolutely spontaneous and part of an endless discipline. The kind of performer I am talking about—like the *shaman,* Artaud's martyr, and Grotowski's Cieslak—discards the buffer of "character." Cieslak does not "play" the Constant Prince; MacIntosh does not "play" Dionysus. Neither "are" they the characters. During rehearsals the performer searches his personal experiences and associations, selects those elements which reveal him and also make an autonomous narrative and/or action structure, strips away irrelevancies and cop-outs, hones what remains until everything is necessary and sufficient. What results is a double structure, not unlike that of the *Hevehe.* The first is the narrative and/or action structure of *The Constant Prince* or *Dionysus in 69.* The second is the vulnerability and openness of the performer. Each performance he risks freshly not only his dignity and craft, but his life-in-process. Decisions made and actions done during performance may change the performer's life. The performance is a set of exchanges between the performer and the action. And of course among all the performers and between them and the audience. "The theatrical reality is instantaneous, not an illustration of life but something linked to *life only by analog.*"[43]

Initiation, a change in status for the participants. This change in who you are flows from the first three qualities. If something has happened here and now, if the actual is made of consequential, irremediable and irrevocable acts and exchanges, and if these involve risk for the performers (and maybe for the spectators too), then there will be changes, new dimensions of integration and wholeness. Change will either be bunched, troubled, difficult—an initiation; or smooth and continuous.

Initiation can be the kernel of a performance. The structure of events will parallel the process stimulated by the events. For example, *The Constant Prince* is a set of initiations both for the Prince and for Cieslak. The performance is made of climactic bursts leading Cieslak from resistance to resignation to sacrifice. The Prince goes one step more, to apotheosis. At each of the first two crossings Cieslak is in crisis, and surrenders to it. His role is passive—to take in all that happens to him. The more he gives up the farther he progresses. When he "dies," he remains still. Other performers apotheosize the Prince, but nothing more happens to Cieslak who merely lends his body to the work of the others. Cieslak's inner movements night to night are not as radical as those proposed for the Prince; but the Prince is a fiction. The narrative of the Prince is a whole and Cieslak is a metaphor. But this does not mean that Cieslak is less whole than the Prince. Cassirer says:

> Whoever has brought any part of a whole into his power
> has thereby acquired power, in the magical sense, over
> the whole itself. . . . The very nature of this magic shows
> that the concept in question is not one of mere analogy, but
> of real identification. If, for instance, a rain-making
> ceremony consists of sprinkling water on the ground to
> attract rain, or rain-stopping magic is made by pouring
> water on red hot stones where it is consumed amid hissing
> noise, both ceremonies owe their true magical sense to the
> fact that the rain is not just represented, but is felt to be
> really present in each drop of water. . . . The rain is
> actually there, whole and undivided, in the sprinkled or
> evaporated water.[44]

Thus, and in precisely that way, Cieslak is there.

The question of efficacy goes to the very heart of theatre's function. The dynamics of ritual have been nicely put by Levi-Strauss

> There is an asymmetry which is postulated in advance
> between profane and sacred, faithful and officiating, dead
> and living, initiated and uninitiated, etc., and the 'game'
> consists in making all the participants pass to the winning
> side by means of events.[45]

Events are the ritual. When it is over initiates have been initiated and everyone is together. If theatre could be an initiatory participatory game, it could be at once entertaining and fateful. But, as Cassirer notes, "word and mythic image, which once confronted the human mind as hard realistic powers, have not cast off all reality and effectuality." Cassirer welcomes this "liberation," hoping that now art will attain "its own self-realization."[46] Artaud wanted to make language "spatial and significant . . . to manipulate it like a solid object.[47] Language is the heated focus of a more general conflict. The ambition to make theatre into ritual is nothing other than a wish to make performance efficacious, to use events to change people. Cassirer's analysis seems old fashioned and Artaud's prophetic.

Space is used concretely and organically. Eliade describes an initiation of Fiji called *Nanda.* For this ceremony a stone enclosure 100 by 50 by 3 feet is built a long way from the village. This is the *nanda* which means "bed." Two years pass between the building of the *nanda* and the first ceremonies, which do not use it. Two more years pass before the second and final ceremony. For weeks before the second ceremony large quantities of food are stored in cabins built near the *nanda*.

> On a particular day the novices, led by a priest, proceed to
> the *nanda* in single file, with a club in one hand and a
> lance in the other. The old men await them in front of the
> walls, singing. The novices drop their weapons at the old
> men's feet, as symbols of gifts, and then withdraw to the
> cabins. On the fifth day, again led by the priests, they once
> more proceed to the sacred enclosure, but this time the old
> men are not awaiting them by the walls. They are then
> taken into the *nanda*. There 'lie a row of dead men, covered
> with blood, their bodies apparently cut open and their
> entrails protruding.' The priest-guide walks over the
> corpses and the terrified novices follow him to the other
> end of the enclosure. 'Suddenly he blurts out a great yell,
> whereupon the dead men start to their feet, and run down
> to the river to cleanse themselves.'[48]

Obviously the mysteries of death and rebirth animate the *Nanda*. But what interests me here is the building of a simple space for one ceremony. This *ad hoc* theatre is built four years before its use. Somehow the elapsed time "prepares" the space. The space is designed by the event performed in it. The walls are high enough to conceal the corpses until the last minute; the *nanda* is large enough to engulf the initiates in the bloody field of death. When the dead rise and race to the river, the initiates are alone in a large fenced-in space.

The *eravo* of the Elema is made for the *hevehe* masks. It grows over the years from rear to front as the masks grow taller. At the culminating moment of the cycle the huge *eravo* doors open and the masks dance out to fulfil their lives. The *eravo* is a womb, and the doors the passageway to life. The *eravo* doors open just once. When the *eravo* is empty of masks, it is left to deteriorate. But, while the masks are growing in the *eravo,* the building is also the men's living quarters and the village meeting house. The womb is comfortable enough to welcome the men easily and naturally.

When the *hevehe* dance through the village and on the beaches, tight circles of women and children numbering around 25 weave around them so that the whole scene is made of as many as 50 dancing groups, each orbiting around a gigantic dancing mask. The space and feel of the *Hevehe* cycle is dynamic and expansive. It moves freely through the village and in spaces around the village. Other elements of the cycle include scaling walls, mock battles fought with lighted torches at night and coconut flakes and sticks during the day. The burning of the *hevehe* takes place near the river, which is tidal. High tide washes the remains of the masks out to sea. Throughout the cycle there is an interplay between the village, the beach, the river, the sea and the bush. Unlike the *Nanda* there is no special stage. The *eravo* is backstage, shop, office and dormitory. Bateson describes how

> the ceremonial house [of the Iatmul] serves as a Green
> Room for the preparation of the show. The men put on their
> masks and their ornaments in its privacy and thence sally
> forth to dance and perform before the women, who are
> assembled on the banks at the sides of the dancing ground.
> Even such purely male affairs as initiations are so staged
> that parts of the ceremony are visible to the women who
> form an audience and who can hear issuing from the
> ceremonial house the mysterious and beautiful sounds
> made by the various secret musical instruments—flutes,
> gongs, bullroarers, etc. Inside, behind screens or in the
> upper story of the ceremonial house, the men who are
> producing these sounds are exceedingly conscious of that
> unseen audience of women. They think of the women as
> admiring their music, and if they make a technical blunder
> in the performance, it is the laughter of the women that
> they fear.[49]

Wherever we turn in the primitive world we find theatre—the interplay among space, time, performers, action and audience. Space is used concretely, as something to be molded, changed, dealt with. The simplest arrangement is, of course, an open area with a performance in the center and the audience on all sides. That is the shape of the Tiwi trial. Or a musical performance from inside to a gathering outside randomly standing, sitting or moving. Or the multiple simultaneous performances of the *hevehe* which cohere into a whole that no one person can see all of. Or the construction of special places as in the *nanda*. Or the building of an entire camp away from the village as in the *bora*. Often space is articulated by the deployment of props or elements, such as a large fire or a hollow log on which the initiates to be circumcised are put, or a throne, or an animal pen where a sacrificial feast-beast is kept. Examples of different spaces can be multiplied at will. Each is made for and is part of a particular ceremony, event or ritual.

Nowhere do we find a permanent theatre or ceremonial place—a single structure whose shape is "neutral" and "adaptable" to all uses. The closest we come to that is an open space for dancing, debating, trading, duelling, trying. Or the whole village which is a stage for everything that goes on in and around it. Throughout the primitive world events make shapes. In many ceremonies the principal architectural element is people—how many there are, how and where they move, what their interactions are, whether they participate or watch or do both. Mead's and Bateson's film *Dance and Trance in Bali*[50] shows some people keenly watching the show, others lounging disinterestedly and several walking through the performance on their way to other business. Our culture is almost alone in demanding uniform behavior from audiences and in clearly segregating audience from performers and audience from others in the area who are neither audience nor performers.

We are also almost unique in using ready-made spaces for theatres. Possibly the development of a theatre as a special place which can accommodate many different kinds of performances is tied to urban cultures where space is expensive and must be clearly marked out for uses. Surely the need for scene design in our theatres is an attempt to overcome the limitations of ready-made space as well as an outlet for mimetic impulses. A strong current of the new theatre is to allow the event to flow freely through space and to design whole spaces entirely for specific performances. Grotowski is a master of this, using very simple elements and combining these with meaningful deployment of the audiences and precise movement of the performers so that the spatial dynamics of the production metaphorise the drama. Thus the audience peeps down at the sacrificial planks on which the Constant Prince is immolated, or sits amid the proliferating crematorium pipes of *Akropolis* or only slightly fills the large open volume of *Apocalypsis*. *Paradise Now* stumbled through the Brooklyn Academy because that large proscenium theatre blocked the flow of the performance.

In the Performance Group's *Makbeth* (1969) I experimented with audience movement through a complicated space. The environment (designer, Jerry Rojo) is not easy to describe. It is an interlocked arrangement of cubic spaces, ladders, a stairway and a long curved ramp. The whole space is 50 by 40 by 20 feet. The lowest level is a trench 6 feet deep and 35 feet long cut below floor level on one side of the space's 50-foot axis. Over it a vertical grandstand of five stories rises from floor to ceiling. On floor level is a table 25 by 12 feet around which audience can sit and on which scenes are played. In three corners of the room are similar but not identical two and three story cubes rising to the ceiling. Along the wall opposite the grandstand is a long ramp rising from the head of the stairs to the top of a corner structure. All the space is open—there are no interior walls, doors or hangings. At the edge of most of the platforms are narrow strips of carpet on which the audience sits. The floor is concrete and the walls of the room white.

The performance occurs throughout the space, often with three or four scenes playing simultaneously. There is no place a spectator can see everything from. On several occasions I met with audiences of around 75 before the show and told them they could move during the performance. "If you are noisy or block the performers' movements, you can bust this thing up. If you take off your shoes so that you are absolutely silent and move from carpeted area to carpeted area, you can intensify your own and our experience. Try to understand the action and go with it. Think of yourselves as witnesses, or people in the street. Something happens—you go to see what. But you can't interfere or change what's happening." The audiences were beautifully cooperative and some impressive things occurred. During the banquet scene the empty table swiftly filled with people who became guests at Dunsinane. The murder of Banquo under a platform was witnessed by a few. During the prophecy scene in the trench where Makbeth learns of Macduff and Birnam Wood, 50 spectators stood or crouched, as around a bear-pit, while Makbeth talked to the Dark Powers who dangled upside down from pipes. Duncan's funeral cortege and Makbeth's coronation parade were augmented by people lining the ramp and joining in the processions. The soldiers advancing through Birnam Wood found allies. In many ways the performance found focus as crowds condensed and dispersed; as a few people showed up here and there; as many silently and swiftly tip-toed stocking-footed through this open but secretive castle. The audience became the soldiers, the guests, the witnesses, the crowds—the powerless but present and compliant public.

Elements exchange, interpenetrate and transform—but there is no hierarchy that permanently or *a priori* puts any life process "above" any other. To dream is as "real" and as "vital" as to eat or dance or make love or war. Different contexts will of course make one activity more important within a given circumstance and time. The model is not ethical or personal—that is, it does not distinguish between right and wrong, good and bad, your taste and mine. Ethics, values and tastes are always making hierarchies—but these are contingent, not fundamental. It has been customary to view theatre hierarchically. For the writer the text is first and most important; to the performer his own presence on stage is the center of the event; the director knows that the theatre would be impossible without him; and every technician will tell you that lights, sets and costumes can make or break a show. Production has been thought of as a blend of many arts and as the "realization" of a text. But it really is a system of equal, independent elements:

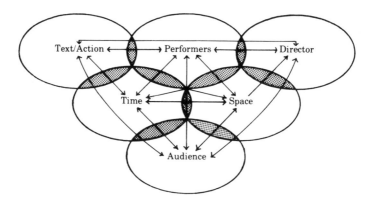

A complicated picture that gets more so the more elements there are. Perhaps an absurd model—for how can the director "transform" or "interpenetrate" or "exchange" with time or space; how can the audience do likewise, and so on? And if I do not mean these operations literally, what do I mean? First I mean that all elements of the theatre are (like experience generally) on the same plane—there is no *a priori* hierarchy, no way of determining before rehearsal what will be the dominating element, if any. Secondly, *all* elements need rehearsal— which means that all elements are capable of radical, total change. Thirdly, in a way that is difficult to explain but which I have experienced, "by a sudden metamorphosis everything may be turned into everything." That is, the director finds himself deeply and personally enmeshed with the performers and their life problems; the environmentalist recognizes that action shapes space and space shapes action; the writer sees his text signify things he never intended; the audience is plunged into the difficulties of the performance so completely that their reactions regulate the tone and flow of the action; the amount of time spent in rehearsals and the immediate timespan of a performance condition the performers' way of working and interactions with each other. These are only a few of the many combinations and outcomes possible.

Mimetic theatre has given us great masterpieces. Mimetic acting is a major tradition. There are other kinds of performances, however. Of these, actuals relate practices among primitive "whole-seeking" peoples and parts of our own population, particularly the young. Parallels can be misleadingly overdrawn. But I think our young are whole-seeking, and in a way and of a scope not experienced in our culture for hundreds of years. What we are undergoing is not a neo-primitive movement, but a post-industrial one. I think it will not be long before we know whether this is a passing phase or a genuine development of lasting power.

Notes

1. Kaprow "Extensions in Time and Space," 154. Kaprow's work, more than any other I know, has the simple quality of "happening"— of something that *is*. By ever so slight a change or heightening he converts everyday actions into "mysteries." See his *Assemblages, Environments and Happenings,* also his "poster-scenarios" which are announcement of his pieces and are also their scenarios.
2. For a popular explanation of Earth Art see Bongartz (1970), 166 ff. Earth Art develops from some very old impulses and is based on two

principles: 1) art includes the arrangement of natural objects or the confrontation between a natural object and a man-made object—for example, draping a cliff for one mile with cloth; 2) art is autonomous and can therefore be "displayed" anywhere, even where it is not likely to be seen by human beings such as under water or deep in a desert.

3. Plato (1945), 323-4.

4. Aristotle's view of the world is organic—he sees all growth and development modeled after what he observed in plants and animals. He believed that every event contained at the beginning the virtuality of its entire career. He believed in "fulfillment" rather than "transformation."

5. Leslie (1960), xi.

6. Lommel (1967), 146.

7. Shamanism has both a technical and broader meaning. Its technical meaning is that of a certain kind of magico-religious leadership originating with hunter peoples in Central Asia. The word is of Siberian origin. The techniques of shamanism spread westward across the northern tier of Europe and to the north shores of the Mediterranean and eastward across Siberia into Alaska and down the west coast of both North and South America. Shamanism in its more general meaning includes all kinds of ceremonial leadership and it is in this wider sense that I use the word.

8. Lommel (1967), 148. Shamanism is not "magic" in our debased sense of that word. It is a rigorous technique that assumes communication and transformation among several kinds of experiences including the reintegration of the past and present, conscious and unconscious, dead and living, dream and waking, individual and group. There are specific techniques to be learned. See Eliade (1970).

9. Eliade (1965), 100.

10. Eliade (1965), 100-1.

11. Rothenberg (1968), 51-2. This is an extraordinary anthology of "sacred poetries" from Africa, America, Asia and Oceania. It includes scenarios and events and a very concise and informative set of commentaries. Rothenberg is a poet and his view of the material is particularly stimulating for artists.

12. Rothenberg (1968), 424.

13. Eliade (1965), 87.

14. Lommel (1967), 138-9.

15. Eliade (1965), 102.

16. Lommel (1967), 139. The techniques of repairing the broken link are not improvised. An identification is made between word and body power and the spirits. Rothenberg comments (in regard to another but similar ceremony): "What's of interest here isn't the matter of myth but the power of repetition and naming (monotony too) to establish the presence of a situation-in-its-entirety. This involves the acceptance (by poet and hearers) of an indefinite extension of narrative

time, and the belief that language (i.e. poetry) can make-things-present by naming them." 385. This is a fundamental part of actualizing.

17. Lommel (1967), 139.

18. Quoted by Rothenberg (1968), 417. It is very hard to show this way of thinking to those who have not thought this way. It is a very fluid way of thinking. All experiences are virtually equal in their claim for attention, combination, transformation, overlap and inter-penetration. The distinctions which we make automatically and abso-lutely, say, between a mental event (a dream) and a physical event (snow falling) are not made. Each situation possibly can equate *any* two (or more) events. This is the "concrete" thinking Levi-Strauss admires and the "poetic" thinking Rothenberg admires.

19. Levi-Strauss (1966), 219-20.

20. Eliade (1965), 4.

21. Eliade (1965), 5-6. The implications of an event happening here and now that is an actualization of a situation which occurred "there and then" are widespread and complicated. There is no doubt that such phenomena are universal. In our own culture, psychoanalysts call these things "acting out" and "abreaction." There is a very rich literature from that point of view—see especially the special issue on acting out of the *Journal of the American Psychoanalytic Association,* Vol. 5, No. 4, 1957. What is involved is treating time concretely and being able to manipulate it so that any time may be any other time. This takes two forms: 1) the living of time A at time B; 2) making time T omnipresent. In both cases an integration of time is accomplished and linear unidirectional time is abolished. This ability to manipulate time is essential for performing. We may also have a metaphorical actualizing—that is, the event actualized is not the "original" event, but a substitute (a displacement or a *pars pro toto).* Or there may be no "original" event but rather a series none of which "came first" and all of which are "available," given the right techniques to evoke them.

22. Williams (1940), 118. Williams's excellent book is unfortunately out of print. It details the whole *Hevehe* cycle.

23. Williams (1940), 356-7.

24. Williams (1940), 361.

25. Williams (1940), 360.

26. Williams (1940), 365.

27. Williams (1940), 367.

28. Williams (1940), 373.

29. Williams (1940), 375.

30. Williams (1940), 376-7.

31. Williams (1940), 373.

32. Williams (1940), 390-1.

33. Eliade (1965), 33.

34. Williams (1940), 364.

35. Williams (1940), 367.
36. Grotowski Lecture at Brooklyn Academy, 1969.
37. Levi-Strauss (1969a), 52.
38. All quotations and descriptions of *The Sky Is Falling* are taken from the manuscript scenario which Ortiz distributed about two weeks before the event which took place at the Middle Atlantic States regional meeting of the American Educational Theatre Association held at Temple University in January, 1970. The event itself was modified the night before performance and some changes were made improvisationally during the performance. I arrived too late to see the performance. I walked through the aftermath in the Ritual Destruction Room and took part in a discussion of the performance. Ortiz told me of the changes made from scenario to performance. Most important of these were: 1) Song-my atrocity posters were distributed on the campus and the piece took on a definite war tone. Interrogations focused on killing and atrocities; the eggs were called "enemy foetuses"; each preliminary act of destruction was identified with killing Vietnamese; initiates were treated as draftees and their participation in the event called "a tour of duty"; the destruction of the piano was identified with the destruction of a Vietnamese village—and the Indian god of destruction Kali was identified with Lt. Calley; 2) When the chickens/babies were delivered the participants divided into two groups, one shouting "Kill the enemy!" and the other, "Let them live!" The chickens were identified as Vietcong babies. The Shamans left the theatre and ran through the campus pursued by the two groups. The goal was to run through the city streets and then back into the Ritual Destruction Room—this goal was achieved and the chickens were not killed; 3) The audience sat in the large Temple University theatre and watched the event over TV—the "six o'clock news," Ortiz calls it. The pursuit of the Shamans with the chickens/babies included climbing over and through the audience watching on TV. Just prior to this a man was brought out and dumped on the stage. He was bloody and his role was to create empathy for his plight as a victim of brutalization. He dragged himself to the edge of the stage. He vomited, drooled, writhed. Brutalizers returned from time to time to lift this man's face, spit in it, throw blood on him. People in the audience thought the man had freaked out. Several demanded that a doctor be called. But no one acted. And when the man tried to crawl off the stage and sit with the audience he was pushed back by people from the audience who said, "There's something wrong with this man—don't let him get off the stage."

Since writing my impressions of *The Sky Is Falling* I have spoken at length to Ortiz. He is interested in provoking "skizoid" reactions in participants in his events—he believes that the "paleologic" of schizoid ritual-making is basic to "visceral acting." He feels that the individual is capable of producing his own private *system;* he makes distinctions between societies that are whole and have social ritual systems and societies, like ours, that are alienating and force people to make their own ritual systems. I hope to examine Ortiz's work in detail soon. I have let my original impressions stand here—but I now believe I undervalued Ortiz's work.

39. Eliade (1965), 134-5.

40. The Dani engage in ritual warfare. See Gardner and Heider (1968) and the excellent movie, *Dead Birds*.

41. Schechner (1970).

42. Grotowski (1968), 125, 123.

43. Grotowski (1968), 118.

44. Cassirer (1946), 92-3.

45. Levi-Strauss (1966), 32.

46. Cassirer (1946), 99.

47. Artaud (1958), 72.

48. Eliade (1965), 33-4

49. Bateson (1958), 128.

50. Mead and Bateson (1938).

Drama, Script,
Theatre and Performance

Part 1

The phenomena called either/all "drama," "theatre," "performance" occur among all the world's peoples and date back as far as historians, archeologists and anthropologists can go.[1] Evidence indicates that dancing, singing, wearing masks and/or costumes, impersonating either other men, animals, or supernaturals, acting out stories, presenting time 1 at time 2, isolating and preparing special places and/or times for these presentations and individual or group preparations or rehearsals are co-existent with the human condition. Of countless examples from Paleolithic times none is more interesting than the cave at Tuc d'Audoubert:

> A sunken river guards the fearsome Tuc d'Audoubert, two
> hundred long underground feet of which one breasts or
> boats upon before the first land; then comes a precarious
> thirty-foot steep shaft up ladders placed there and slippery
> pegs; and next a crawl through claustrophobic low
> passages, to reach the startling footprints of ancient
> dancers in bare feet and the models of copulating bisons, in
> clay on the floor beyond.[2]

This cave is not the only one to make difficult, if not altogether inaccessible, its performance space. These earliest theatres—or shall I call them temples?—are hidden in the earth, lit by torch; and the ceremonies enacted apparently concerned hunting-fertility. It is clear why the two are associated: even today, among the hunters of the Kalahari Desert, for example, when large game is taken a brief ceremony entreats the gods for replenishment of "so large a life" converted into meat by the thrusting of spears.[3] Hunters do not breed cattle—they depend on what game is available; the more prolific the species hunted the better the hunting.

But it was not only animal fertility that Stone Age humans celebrated. Figures, carvings, paintings and symbols depict human fertility as well. The most ancient are of enlarged vulvas and/or huge buttocks (not unlike what females of some species of monkeys and apes display during estrus), or of pendant, milkful breasts.[4] Then the ubiquitous phallic symbols, many of them exaggerated replications of the original, others more far-fetched. Associated with these human fertility figures are dances, some of them persisting into historical times. One has to think only of the erotic sculptings at Konarak (Orissa, 13th century) to recall how the association among fertility, dancing and music has continued over the millennia. The sheer fecundity of the Konarak figures is overwhelming; and many of the copulatory and fondling poses are also dance positions. This is also true of Paleolithic cave art.[5] Nothing I know more succinctly shows the association in the mind/behavior of humans between fertility-sexuality, fertility-hunting and performance than the second vestibule of the cave at El Castillo. There one sees "five bell-shaped signs. They have long been recognized as representing the vulva. They are red and very large (ca. 45 cm.) and are divided by a short vertical stroke. Between them is an (80 cm.) upright black line, feathered at the end. [. . .] The red female symbols and the single black male symbol are spectacularly situated within a slightly raised part of the so-called second vestibule of the cavern of El Castillo. Below the smoothened surface of the niche which they occupy is a small table-like projection of the rock, beside which fall the folds of a curtainlike rock formation. [. . .] Parts of this rock curtain show signs of having been rubbed smooth by long usage."[6] In India it is common practice to rub the representations of both phallus and vulva when one passes by them in a temple. Everywhere cult items are fondled; curing and blessing is commonly practiced by the "laying-on" of hands.

We know nothing of the scripts used by the dancer-shamans of the Paleolithic temple-theatres. I don't say "texts," which mean written documents. I say "scripts," which mean something that pre-exist any given enactment, which act as a blueprint for the enactment, and which persist from enactment to enactment. Extrapolating from the existing evidence and modern experience I assume that the dancing took a persistent (or "traditional") shape which was kept from one event to another; that this shape was known by the dancers and by the spectators (if there were any), and that the shape was taught by one group of dancers to another.[7] Furthermore, the script was important: maintaining it contributed to the efficacy of the rite; abandoning it endangered that efficacy. Even more: the efficacy was not "a result of" dancing the script but "contained in" dancing the script. In other words, in prehistoric ritual theatre, as in contemporary ritual, the doing is a *manifestation* more than a communication.

However, the manifestation is merely implicit, or potential, in the script; it is not until much later that power is associated with the written word. To conceive of these very ancient performances—some as far back as 25,000 years ago—one has to imagine absolutely non-literate cultures: unliterate is probably the better word. Drawings and sculptings, which in the modern world are associated with "signs" and "symbols" (word-likeness), are in Paleolithic times associated with doings. Thus, the "scripts" I am talking about are patterns of doing, not modes of thinking. Even talking is not originally configurated (words-as-written) but sounded (breath-noise). Ultimately, long after writing was invented, drama arose as a specialized form of scripting. The potential manifestation that had previously been encoded in a pattern of doings was now encoded in a pattern of written words. The dramas of the Greeks, as Aristotle points out, continued to be codes for the transmission of action; but action no longer meant a specific, concrete way of moving/singing—it was understood "abstractly," a movement in the lives of men. Historically speaking, in the West, drama detached itself from doing. Communication replaced manifestation.

From the Renaissance until very recently, concomitant with the rapid extension of literacy, the ancient relationship between doing and script was inverted. In the West the active sense of script was forgotten, entirely displaced by drama; and the doings of a particular production became the way to present a drama in a new way. Thus, the script no longer functioned as a code for transmitting action through time; instead the doings of each production became the code for re-presenting the words-of-the-drama. Maintaining the words intact grew in importance; how they were said, and what gestures accompanied them, was a matter of individual choice, and of lesser importance.

Thus, we are accustomed to concentrating our attention on a specialized kind of script called drama. But the avant-garde in the West, and traditional theatres elsewhere, refocuses attention on the doing-aspects of script, and beyond script altogether to "theatre" and "performance." Before attempting a concrete, taxonomical presentation of these words I must acknowledge the difficulty of using them. Words like "script," "drama," "theatre" and "performance" are loaded, and none have neutral synonyms. My choice is either to invent new words, which no one will pay attention to, or to use the old words in as precise a manner as I can, hoping to introduce regions of restrictive meaning into the more general areas covered by these words. To help in this task of definition/classification I offer a model of concentric, overlapping circles; a set of four discs with the largest on the bottom, each of the others resting on the one immediately larger than itself.

The increase in size is meant literally, in time/space, and conceptually in the idea-area covered. Generally speaking, though not in every case, the larger disc contains all those smaller than itself.

Drama: the smallest, most intense (heated-up) circle. A written narrative text, score, scenario, instruction, plan or map. The drama can be taken from place to place or time to time independent of the person who carries it.

Script: all that can be transmitted from time to time and place to place; the basic code of the event. The script is transmitted person to person and the transmitter is not a mere messenger; the transmitter of the script must know the script and be able to teach it to others.

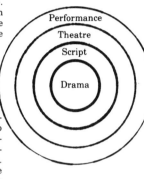

Theatre: the event enacted by a specific group of performers; what actually occurs to the performers during a production. The theatre is concrete and immediate. Usually the theatre is the response of the performers to the drama and/or script; the manifestation or representation of the drama and/or script.

Performance: the broadest, most ill-defined disc. The whole constellation of events, most of them passing unnoticed, that takes place in both performers and audience from the time the first spectator enters the field of the performance—the precinct where the theatre takes place—to the time the last spectator leaves.

Drama is the domain of the author, composer, scenarist; script is the domain of the teacher, guru, shaman, master; theatre is the domain of the performers; performance is the domain of the audience. Clearly, in many situations, the author is also the guru and the performer; in some situations the performer is also the audience. The boundary between the performance and everyday life is arbitrary; different cultures mark the boundaries differently. Preparations may begin anywhere from minutes before a performance (an improvised guerrilla theatre action) to years before (the Hevehe cycle play of the Orokolo). However, wherever the boundaries are set, it is within the broad region of performance that theatre takes place; at the center of the theatre is the script, sometimes the drama. Just as drama may be thought of as a specialized kind of script, so theatre can be considered a specialized kind of performance. Thus another model can be generated, one of oppositional pairs: Drama/Script——Theatre/ Performance. Cultures which emphasize the dyad drama-script deemphasize theatre-performance; and vice-versa. In general terms, Asian, Oceanic and African cultures emphasize theatre-performance and Western cultures emphasize drama-script. However, a strong Western influence is felt in non-Western nations; and an equally strong non-Western influence is felt within the Western avant-garde.

But however de-emphasized the script is in relative terms, it still dominates Western performances, even in the avant-garde. What is happening is an increasing attention to the *seams* that apparently weld each disc to the others. Illusionistic theatre, or mimetic theatre, is based on hiding the seams joining drama to script to theatre to performance. Stanislavsky goes so far as to deny the existence of the performance altogether; that is the import of his famous assertion that going to the theatre ought to be like visiting the Prozorof household, with the fourth-wall removed. Many years, and much theatrical activity, has intervened between Stanislavsky's assertion and now; at least since Meyerhold and Vakhtangov the performance has been admitted to consciousness. Brecht concentrated his work on exposing the seam between the theatre and the script: his *V-effekt* is a device revealing the script as of a different conceptual order than the theatre event in which it is contained. Currently persons like Richard Foreman and Robert Wilson explore the disjunctions between script and drama.

I don't know why the seams, which traditionally have held the four elements together, are now being explored in ways that break them apart. It directs the attention of the audience not to the center of any event but to those structural welds where the presumed single event can be broken into disparate elements. Instead of being absorbed into the event the spectator is given the chance to observe the points where the event is "weak" and disjunctive. This breaking apart is analogous to the process of de-figuration and abstraction that happened earlier in painting, and which has left a permanent mark on all the arts.

In rehearsing Sam Shepard's *The Tooth of Crime,* The Performance Group opened the seam between performance and theatre. Ultimately these were experienced by performers and spectators alike as *separate systems*. The opening of the performance-theatre seam was facilitated by an environment that not only is dominated by a central construction that makes it impossible for a spectator to see everything from a single vantage, but which also requires the scenes to move from place to place, audience following; as this movement became orchestrated during months of rehearsal and performance, the Performing Garage environment clearly developed two sides, a public side and a private side. This division into spatial-emotional areas strongly contributed to opening the performance-theatre seam. In a condensed and reduced way, TPG's *Tooth* was like a medieval pageant play; the actual progression of events in space matched the awakening of consciousness on the part of the drama's protagonist, Hoss.

The concentration on the seam between performance and theatre, the inclusion of the audience in the performance as the major collective architect of the action, stems partly from my lack of interest as a director in character work. I make no attempt to harmonize the feelings of the performers with the alleged feelings of the characters; I try not to question performers about what they are feeling. I am more interested in patterns of movement, arrangements of bodies, "iconography," sonics and the flow of audience throughout the environment. The criteria I use for evoking, guiding and selecting patterns are complicated; but the "demands" of the drama are of low priority.

It is this that Shepard doubtlessly senses. He hasn't seen TPG's *Tooth*. He saw one rehearsal in Vancouver and helped us considerably then by giving a rendition of speaking-style he wanted in the Hoss-Crow fight. It is to his credit, and a testimony to the faith he has in his drama, that he never interfered with our work. He and I have had a reasonably extensive correspondence about *Tooth;* most of it is about basic tones, and very little about specific staging. In May, 1973, Shepard wrote:

> I can see from the reviews, eyewitness accounts from some of my friends and your public writings [. . .] that the production is far from what I had in mind. But I never expected it to be any different and I don't see why you should expect my vision of the play to change. [. . .] I've laid myself open to every kind of production for my plays in the hope of finding a situation where they'll come to life in the way I vision them. Out of all these hundreds of productions, I've seen maybe five that worked. [. . .] For me, the reason a play is written is because a writer receives a vision which can't be translated in any other way but a play. It's not a novel or a poem or a short story or a movie but a play. It seems to me that the reason someone wants to put that play together in a production is because they are pulled to its vision. If that's true then it seems they should respect the form that vision takes place in and not merely extrapolate its language and invent another form which isn't the play. It may be interesting theatre but it's not the play and it can never be the play. [. . .] I'm sure that if you attempt other plays by living writers you're going to run into the same situation. It's a question you should really look into rather than sweep it (sic) aside as being old-fashioned or even unimportant.

TPG's production results in a dissociation between drama-script and theatre-performance, as well as a further dissociation between theatre and performance. The model can be re-drawn into utterly discrete units, each of which may be in opposition to one or more of the others. (See page 42.) It is this process of dissociation, and its consequent tensions, ambivalencies and novel combinations that characterizes the contemporary avant-garde, including The New Dance.

A side issue of importance raised by Shepard in his May letter is what to do with the author's "vision"? To what degree must the drama determine the script, theatre and performance? The issue has mainly been avoided over the last 15 years because those most deeply into dissociating elements have either written their own dramas (Foreman, Wilson), brought dramatists into their theatres and controlled their

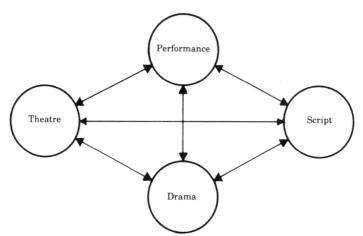

visions (Chaikin-van Itallie, Brook-Hughes), or worked from existing public domain material that has been restructured according to need (TPG, Polish Laboratory Theatre). But I, for one, want to work with writers, and must therefore find a way of dealing with their "vision."

I assume that plays "present" themselves to their authors as scenes, that this scening is coexistent with playwriting. (Beckett, with his ear for music and sense of wordness, may be an exception; he may not "see" his plays but "hear" them.) The act of playwriting is a translation of this internal scening into dialogue + stage directions. The stage directions are vestiges and/or amplifications of the internal scening. The whole scening process is, in my view, a scaffold that is best dismantled entirely once the play takes shape as dialogue. This was the Classical and Elizabethan convention; I think the survival of many of those plays is due to the fact that later generations have been spared stage directions and character descriptions. The work of those doing the production is to re-scene the play not as the writer might have envisioned it but as immediate circumstances reveal it. Generally, it is not possible to do the play in the author's vision anyway. Either that vision is unknown, as with most pre-modern writers; or the play is produced in a culture outside that of origin; or the conventions and architecture of the theatre make it impossible. Re-scening is inevitable because the socio-cultural matrix of the play-as-visioned soon changes. The drama is, by definition, that which can be passed on through successive socio-cultural transformations. The original vision is tied to the original matrix, and decays with it. I don't think that even the first production of a drama is privileged in this regard—unless the author stages the play himself.

In TPG's *Tooth,* the environment developed into two interrelated spaces, each of which sponsored a special kind of interaction between performers and spectators. The private side featured intimacy, one-to-one scenes, sharply focused and defined lighting areas, soft-speaking, direct contact between performers and spectators (ad-libs and asides). The public side featured big numbers, agonistic stances, bright, general lighting, formal inclusion of the audience in a contest. The kinetic activity of the audience encourages a detachment, a critical attitude. Each spectator is self-conscious enough to move to where the action is, station himself in an advantageous position to see, and decide what his relationship to the theatre is to be. Often enough people change places in mid-scene. This is not participation in the *Dionysus* sense. It is each audience educating itself concerning the difference between performance and theatre. The theatre event they see remains the same regardless of what perspective spectators adapt. Instead of being in a predetermined relationship to the theatre event, each spectator determines this relationship point by point. The determination is not thought out, but usually automatic. *And in moving, the spectator discovers his attitude regarding the play.* He learns that he controls the performance, even if the performers control the theatre. As every member of TPG can testify, performances of *Tooth* vary widely, much more so than performances of *Commune*. This is so because the performance control aspect of the audience is activated in *Tooth*. The mood of the audience—as directly conveyed in how they move, position themselves and react to scenes (and sometimes these signals are communicated very subtly) firmly controls the entire production.

Pirandello's plays are an attempt to integrate into the dramatic mode dissociations between drama and script. Genet's *The Maids* is a deeper elaboration of this theme. The action of *The Maids* is the drama, and the fantasy-life of the characters is the script. Claire/Madame and Solange/Claire ultimately convert their script into the drama, playing out once-and-for-all the murder of Madame. Genet turns the screw an extra time in Solange's epilogue where she confesses that the whole enterprise has been a drama; and the example itself is suspicious because the riddle is contained in Genet's drama and hardly needs a performance to explicate it.

In Bali, theatre and drama are fixed and the script floats in relation to them. The minute gestures of a trance dance—the movement of fingers and hands, the way a torso is held and bent, the facial expression (or lack of it, the famous Balinese "away" look)—are fixed; so is the traditional story or story fragment: often a contest between good and bad demons or a fragment from the Ramayana epic. But how long the theatrical gestures will be performed; how many repetitions of cycles of movement; what permutations or new combinations occur— these things are unknown, and depend on the "power" of the trance. In Carnatic music, the progression of the raga is known; this progression is the "drama" of the music. But how a specific performer or group will proceed from one phase or note of the raga to the next, and how the progression will be organized (how many repetitions, sequences, speed, volume) are not known in advance, not even by the performer: the script evolves on the spot out of a relationship between the drama (raga) and the theatre (particular skills of the specific performer). In both the Balinese and Indian examples, the Western distinction between "author" and "performer" does not apply. Dancer and musician did not author the trance dance or the raga; neither are they conforming to an exact prior script or drama. Most Western improvisatory theatre is *not* a version of Asian theatre but a means by which the performers function as dramatists, ultimately arriving at a very orthodox form that is repeated night after night with little or no immediate invention or permutation.

To summarize thus far: the drama is what the writer writes; the script is the interior map of a particular production; the theatre is the specific set of gestures performed by the performers in any given performance; the performance is the whole event, including audience and performers (technicians too, anyone who is there). It is hard to define "performance" because the boundaries separating it on the one side from the theatre and on the other from everyday life are arbitrary. For example, in Vancouver TPG did two "real time" performances of *Commune* in which audiences were invited to come to the theatre at the same time that the performers did. About 12 people showed up at 6 P.M., watched the Group clean up, set props, get into costume, do warm-ups, establish the box office, admit the regular audience, do the play, chat with spectators, remove costumes, clean up and shut the theatre. Two different performances occurred simultaneously those nights: one for the "real time" audience and one for the "regular" audience; for the "real time" audience the "regular" audience was part of the show, as were a number of events not normally included in the production of *Commune.*

My work in this area has been an attempt to make both performers and audiences aware of the overlapping but conceptually distinct realities of drama, script, theatre and performance. Also to make myself more aware and definite. Others have gone further than I in the process of dissociating one reality from another, but usually at the expense of one system or another. I want to find ways of keeping three or all four in tension. I believe that none has precedence over the others.

In many rural areas, especially in Asia and Africa, what is important is the performance: the whole panoply of events at the center of which is theatre, or maybe a drama. (I distinguish a "performance" from a simple "gathering," such as for a party, by the presence in a performance of a theatrical event—something planned and designed for presentation.) Party games are proto-theatrical but not sufficient to convert a party into a performance. On the other hand, the dancing of a Kathakali sequence by a professional troupe at an Indian wedding is enough to make the wedding-gathering into a performance. I know these distinctions are arbitrary. Taxonomy in a social science is based on structures that tend to blend into each other on a continuum rather than exist as compartments of "species" of events. Thus, the exact point at which a boundary is set marking one structure off from another is arbitrary. However, the center of each kind of structure is very different from the center of any other.

I attended a pig-kill, dance and meat-exchange at Kurumugl in the Highlands of Eastern New Guinea. Although the dancers exhibit considerable skills, and the music is vigorous, no one is much interested in appreciating these as such. At one time or another everyone is dancing/singing; the move from the audience realm to the performer realm is an easy one. This ease of movement between these two realms is one of the characteristics of performance as distinct from theatre or drama where knowing particular techniques in an exact sequence/context makes movement between realms difficult. The climatic event of the two-day celebration at Kurumugl was the invasion of the "council grounds"[8] by one group in order to get meat being given to them by another group. This invasion took four hours during which armed dancers from both groups confronted each other. The men charged at each other, raising their spears and arrows as if to throw or shoot. Then, they began a rapid, kicking from the knee, dancing; a running in place accompanied by fierce shouting and whooping. With each charge by the invading (guest) group, the resisting (host) group retreated a few yards. Ultimately the invaders arrived at the center of the council grounds where the women and some men had assembled a huge, tangled pile of meat 75 feet in diameter, three feet deep. After a half-hour of running in a big circle around the meat, shouting in high-pitched tones in which guests and hosts fused into one unit of about 1,200 men, orations began. Men climbed into the pile of heads, torsos, flanks, legs, foreparts of pig and cow and tugged at specific morsels, declaiming and exhibiting the meat. In the Highlands meat is rare and valuable; so much meat in one place is a collection of terrific wealth, a focus of ecstatic energy. To one side were three white goats, still living, tethered to a small tree. These were not slaughtered; I don't know what happened to them. Slowly the meat was distributed; small groups departed for their home villages singing and carrying meat shoulder high on stretchers made from bamboo, vines and leaves.

Such a celebration as that at Kurumugl is pure performance. There is no drama; the script is vague and shifting; no one cares much about the quality of the theatrical gesturing. But there are definite dance steps and shouts, a known style of singing, an over-all pattern consisting of accepted sequences of events. The dancing, mock-battling, circle dance, orating, distributing of meat and recessional constitute, in Erving Goffman's rich phrase, a way in which the Highlanders "perform their realities."

Joan MacIntosh and I attended on January 15–16, 1972, a Thovil ceremony in Koratota, a Sri Lankan village about an hour's drive from Colombo. A. J. Gunawardana took us there. The occasion was the fulfillment of an oath made six months before when an outbreak of chicken pox passed harmlessly. The performance took more than 30 hours and I saw about 14 hours of it. It consisted of dances, songs, chants, ritual observances, partying, gambling, clowning and story-telling. These occurred sequentially rather than simultaneously. The main performing area was an oval about 80 feet by 60 feet, rising slightly to a 15-foot-high roofed shed enclosed on three sides containing an altar; five other altars scattered around the oval; a chair with ritual implements (flowers, incense, cup); and other decorations. The audience varied from less than 50 to more than 400 during the late-night trance dance. Some of the performers—such as the trance dancer, the musicians and some of the other dancers—were professionals; others were local people. Appeals for money were interspersed with the performance. As Westerners and outsiders we were given a special place to view the performance, inside the oval, almost part of the show. (As indeed we were, openly for the village children, and more discreetly for the adults.)

The portion of the Thovil I saw had five parts: (1) arrival and set up, (2) events before supper, (3) main dances and events until midnight, (4) intermission, side-events, slow-down until 4:25, (5) an hour-long trance dance. Gunawardana told me that the events of the following day would include more singing and dancing, and closing ceremonies. Each part of the Thovil had theatrical elements embedded in a performance matrix. There was no drama, and the script was very loose, adjusting itself for example to our arrival. Many of the early dances were danced to us, directly in front of our mat; the officiating priest took time to explain to us what he was doing. These were alterations of the script. The crowd's appreciation was divided between simply enjoying each other, a good-time-at-a-party feeling, and evaluating the quality of the dancers. At one point a local obvious amateur began dancing. No one stopped him or derided him, but he was studiously ignored, which in Sri Lanka society is a distinct put-down. He was drunk or I'm sure he would have ended his dance even more abruptly than he did. On the other hand, a very old man who, I was told, was the village's chief "devil dancer" executed a few steps and sang a chant to the full appreciation of a very quiet crowd. The old man had no skills in the usual theatrical sense; he was thought to have "power," and was deeply respected, even feared, for this. His presence, not his theatrical ability, got attention.

Preparations for the trance dance began a little before 4 A.M. The Thovil had come almost to a complete halt before then. The musicians were drunk, most of the village was asleep except for about a dozen men who were gambling in a shelter about 50 feet from the oval. The trance dancer was a young medical technician from Colombo and we had driven to Koratota with him. On our way out I questioned him:

How did you become a trance dancer?
My teacher taught me.
Why do you do it?
I like it. I earn extra money.
Does your dancing conflict with the 'scientific ideas' of your work?
No. Why should it?

The preparations for the trance dance are very simple. The man sits in a chair behind the shelter containing the main altar. He looks at himself in a hand-mirror. Two assistants wrap his torso with a bandagelike cloth, very stiffly. (This is very much how young trance dancing girls are wrapped in Bali.) When he is firmly wrapped, incense is lit, and he takes very deep draughts of it, holding the incense tray directly below his nose. Finally, he puts on his headdress, which is a turbanlike thing. After about 20 minutes his assistants lift him from the chair and place him at the edge of the oval. A large crowd of about 400 has gathered, and they are very quiet. The musicians—two drummers, a flute player, and several singers—are sitting on their mats.

Very suddenly the drums begin a very loud, very fast beat and the dancer leaps to the center of the oval. I say *leaps*—the dance is incredibly athletic and consists of several parts. Some of it is sheer running up and down and around the oval. At another time the dancer lifts his knees very high, almost to his chest. The most spectacular part of the dance involves "fire-throwing." One of his assistants pursues him carrying a large pot of "fire dust," some kind of highly inflammable resin. The dancer is carrying one, sometimes two, kerosene soaked burning torches. Without looking at the assistant, the dancer reaches into the pot, takes a fistful of fire dust, hurls it into the air, and ignites it. The flash explosion, and whoosh noise, generates exciting heat, light, sound.

For more than an hour—until 5:35—the trance dancer never broke rhythm; he never rested. The trance dances of Bali are often quiet, meditative affairs (the exception being the Barong kris-dance). But this Thovil was fierce. Finally, his two assistants enter the oval, the drumming stops and they wrestle the dancer to the ground, unclenching his fists to pry the torches from him. It is an actual fight to get him to stop dancing. Then, as suddenly as he started, he relaxes; he is not even breathing heavily. He kneels, says a prayer. He is absolutely relaxed, alert, not tired. Not even sweating. As soon as the dance ends people disperse. The next morning we drive back to Colombo.

The Thovil is pure theatre. There is no drama, little script. There are certain steps to be done but these may be varied according to the strength of the possession. The thing the crowd loves most is the fire-throwing. They appreciate that with ooh's and ahh's; they are thrilled by the dancer's stamina and energy. The spectators do not participate in the event, they simply watch; the dancer is totally oblivious to them. He is even, apparently, oblivious to his own assistants—though he has enough presence of mind to reach into the fire dust pot. But when the time comes to end the dance he must be wrestled out of trance. This is not a gradual process, as going into trance seems to be; but a sudden re-emergence, a letting go of the trance and a falling directly into full, relaxed ordinary consciousness. It is my belief that Western culture is generally unable to enjoy trance dancing because of our insistence on drama and scripts. However, in black and Pentecostal churches—revivals, healing, chants and responses, talking in tongues, snake-charming and the like—there is ample evidence that trance is a viable mode for theatre in the West, if we so choose.

Structurally, the Thovil presents a complicated picture. Entertainment, ritual, athletics, partying, gambling, spirit-possession are all mixed. There is no exact progression of events, and yet there is a special kind of building toward the trance dance that joins the darkest, stillest hour of night to dawn. What holds the Thovil together is a sequence of punctuations—ritual chants, further decoration of the performance oval, expected dances and farces—that keep up the people's interest. Between these punctuations the space/time is open, and a variety of events transpire. Men move from gambling to watching dances and back; alcohol is dispensed; children play games to the side of the oval and then return for the farces; women watch, go away to prepare meals or nurse infants, then return. Even the musicians wander in and out so that sometimes the full orchestra is playing and sometimes only a single drummer.

Drama is tight, verbal, narrative; it allows for little improvisation; it exists as a code independent of any individual transmitter; it is a text. A script is either a traditional plan for a theatre event such as the Koratotan Thovil or the Kurumugl pig-kill, or it is developed during rehearsals to suit a specific text as in orthodox Western theatre. The theatre is the visible/sonic set of events consisting either of well-known components, as in Bali, or of a score invented during rehearsal, as in the West. To some degree the theatre is the visible aspect of the script, the exterior topography of an interior map. But script and theatre do not necessarily relate in this way; a script may be the cause of the theatre, and the theatre may influence the shape of a script. Performance is the widest possible circle of events condensing around theatre. The audience is the dominant element of any performance.

Drama, script, theatre and performance need not all exist for any given event. But when they do, they enclose one another, overlap, interpenetrate, simultaneously and redundantly stimulating and using every channel of communication. This kind of behavior eventuates in many modes, even art.

Part II

I began this essay by describing some Paleolithic caves; I indicated that ancient humans associated themselves with animals, connecting hunting with the need to replenish the hunted species. A parallel connection apparently was made between human and animal fertility; and initiation rites, which are closely associated with human fertility, were also often totemistic/animist in their essence and practice. I now want to return to those themes and elaborate on them in a direction that will link up to what has thus far been the main subject of my essay.

More than in the first part of my essay I caution now against accepting my remarks as definite. About performing I know something, having made many careful observations; about playing in man and some other primates I know very little, and hardly anything from observation. I present my speculations in the spirit of those 16th-century cartographers who drew hilarious maps of the New World. All succeeding maps were revisions, not rejections, of those first shapes drawn on vellum: the New World existed, it had a definite shape, it remained to measure it accurately.

One can only speculate, and many have, about the origins, structure and functions of totemism and animism. What is very clear is that men identify themselves with animals, dress in animal skins and heads and develop specific ceremonies and observations to keep intact links connecting animal species to humans. Such phenomena are not new. In the Hall of Hieroglyphs at Pech-Merle "is the earliest known representation of the fusion of a human being with an animal"—a bird-headed woman apparently in some dancing attitude.[9] Also "the celebrated 'Dancing Sorcerer' or 'Reindeer Shaman' of Trois Frères wears the antlers of a stag, an owl mask, wolf ears, bear paws and a horse-tail, but is otherwise a nude human male dancing, perhaps wearing streaks of body paint."[10] La Barre (1972) emphasizes that shamanistic animal cults can be traced from contemporary subarctic cultures back to the Stone Age. "Similarities in European Paleolithic and Asiatic Paleosiberian shamanism, indeed, are present even down to arbitrary details. For example, the Old Stone Age had both bird and reindeer shamans quite like those of Paleosiberian tribes. [. . .] The reindeer shaman shows an extraordinary continuity in Europe down to proto-historic and modern ethnic times; the bird shaman can be traced from Magdalenian to modern Siberian times."[11] There is hard evidence about dancing ceremonies accompanying the visual representations in the paleolithic caves. "Near the final chamber [of the cavern of Le Tuc d'Audoubert], which contains the high relief of two bison, footprints of the Magdalenian age have been preserved beneath a layer of crystalline lime deposit."[12] These are interpreted as footprints of dancers.

If ancient man drew and carved beings who combined the physical attributes of humans and animals can we not assume that actual costumes were created; and if the artistic representations on the cave walls are of dances can we not assume that these men danced? We don't know the structure of these dances, except as we may extrapolate from historic times. The dances were probably both evocations of animal spirits and emulations of animal movements. The ancient hunters who felt such a dependency on the animal world knew also of similarities between that world and their own. Generally those similarities extended animal nature into the realm of human life. Always it is the human who is adorned, who shows how he is like an animal. No animal dances wearing human skin, or puts over its head the face of a man. But there are connections I believe we can make without falling into the error of anthropomorphism.

Jane van Lawick-Goodall describes this scene in her masterful study of chimpanzee life in the wild:

> At about noon the first heavy drops of rain began to fall. The chimpanzees climbed out of the tree and one after the other plodded up the steep grassy slope toward the open ridge at the top. There were seven adult males in the group [. . .] several females, and a few youngsters. As they reached the ridge the chimpanzees paused. At that moment the storm broke. The rain was torrential, and the sudden clap of thunder, right overhead, made me jump. As if this were a signal, one of the big males stood upright and as he swayed and swaggered rhythmically from foot to foot I could just hear the rising crescendo of his pant-hoots above the beating of the rain. Then he charged flat-out down the slope toward the trees he had just left. He ran some thirty yards, and then, swinging around the trunk of a small tree to break his headlong rush, leaped into the low branches and sat motionless.

> Almost at once two other males charged after him. One broke off a low branch from a tree as he ran and brandished it in the air before hurling it ahead of him. The other, as he reached the end of his run, stood upright and rhythmically swayed the branches of a tree back and forth before seizing a huge branch and dragging it farther down the slope. A fourth male, as he too charged, leaped into a tree and, almost without breaking his speed, tore off a large branch, leaped with it to the ground, and continued down the slope. As the last two males called and charged down, so the one who had started the whole performance climbed from his tree and began plodding up the slope again. The others, who had also climbed into trees near the bottom of the slope, followed suit. When they reached the ridge, they started charging down all over again, one after the other, with equal vigor.

> The females and youngsters had climbed into trees near

the top of the ridge as soon as the displays had begun, and
there they remained watching throughout the whole
performance. As the males charged down and plodded back
up, so the rain fell harder, jagged forks or brilliant flares of
lightning lit the leaden sky, and the crashing of the
thunder seemed to shake the very mountains.

My enthusiasm was not merely scientific as I watched,
enthralled, from my grandstand seat on the opposite side of
the narrow ravine, sheltering under a plastic sheet. [. . .] I
could only watch, and marvel at the magnificence of those
splendid creatures. With a display of strength and vigor
such as this, primitive man himself might have challenged
the elements.[13]

But don't confuse "primitive man" with chimps. The chimps are not
forerunners of man—chimps have been around as long or longer than
man. Possibly both man and chimp have a common ancestor, the
evolutionary tree branching some millions of years ago; since then
homo sapiens has developed in one way, *pan troglodytes* in another.
Thus, chimp performance is not a prototype of human performance,
but a parallel. As such it is even more interesting than as a prototype.
A prototype tells us nothing more than that human performing has
antecedents; a parallel means that another species, developing in its
own track, is engaged in deliberate, conscious, chosen activity that
can best be described as "performing." If this is true, so-called "aesthetics" is not the monopoly of humans; and theories about aesthetics
that talk about art as a "luxury," or a function of "leisure," are put
into question. Instead one ought to seek for the *survival value* of performance; what purpose does it serve in the behavior scheme of
chimps and man, and possibly other species too? It is necessary for the
reader to study some of the literature on primate behavior to understand that I am not using words like "deliberate," "conscious," "chosen" and "survival value" in any but the strict sense.

Examples abound of "animal rituals"[14] or "playing," which, viewed
from a human perspective, appear to be performances. But these patterns of instinctive behavior are automatic and cannot be thought of
as performance in the sense that human and chimpanzee displays are.
However, even events as regulated by instinct as the "triumph dance
of geese," or the offering of the throat by a vanquished wolf to the
victor, can indicate the bio-antiquity of behavior in which status,
territory and sexual priorities are mediated by rituals rather than by
direct combat which, in most cases, would severely deplete at least the
male population of many species. In the opinion of Lorenz (1967),
Tinbergen (1965) and other ethologists, an instinctive animal ritual is
an alternative to violent behavior; the rituals developed—were
"selected" evolutionarily speaking—because those individuals within
a species that had the rituals bred in survived. In time, entire species

instinctively respond to stimuli that evoke the rituals. In my terms, performance is something else, more conscious, and probably belongs only to a few primates, including man. The rituals of lower animals are indeed prototypes for primate performances. What humans do consciously, by choice, lower animals do automatically; the displaying peacock is not "self-conscious" in the way an adolescent male human is on Saturday night. The behavior of peacock and boy may be structurally identical; but self-consciousness and the ability to change behavior according to self-consciousness (and not just outside stimulation) sets animal ritual off from primate and human performance.

However, before examining some of the conscious behavior I call performance, I think it is necessary to scan the more ancient patterns of ritual behavior. These patterns involve display, fight-flight, turf and mating. Many animals put on shows in order to demonstrate status, or to claim and defend territory, or to prepare for mating; these displays are aggressive. When challenged, the animal will either continue the display, transform it into a submissive gesture, flee or fight. According to Lorenz, it was Julian Huxley who first called this kind of behavior "ritual."

> [Huxley] discovered the remarkable fact that certain movement patterns lose, in the course of phylogeny, their original specific function and become purely "symbolic" ceremonies. He called this process ritualization and used this term without quotation marks; in other words, he equated the cultural processes leading to the development of human rites with the phylogenetic processes giving rise to such remarkable "ceremonies" in animals. From a purely functional point of view this equation is justified, even bearing in mind the difference between the cultural and phylogenetic processes.[15] [. . .] The triple function of suppressing fighting within the group, of holding the group together and of setting it off, as an independent entity, against other, similar units, is performed by culturally developed ritual in so strictly analogous a manner as to merit deep consideration.[16]

Ritualized behavior extends across the entire range of human action; but performance is a particularly heated arena of ritual, and theatre, script and drama are heated and compact areas of performance. However, something else is involved in performance, and this is *play*. Play also occurs in many species, but nowhere is it so extensive, nowhere does it permeate so many activities, as in human beings. This is only relatively less true of chimpanzees, and so on down the primate ladder. A tentative definition of performance may be: *Ritualized behavior conditioned/permeated by play.* The more "freely" a species plays, the more likely performance, theatre, scripts and drama are to emerge in connection with ritualized behavior. Some animals, such as bees and ants, are rich in ritualized behavior but absolutely bereft of play. No species that I know of plays without also having a wide repertory of ritual behavior. But it is only in the primates that play and ritual coincide, mix, combine; it is only in man and closely related species that the aesthetic sense is consciously developed. The only theory of aesthetics that I can tolerate is one in which aesthetics is considered a specific coordination of play and ritual.

What is play? What are its characteristics, functions and structure? Huizinga defines play as

> a free activity standing quite consciously outside
> "ordinary" life as being "not serious," but at the same time
> absorbing the player intensely and utterly. It is an activity
> connected with no material interest, and no profit can be
> gained by it. It proceeds within its own proper boundaries
> of time and space according to fixed rules and in an orderly
> manner. It promotes the formation of social groupings that
> tend to surround themselves with secrecy and to stress
> their difference from the common world by disguise or
> other means.[17]

Just as the 1908 publication of Van Gennep's *Les rites de passage* introduced a way of classifying and therefore understanding rituals, so the 1938 publication of Huizinga's *Homo Ludens* made it possible to speak of play in a full variety of cultural contexts. Huizinga connects playing to ritual, and stresses the idea of sacred time and place, and of contest *(agon)*. But, unfortunately, he rejects all ideas of function, believing that to discuss the function of play is to deny its unique nature, its "in-itselfness." I agree with Huizinga that play is coexistent with the human condition; but I think an examination of its biological function—its survival value—will add to our understanding of its structure, and point the way to relating primate play behavior to human performances.

Loizos' (1969) review of the functions of play in non-human primates identifies the following:

1.   As schooling or practice for the young;
2.   As an escape from or alternative to stress;
3.   As a source of "vital information" about the environment;
4.   As exercise for muscles involved in agonistic and reproductive behavior.

Loizos rejects these functions as not being either sufficient or necessary; but she maintains nevertheless that play has survival value. Instead of suggesting more functions she extrapolates from observations of primate behavior certain characteristics of play:

> One of [play's] immediately noticeable characteristics is
> that it is behavior that borrows or adopts patterns that
> appear in other contexts where they achieve immediate
> and obvious ends. When these patterns appear in play
> they seem to be divorced from their original motivation

and are qualitatively distinct from the same patterns
appearing in their originally motivated contexts. [. . .] The
[similarity between human and other primate play] lies in
the exaggerated and uneconomical quality of the motor
patterns involved. Regardless of its motivation or its
end-product, this is what all playful activity has in
common; and it is possible that it is all that it has in
common, since causation and function could vary from
species to species.[18]

Loizos recounts that there is an ontogeny of play in chimps. At a very
early age the animals begin "exploration and manipulation"; later
comes "organized play, or play behavior that has a logical sequence to
it"; then comes "bodily activity" in which things like acrobatics are
practiced; and finally there is "social play," such as threatening and
swaggering, which needs playmates to be effective. The addition of
new ways of playing does not eliminate old ways; playing is additive
and all kinds can be combined to form very complex activities.

What is particularly significant about Loizos' observations is that
she says that play apparently derives from "behavior that appeared
earlier phylogenetically and for purposes other than play." In other
words, in her view, play is not rehearsal for life situations but a derivation from life situations, a ritualization and elaboration of "patterns of fight, flight, sexual and eating behavior." And insofar as these
patterns are specific to each species so will play be species-specific.

An interesting sidelight that most probably applies to human behavior as well as chimps is that experiments show that a reduction of
sensory input, particularly deprivation in the mother-infant relationship, "increases the likelihood of repetitive, stereotyped behavior."
And that the "most damaging and least reversible of sources of
stereotyping occurs in primates raised in restricted and, in particular,
socially restricted circumstances."[19] The smaller the cage, the less
interaction, the more the stereotyping. Also, by and large, labora-
tory-reared chimps are more stereotyped in their behavior, less given
to creative play, than chimps in the wild.

Primate studies disclose more interesting aspects of play. According
to Carpenter (1964), social play is a main means by which young
monkeys find their place in the group. The agonistic nature of play
itself establishes a dominance scale; and the practice of play prepares
the young animal for similar kinds of ranking as an adult. Also,
sexual elements make their appearance early in the play of primates.
However, as animals approach adulthood many kinds of play seen in
childhood give way to other activities like social grooming, actual
mating or hunting. It is difficult to say that the swaggering and displays characteristic of maintaining social order in a troop of chimps is
anything but play; whatever the function and consequences of these
displays they are not actual combats. Ultimately, "play between fully
grown adults is rare."[20] Here man is the spectacular exception.

Loizos speculates that "the more rigid the social hierarchy in a primate species, the less likely it is that play will occur among the *adults* of that species."[21] I am inclined to disagree as far as humans are concerned. I see no evidence indicating that democratic, flexible human societies play more than rigid societies. In fact, many rigid societies are given to great ritual displays; and if the connection between play and ritual is accepted the argument from apes to humans does not apply here. What I think can be said is that rigid social systems tend to generate events that concentrate on theatre and performance, on spectacular confirmations of existing social order; and flexible social systems tend towards drama, the expression of individual opinion as definitely set down in words. The impulse toward collectivity, groupness, identification with others leads toward theatre and performance; the impulse toward individuality, personal assertiveness and confrontation between individuals leads toward drama. In certain periods—such as the heydays of Greek and Elizabethan theatre/drama—a palpable tension is felt between two contradictory modes. In the Greek, the tension is between the shamanistic and collective modes of celebration represented directly in the satyr plays and the Eleusinian mysteries and other Orphic ceremonies and a newly emerging rationalism and individuality. In the Elizabethan era, the tension arises between the variety of medieval collectives (guilds, feudalism, Catholicism) and a surging Renaissance spirit of rationalism and individuality (self, cities, Protestantism). I won't elaborate these theories here. But studies of primate behaviors is not incidental to understanding patterns of human culture.

I want to say a few words in favor of another theory of the function of play. It is not a new theory, and my contribution to it is to connect it to the whole field of performance; for I believe play is the factor that literally organizes performance, makes it comprehensible. If the distinction I made earlier between play and ritualized behavior is kept in mind, then clearly play belongs mainly to carnivorous and omnivorous species: hunters. It belongs to species that depend on other species for life, and in fact on stalking, attacking, killing prey. Furthermore, not only among lions, but also with chimps and certainly with man, hunting is group activity. Goodall says that "sometimes it appears that the capture of a prey is almost accidental. [. . .] On other occasions the hunting seems to be a much more deliberate, purposeful activity, and often at such times the different individuals of a chimpanzee group show quite remarkable cooperation—as when different chimpanzees station themselves at the bases of trees offering escape routes to a cornered victim."[22]

Hunting demands not only cooperation but sudden bursts (climaxes) of energy balanced by extended periods of stealth; and a great deal of practice. This is where play comes in—especially creative or "free" play. One of the qualities of play in higher primates in the wild is its improvisational manner, and yet its orderliness: in fact, play is improvisational imposition of order, the making of order out of disorder. And where play is not autistic it is outer-directed, ultimately involving playmates. Although play prepares a young primate for more than hunting, hunting is a particularly full application of play activity. The main difficulty in hunting comes when the prey is intelligent and strong. To hunt baboons effectively chimps must develop strategies that take into account the formidable qualities of the resourceful baboon. Such strategy is actively futurist; the present moment is conditioned by what is to come next.[23] The hunter must know what the prey is going to do, or the hunt will fail. What develops is a game in the true sense. This game involves the hunter, or hunting group, the prey and the environment.

Hunting is inherently, not metaphorically, theatrical/dramatic. A script is necessary in order to develop strategies that culminate in a climactic attack-event; agonistic and cooperative behaviors combine in a complicated way so that a "we and them" mentality is heightened; signals are given that not only express feelings but direct actions; there usually is a leader of the hunt and a single, identifiable prey so that activity focuses toward a swift, violent, climactic confrontation during which the issue is settled; the activity that builds to a climax is itself active (this is the difference between hunting and trapping); after the kill there is a feast with meat being shared according to strict rules (a communion); and after the feast, total relaxation.

One aspect of the functional theory of play needs, I think, special elaboration because of its relationship to theatre. Most animals that play also engage in activities that call for sudden expenditures of kinetic energy: crises. This energy is spent on fighting, fleeing, hunting, mating, maintaining dominance and defining and/or protecting turf. In the energy economy of any animal these crises arise relatively infrequently; but when a crisis arises an animal that cannot command great energy is doomed. An energy "bank" is necessary for survival. This bank has two primary "accounts," erotic and combative; and several secondary (displacement) accounts: display, dominance-submission gestures, marking (deposit of urine or feces, scratches on trees, etc.). But I use the word "bank" only metaphorically. The metabolisms of higher animals are ill-equipped for long-term storage. Instead, play maintains a regular, crisis-oriented expenditure of kinetic energy. In play, energy is spent in behavior that is not only harmless but fun. Kinetic potential is maintained not by being stored but by being spent; and the activity of play is also adaptive in the "creative" ways mentioned earlier. When a crisis arises, the animal is able to meet it by switching play-energy into fight-energy, for example. The problem remains: How do animals (and persons) tell the difference between play and "for real"? Ritualized behavior, including performances, are means of continually testing the boundaries between play and "for real." The "special ordering of time and place" most observers note in play—even animal play—are signals that the behavior taking place within such brackets are "only play." Even so, confusions happen, and placative gestures, or the presence of a referee, are necessary to keep play in hand.

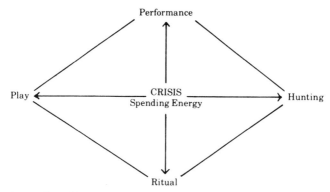

Crisis, the spending of kinetic energy, is the link between performance, hunting, ritual and play. Each gives rise to the others; together they comprise a system through which the animal maintains an ability to speak kinetic energy irregularly, according to needs.

What might be the relationship between hunting and play, hunting and ritual, ritual and play, play and theatre? At the outset of this essay I suggested some connections between Paleolithic cave art and hunting/fertility rituals; also between these rituals and theatre. Now I want to argue from a structural basis what I previously adduced from prehistory. To do so I assume a homology between the behavior of the higher primates and humans.

Recall that Loizos argues that "playful patterns owe their origin to behavior that appeared earlier phylogenetically and for purposes other than play." She describes "some of the ways in which motor patterns may be altered and elaborated upon when transferred to a playful context."

1. The sequence may be *re-ordered.*
2. The individual movements making up the sequence may become *exaggerated.*
3. Certain movements within the sequence may be *repeated* more than they would normally be.
4. The sequence may be broken off altogether by the introduction of irrelevant activities, and resumed later. This could be called *fragmentation.*
5. Movements may be both *exaggerated and repeated.*
6. Individual movements within the sequence may never be completed, and this incomplete element may be repeated many times. This applies equally to both the beginning of a

movement *(the intention element)* and to its ending *(the completion element)*.[24]

These qualities are characteristic of "creative" or "free" play. In such play the animal is not bound by circumstances to stick to a pattern that will yield results. A cat playing with a crumpled-up paper ball may "hunt" it for a few moments and then stop; a chimp may chase a playmate through the tree tops and stop before making contact; humans involve themselves in dozens of momentary, incomplete play activities each hour. In fact, the more advanced the animal, the more likely that each of the six play elements will be used. Behavior is re-combined in new ways, exaggerated, repeated, fragmented, short-circuited. In lower animals, the flow of behavior is mostly one-directional; it is clear whether or not the animal is playing. But, as organisms grow more complicated, the flow becomes two ways. A cat with a captured mouse is "playing" with its prey; it is also completing the hunting process. Chimps will convert play behavior into serious behavior and back again, so that a play chase suddenly erupts into a fight, the fight is resolved by gestures of dominance and submission, this "contract" is "ratified" by mutual grooming and soon enough there is another playful chase.

In humans, the situation is the most complicated. First off, humans hunt other humans with the same diligence that other species reserve for inter-specific warfare. But if human aggression is non-specific, so is human inventiveness. So-called "serious" work in humans is treated playfully, so-called play becomes a very serious matter. Humans can speak truthfully of "war games" and "theatres of war"; and great issues can be carried on the shoulders of athletes or actors who become very important ambassadors indeed. I will not elaborate these ideas here except to insist that Huizinga is wrong when he decries the "deterioration" of play because serious issues get included in it. Serious issues are always involved in play; just as, in humans, play is inextricably combined into all serious work. When through industrial or other means the play elements are taken out of work, work becomes drudgery and less efficient, not more; and when the seriousness is taken away from play, the playing grows sloppy and dull, not fun.

But what is "fun"? Everyone agrees that playing is fun. Certainly this is so for humans, and it appears to be so for animals too. I think it is wrong to say that play is "free," if Loizos is correct in saying that play is a restructuring of other behavior. Also, we know that the "rules of the game," which orders an otherwise chaotic situation, adds to the fun while taking away from freedom. Playful activity constantly generates rules, and although these may change swiftly, there is no play without them. In other words, to use terms developed earlier, all play is "scripted." Thus, "fun" is not being "free from rules." It is something else. Let me again return to the hunt, which I think has particular significance regarding theatre. Hunting is not play when it eventuates in a kill. The actual killing, which is the climax of the hunt, expends more energy more swiftly than anything else in the animal's life (with the possible exception of fleeing from other hunters). In play this actual killing is avoided. If, "by accident," actual killing occurs, the hunt is no longer play. The difference in kinetic energy spent in actually killing and in playing is precisely what is felt as "fun." Fun is surplus kinetic energy. Fun is playing at killing.

Not all playing, but that which is related to hunting behavior. And it is this kind of playing that is also related to that kind of performance that has become drama. Drama, as distinct from performance and theatre, is not universal. It arises often in connection with hunting cultures and/or among peoples who engage in human sacrifice.[25] The dynamics of the relationships between hunting, playing, ritual and drama might be modeled in this way:

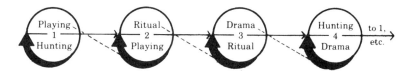

The bottom half of each circle is the "source" of the top half, although there is a significant amount of feedback from the top. The bottom is, in psychological terms, "unconscious" and the top "conscious." The top half of each transaction becomes the bottom half in another transaction. All of the transactions exist in any culture that has one of them. Ecological and social circumstances determine which transaction is dominant in a given culture.

My thesis is that the play behavior of cultures with extensive hunting activity is of a special kind that is adapted from hunting; it also influences hunting. This kind of playing is strategic, futuristic, crisis oriented, violent and/or combative; it has winners and losers, leaders and followers; it employs costumes and/or disguises (often as animals); it has a beginning, middle and end; and its underlying themes are fertility, prowess and animism/totemism. Also this kind of playing emphasizes individual or small-group action and teamwork. In time, playing and hunting behaviors generate secondary symbolic activities called rituals and dramas (scripts). This transformation may be a function of what Lorenz calls "displacement activity"—when two conflicting impulses prevent each other from being activated, a third action results. In animals, displacement activity is often ritualized behavior. In humans, the conflicting impulses may be the wish to hunt people versus love bonds for members of one's own species or culture group. The displacement activity is a ritual or drama in which humans kill humans—but only "in play." Or the hunting of loved ones may become scarring, circumcising, marking: some disfiguration or permanent alteration of the body. Through the ordeal of being prey, the initiated gains the status of hunter.

Like the behaviors they derive from and elaborate, rituals and dramas are violent and crisis oriented; they test individual courage, stamina and ingenuity; participation in them is in itself status-raising; they occur within special times/places; they operate according to rules, traditions, strategies. Agricultural societies develop spectacles organized around proprietory ceremonies whose function it is to entreat the regularity of the seasons, the falling of rain, the warming of sun. Agricultural ceremonies emphasize what I have been calling performance and theatre; hunting rites emphasize script and drama.

I think drama as it developed in ancient China, Japan, Korea, India, America and Greece derived from circumpolar hunting cultures (the remnants of which still exist in Siberia and in pockets throughout the Americas) that also developed shamanism. These cultures very early associated hunting-killing, fertility, animality, curing, spirit-possession and crisis initiation through man-made ordeals. Most significantly, they translated strategic, futuristic hunting behavior into strategic, futuristic language: storytelling. This storytelling was done not merely through words but through songs, chants, dances, drumming and "settings" (such as the caves). Ultimately, drama arose as a playful combination of strategic behaviors.

I don't speak of Africa because I know little about Africa. But if I'm right, then African drama will also be associated with hunting. As for Australian, Melanesian and Polynesian cultures, these deserve special discussion but from what I know, and what I've observed in New Guinea, I think my thesis will hold up. *It is my belief that performance and theatre are universal, but that drama is not.* I think that drama may develop independently of performance and theatre, as a special instance of performance and theatre. (All performance events have "scripts.")

A particular difficulty arises in modern times. The world, which used to be made up of thousands of distinct cultures, is fast becoming global. The change is not merely technological; and the consequences of the change are barely known. In industrialized societies—East and West—"workshop" has developed as a way of recreating, at least temporarily, some of the security and circumstances of small, autonomous cultural groups. The workshop is a way of playing around with reality, a means of examining behavior by re-ordering, exaggerating, fragmenting, recombining and adumbrating it. The workshop is a protected time/space where intra-group relationships may thrive without being threatened by inter-group aggression. In the workshop special gestures arise, definite sub-cultures emerge. The workshop is not restricted to theatre, it is ubiquitous. In science, it is the "experimental method," the laboratory team, the research center, the field-work outpost. In psychotherapy, it is the "group," the rehabilitation center, the "therapeutic community." In living styles, it is the neighborhood, the commune, the collective. (When the workshop is repressive rather than facilitative, as in most "total institutions," asylums, prisons, hospitals and schools, it is the most completely abusive way possible of treating human beings.) The aim of the workshop is to construct an environment where rational, a-rational and irrational behavior exist in balance. Or, to put it biologically, where cortical, brain-stem, motor and instinctive operations exist in balance, and lead to expressive, symbolic, playful, ritualized, "scripted" behavior. It is my opinion that workshops are more important than most people dream of.

And if I may end on a somewhat fanciful note: I associate the workshop environment with those ancient, decorated caves that still give evidence of singing and dancing, people celebrating fertility in risky, sexy, violent, collective, playful ways.

Notes

1. See La Barre (1972), 387-432, and Giedion (1962). These, in turn, are copiously documented.
2. La Barre (1972), 397.
3. The film, *The Hunters* (NYU Film Library), depicts the giraffe hunt of a small group of Kalahari tribesmen.
4. Note that contemporary sexual aesthetics prefer upright (dry) breasts; nor is sheer fecundity a value among us.
5. See Giedion (1962) for many photographs supporting this assertion.
6. Giedion (1962), 190-2.
7. Most probably this teaching was not formal, but through imitation. However, a case could be made that the inaccessibility of the caves indicates an esoteric cult, and that the "secrets" of the cult would be definitely and formally transmitted.
8. A council grounds is a temporary village established by government authorities to facilitate cooperation and exchange rather than combat which had been the principle means of contact among many Highlands groups. Several forms of Asian drama and meditation have been derived from martial training. The dancing at Kurumugl was a direct adaptation of fighting modes; a conscious inhibition of combat which led to a transfer of energy from thrusting shoulders (shooting arrows or throwing spears) to the thighs and legs: the unique, knee-kicking, dancing-running-in-place.
9. Giedion (1962), 284.
10. La Barre (1972), 410.
11. La Barre (1972), 410.

12. Giedion (1962), 284.
13. Goodall (1972), 66-7.
14. Lorenz (1967), 54-103.
15. Lorenz (1967), 54-5.
16. Lorenz (1967), 74.
17. Huizinga (1955), 13.
18. Loizos (1969), 228-9.
19. Loizos (1969), 252. There are cases of autism developing in chimps because of isolated rearing.
20. Loizos (1969), 269.
21. Loizos (1969), 270.
22. Goodall (1972), 205.
23. Hunting is more strategic than farming. Farming involves the simplest strategies only; most of it is hoping that the right combination of rain and sun will bring the crop to fruition. The smaller the farm the less strategy needed; and the activity called "gathering" is the most passive of all.
24. Loizos (1969), 229.
25. I know that traditional scholarship identifies sacrifice with agriculture, particularly agriculture in ancient Egypt and the mid-East; but I think it could also be connected to hunting. Furthermore, I believe that warfare is mainly an adaptation of hunting behavior, and in this sense all human societies are hunting societies, since all make war.

From Ritual
To Theatre and Back:
The Structure/Process of the
Efficacy-Entertainment Dyad

The *kaiko* celebration of the Tsembaga of Highlands New Guinea is a year-long festival culminating in the *konj kaiko*—pig *kaiko*. *Kaiko* means dancing, and the chief entertainments of the celebrations are dances. During 1962 the Tsembaga entertained thirteen other local groups on fifteen occasions.[1] To make sure that the *kaiko* was successful young Tsembaga men were sent to neighboring areas to announce the shows—and to send back messages of delay should a visiting group be late: in that case the entertainments were postponed. The day of dancing begins with the dancers—all men—bathing and adorning themselves. Putting on costumes takes hours. It is an exacting, precise and delicate process. When dressed the dancers assemble on the flattened, stamped-down grounds where they dance both for their own pleasure and as rehearsal in advance of the arrival of their guests. The visitors announce their arrival by singing—they can be heard before they are seen. By this time many spectators have gathered, including both men and women from neighboring villages. These spectators come to watch, and to trade goods. Finally,

> the local dancers retire to a vantage point just above the
> dance ground, where their view of the visitors is
> unimpeded and where they continue singing. The visitors
> approach the gate silently, led by men carrying fight
> packages,[2] swinging their axes as they run back and forth
> in front of their procession in the peculiar crouched
> fighting prance. Just before they reach the gate they are
> met by one or two of those locals who have invited them
> and who now escort them over the gate. Visiting women

> and children follow behind the dancers and join the other
> spectators on the sidelines. There is much embracing as
> the local women and children greet visiting kinfolk. The
> dancing procession charges to the center of the dance
> ground shouting the long, low battle cry and stamping
> their feet, magically treated before their arrival . . . to
> enable them to dance strongly. After they charge back and
> forth across the dance ground several times, repeating the
> stamping in several locations while the crowd cheers in
> admiration of their numbers, their style and the richness of
> their finery, they begin to sing.[3]

The performance is a transformation of combat techniques into entertainment. All the basic moves and sounds—even the charge into the
central space—are adaptations and direct lifts from battle. But the
Tsembaga dance is a dance, and clearly so to everyone present at it.
The dancing is not an isolated phenomenon—as theatre-going in
America still is usually—but a behavior nested in supportive actions.
The entry described takes place late in the afternoon, and just before
dusk the dancing stops and the food which has been piled in the center
of the dancing ground is distributed and eaten. It might be said, literally, that the dancing is *about the food*, for the whole *kaiko* cycle is
about acquiring enough pigs-for-meat to afford the festival.

> The visitors are asked to stop dancing and gather around
> while a presentation speech is made by one of the men
> responsible for the invitation. As he slowly walks around
> and around the food that has been laid out in a number of
> piles, the speechmaker recounts the relations of the two
> groups: their mutual assistance in fighting, their exchange
> of women and wealth, their hospitality to each other in
> times of defeat. . . . When the speech of presentation is
> finished they gather their portions and distribute them to
> those men who came to help them dance, and to their
> women.[4]

After supper the dancing resumes and goes on all night. By dawn
almost everyone has danced with everyone else: and this communal-
ity is a sign of a strong alliance.

With dawn the dancing ground is converted into a market place.
Ornaments, pigs, furs, axes, knives, shells, pigments, tobacco are all
traded or sold (money has come into the Tsembaga's economy).

> The transactions that take place on the dance ground are
> completed on the spot; a man both gives and receives at the
> same time. . . . At the men's houses, however, a different
> kind of exchange takes place. Here men from other places
> give to their kinsmen or trading partners in the local group
> valuables for which they do not receive immediate return.[5]

This orchestrated indebtedness is at the heart of the *kaiko*. At the start of the celebration the hosts owe meat to the guests and the guests owe items of trade to the hosts. In the first part of the *kaiko* the hosts pay meat to the guests; in the second part of the *kaiko* the guests pay the hosts trade items. But neither payment ends in a balance. When the *kaiko* is over the guests owe the hosts meat, and the hosts owe the guests trade items. This symmetrical imbalance guarantees further *kaikos*—continued exchanges between groups. Often trade items are not given back directly, but traded back through third or fourth parties. After the public trading and the gift-giving, some dancing resumes which ends by midmorning. Then everyone goes home.

The *kaiko* entertainments are a ritual display, not simply a doing but a *showing of a doing*. Furthermore, this showing is both actual (=the trading and giving of goods resulting in a new imbalance) and symbolic (=the reaffirmation of alliances made concrete in the debtor-creditor relationship). The entertainment itself is a vehicle for debtors and creditors to exchange places; it is also the occasion for a market; and it is fun. The *kaiko* depends on the accumulation of pigs and goods, and on a willingness to dress up and dance; neither by itself is enough. The dancing is a performance—and appreciated as such, with the audience serving as frequently acerbic critics—but it's also a way of facilitating trade, finding mates, cementing military alliances and reaffirming tribal hierarchies.

> The Tsembaga say that "those who come to our *kaiko* will also come to our fights." This native interpretation of *kaiko* attendance is also given expression by an invited group. Preparations for departure to a *kaiko* at another place include ritual performances similar to those that precede a fight. Fight packages are applied to the heads and hearts of the dancers and *gir* to their feet so that they will dance strongly, just as, during warfare, they are applied so that they will fight strongly.... Dancing is like fighting. The visitors' procession is led by men carrying fight packages, and their entrance upon the dance ground of their hosts is martial. To join a group in dancing is the symbolic expression of willingness to join them in fighting.[6]

The *kaiko* dance display is a cultural version of territorial and status displays in animals; the rituals of the Tsembaga are ethological as well as sociological. They are also ecological: the *kaiko* is a means of organizing the Tsembaga's relationships to their neighbors, to their lands and goods, to their gardens and hunting ranges.

A *kaiko* culminates in the *konj kaiko*. The *kaiko* lasts a year, the *konj kaiko* a few days, usually two. Kaiko years are rare. During the fifty to sixty years ending in 1963 the Tsembaga staged four *kaikos*, with an average of twelve to fifteen years between festivals.[7] The whole cycle is tied to the war/peace rhythm which, in turn, is tied to the fortunes of the pig population. After the *konj kaiko*—whose major event is a mass slaughter of pigs and distribution of meat—a short peace is followed by war, which continues until another *kaiko* cycle begins. The cycle itself lasts for enough years to allow the raising of sufficient pigs to stage a *konj kaiko*. The *konj kaiko* of November 7 and 8, 1963, saw the slaughter of 96 pigs with a total live weight of 15,000 pounds, yielding around 7,500 pounds of meat; eventually about 3,000 people got shares of the kill.[8] What starts in dancing ends in eating; or, to put it in artistic-religious terms, what starts as theatre ends as communion. Perhaps not since classical Athenian festivals and medieval pageants have we in the West used performances as the pivots in systems involving economic, social, political and religious transactions. With the re-advent of holism in contemporary society at least a discussion of such performances becomes practical. It is clear that the *kaiko* dances are not ornaments or pastimes or even "part of the means" of effecting the transactions among the Tsembaga. The dances both symbolize and participate in the process of exchange.

The dances are pivots in a system of transformations which change destructive behavior into constructive alliances. It is no accident that every move, chant and costume of the *kaiko* dances are adapted from combat: a new use is found for this behavior. Quite unconsciously a positive feedback begins: the more splendid the displays of dancing, the stronger the alliances; the stronger the alliances, the more splendid the dancing. Between *kaikos*—but only between them—war is waged; during the cycles there is peace. The exact transformation of combat behavior into performance is at the heart of the *kaiko*. This transformation is identical in structure to that at the heart of Greek theatre (and from the Greeks down throughout all of Western theatre history). Namely, characterization and the presentation of real or possible events—the story, plot or dramatic action worked out among human figures (whether they be called men or gods)—is a transformation of real behavior into symbolic behavior. In fact, transformation is the heart of theatre, and there appear to be only two fundamental kinds of theatrical transformation: (1) the displacement of anti-social, injurious, disruptive behavior by ritualized gesture and display, and (2) the invention of characters who act out fictional events or real events fictionalized by virtue of their being acted out (as in documentary theatre or Roman gladiatorial games). These two kinds of transformation occur together, but in the mix usually one is dominant. Western theatre emphasizes characterization and the enactment of fictions; Melanesian, African and Australian (aborigine) theatre emphasize the displacement of hostile behavior. Forms which balance the two tendencies—Nō, Kathakali, the Balinese Ketchak, medieval moralities, some contemporary avant-garde performances—offer, I think, the best models for the future of the theatre.

Much performing among communal peoples is, like the *kaiko,* part of the overall ecology of a society. The *Engwura* cycle of the Arunta of Australia, as described by Spencer and Gillen in the late 19th century,[9] is an elegant example of how a complicated series of performances expressed and participated in a people's ecology. The fact that the *Engwura* is no longer performed—that the Arunta, culturally speaking, have been exterminated—indicates the incompatibility of wholeness as I am describing it and Western society as it is presently constituted. Insofar as performing groups adapt techniques from the *kaiko* or *Engwura* they are bound to remain outside the "mainstream." But the chief function of the avant-garde is to propose models for change: to remain "in advance." The *Engwura* was an initiation cycle that spanned several years; the last phase consisted of performances staged sporadically over a three-to-four-month period. Each phase of the *Engwura* took place only when several conditions meshed: enough young men of a certain age gathered in one place to be initiated; enough older men willing to lead the ceremonies (particularly important in a non-literate culture); enough food to support celebration. Then the sacred implements and sacred grounds were prepared painstakingly and according to tradition. Finally, there had to be peace among neighboring tribes—but the announcement of a forthcoming *Engwura* was sometimes enough to guarantee a peace.

The daily rhythm recapitulated the monthly rhythm: performance spaces were cleared, implements repaired and laid out, body decorations applied, food cooked. Each performance day saw not one but several performances, with rest and preparations between each. Each performance lasted on an average ten minutes, and was characteristically a dance accompanied by drumming and chanting. Then the performers rested for about two hours; then preparations for the next performance began, and these preparations took about two hours.[10]

The whole cycle recapitulates the life cycle of the Arunta male; and during his life he could expect to play roles co-existent with his status in society: initiate, participant, leader or onlooker. Thus on each day performers enacted condensed and concentrated versions of their lives; and the three-to-four-month culminating series of performances also replicated the life cycle. The whole cycle was, in fact, an important—perhaps the most important—set of events in an Arunta life.[11] Each phase of the cycle was a replication (either an extension or a concentration) of every other phase.

The subject matter of each brief dance-drama was life events of mythical Dreamtime beings who populated the world "in the beginning."[12] These mythic events were very important to the Arunta and constituted for them a history and, since each Dreamtime event was connected to specific places and landmarks, a geography.[13] The rituals are a concrete symbolization and reenactment of Dreamtime events, and to this extent the *Engwura* is familiar to us: it is not unlike our own drama except that we accept the reactualization of past events only as a convention. The Arunta, like the orthodox Catholic taking the Eucharist, accepted the manifestation of Dreamtime events as actual.

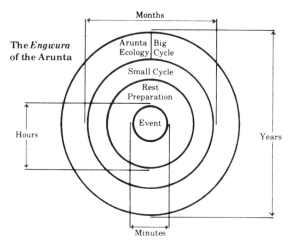

The overall structure of the *Engwura* is analogic, while its interior structure is dramatic. The two structures are integrated because the Arunta believed concretely in the Dreamtime and experienced their own lives as divided between "ordinary" and "super-ordinary" realities. They experienced an interaction between these realities, and *Engwura* performers were the navel, or link, or point-of-time-and-place where the two realities meshed.

I saw an ecological ritual similar to the *konj kaiko* (but much less inclusive than the *Engwura*) in March, 1972, at Kurumugl in the Eastern Highlands of New Guinea.[14] Surrounding the performance of the *kaiko* is no special self-conciousness—that is, the ritual functions without the Tsembaga being explicitly aware of its functions; and aside from commendatory or critical comments on the dancing no aesthetic judgments are passed. In other words there are neither performance theorists nor critics among the Tsembaga. At Kurumugl the people know what the ritual does and why it was established—to inhibit warfare among feuding groups. The ritual at Kurumugl is already traveling along the continuum toward theatre in the modern sense. Knowing what the ritual does is a very important step in the development of theatre from ritual.

It's my purpose to outline a process through which theatre develops from ritual; and also to suggest that in some circumstances ritual develops from theatre. I think this process ought to be documented from contemporary or near-contemporary sources because so often the jump from ritual to theatre is assumed, or attributed to ancient events the evidence for which is suspect.[15]

Unlike the *kaiko* dancing grounds, the "council grounds" (as they are called) at Kurumugl are near no regular village. The colonial Australian government set them up as a place where former enemies assemble to *sing-sing* (pidgin for drama-music-dance). The difference between the Tsembaga and the people at Kurumugl is that the *kaiko* brought together traditional allies while the Kurumugl *sing-sing* assembles traditional enemies. The performances at Kurumugl are always in danger of tipping over into actual combat, even though the performances are very much like those of the *konj kaiko*: dance movements adapted from combat, war chants, the arrival of a guest group at a dance ground piled high with freshly slaughtered, cooked pork. The celebration at Kurumugl that I saw took two days. The first consisted of arriving, setting up temporary house inside long rectangular huts, digging cooking ovens. All the people gathered—about 350—were of one tribal group. They awaited the arrival of their guests, a group comparable in size, but recently their enemies. The second day began with the slaughter of about two hundred pigs. These are clubbed on the snouts and heads. As each owner kills his animal he recites—sings—a speech telling how difficult it was to raise the pig, who it is promised to, what a fine animal it is, etc. The *pro forma recitatives* are applauded with laughs and roars, as they often contain jokes and obscene invective. The orations are accompanied by the death squeals of the pigs. Then the animals are gutted, butchered and lowered in halves and quarters into earth ovens to cook. Their guts are hung in nets over the ovens and steamed. Their bladders are blown into balloons and given to the children. The sight and smell of so much meat and blood excites the people, including me. No special clothes are worn for the killing. The only ritual element I detected was the careful display of pig jawbones on a circular altar-like structure in the middle of the dance grounds. From each jaw flowers were hung.

As the cooking starts, the men retire to the huts to begin adorning themselves. From time to time a man emerges to try on a towering headdress of cassowary and peacock feathers. The women cook and tend to the children. After about four hours the meat, still nearly raw, is taken from the ovens and displayed in long rows. Each family lays out its own meat—the women doing most of the work—like so much money in the bank: pork is wealth in the Highlands. As more and more men finish dressing they emerge from the huts to show off and admire each other in a grudging way—the adorning is very competitive. Some women also adorned themselves, dressing much like the men. I couldn't determine if this was traditional or an innovation. A man invited Joan MacIntosh[16] and me into his hut to watch him put on his makeup. He set out a mirror and tins of pigment (bought from a Japanese trading store) and then applied blue, red and black to his torso, shoulders, arms and face. He painted half his nose red and the other half blue. I asked him what the patterns meant. He said he chose them because he liked the way they looked. The Australian aborigines, by contrast, adorn their bodies with patterns each detail of which is linked to ancestral beings, sexual magic or recent events. Aborigine body painting is map-making and myth-telling.

Our performer showed us his headdress of four-foot-long feathers, and stepped outside to try it on. As he emerged from the hut his casual air dropped and he literally thrust his chest forward, gave a long whooping call, put on his headdress and displayed himself. He was costumed for a social not a dramatic role—that is, not to present a fictional character whose life was separable from his own, but to show himself in a special way: to display his strength, his power, his wealth, his authority. It is not easy to distinguish between these kinds of roles, except that in drama the script is already fixed in its details, the precise gestures of the role are rehearsed for a particular occasion (and other occasions, other "productions," might eventuate in different gestures), while "in life" the script is "replaced by an ongoing process, this process is set in motion by the objective demands of the role, and the subjective motives and goals of the actor."[17] An awareness that social and dramatic roles are indeed closely related to each other, and locating their points of convergence in the mise-en-scène rather than in the mind of the playwright, has been one of the major developments in contemporary theatre. This development has been helped by film and television—by film because it presents dramatic actions on location, as if in "real life," and by TV because all so-called news is staged. It is staged not only by the obvious editing of raw footage to suit TV format and the need to sell time (that is, to hold the viewer's attention), but also as it is actually made. Many guerrilla activities, terrorist raids, kidnappings, assassinations and street demonstrations are theatricalized events performed by groups of people in order to catch the attention of larger masses of people by means of TV. This is the main way today in which powerless groups get a hearing. In response, the authorities stage their repressive raids, their assaults and their reprisals: to show the world how the insurgents will be dealt with, to display the power of authority and to terrorize the viewer. Thus an apparent two-person exchange between activist and authority is actually a three-person arrangement with the spectator supplying the vital link. Thus are we continually being educated to the histrionic structure of communication.[18]

The seeds of this histrionic sense are at Kurumugl. As these people are "technified" (already they have planes before cars, TV before newspapers) they will leap not into the 20th century but beyond, going directly from pre-industrial tribalism to automation-age tribalism. The big difference between the two is that pre-industrial tribalism scatters power among a large-number of local leaders, there being no way for people to maintain themselves in large masses; automation-age tribalism is a way of controlling megalopolitic masses. I mean by tribalism the shaping of social roles not through individual choice but by collective formation; the substitution of histrionic-ritualized events for ordinary events; the sacralization or increasingly closely codified definition of all experience; and the disappearance of solitude and one-to-one intimacy as we have developed it since the Renaissance. Automation-age tribalism is medievalism under the auspices of technology. Such tribalism is good for the theatre—if by good one means that most social situations will be governed by conventional, external gestures loaded with metaphoric/symbolic significances. Anomie and identity crisis are eliminated and in their places are fixed roles and rites of passage transporting persons not only from one status to another but from one identity to another. These transportations are achieved by means of performances. I call these kinds of performances "transformances" because the performances are the means of transformation from one status, identity or situation to another.

When the performer at Kurumugl stepped outside his hut he joined a group of envious males whose costumes were, like his, peculiar amalgams of traditional and imported stuff: sunglasses and bones stuck through the septum; cigarette holders and homemade tobacco pipes; khaki shorts and grass skirts. But despite the breakdown in traditional costume an old pattern was being worked out. An ecological ritual where the pig meat was a "payback" (pidgin for fulfilling a ritual obligation) from the hosts to the guests. As among the Tsembaga every adult male at Kurumugl was in a debtor relationship to persons arriving in the afternoon of the second day. The nature of the payback is such that what is given back must exceed what is owed. (This is true even of war, where a perpetual imbalance in casualties must be maintained.) The payback ceremony involves an exchange of roles in which creditors become debtors and debtors become creditors. This insures that more ceremonies will follow when the new debtors accumulate enough pigs. Never is a balance struck, because a balance would threaten an end to the obligations, and this would lead to war. As long as the obligations are intact the social web transmits continuous waves of paybacks back and forth. The visitors approaching Kurumugl came not as friends but as invaders. The afternoon's performance was not a party but a ritual combat with the guests assaulting Kurumugl in a modified war dance, armed with fighting spears, and the campers at Kurumugl defending their ground and the immense pile of meat piled in the center of it. Instead of a secret raiding party there were dancers; instead of taking human victims, they took meat. And instead of doubt about the outcome everyone knew what was going to happen. Thus a ritualized social drama (as war in the

Highlands often is) moves toward becoming an aesthetic drama in which a script of actions is adhered to—the script being known in advance and carefully prepared for.

Again, differences between social and aesthetic drama are not easy to specify. Social drama has more variables, the outcome is in doubt—it is more like a game or sporting context. Aesthetic drama is almost totally arranged in advance, and the participants can concentrate not on strategies of achieving their goals—at Kurumugl, to penetrate to where the meat was, or to defend the meat pile—but on displays; aesthetic drama is less instrumental and more ornamental than social drama. Also, it can use symbolic time and place, and so become entirely fictionalized.

Early in the afternoon of the second day I heard from outside the camp the chanting and shouting of the invaders. The people in camp returned these shouts so that an antiphonal chorus arose. Then the men in camp—and a contingent of about twenty women who were fully armed—rushed to the edges of Kurumugl and the ritual combat began. Both sides were armed with bows and arrows, spears, sticks and axes. They chanted in a rhythm common to the Highlands—a leader sings a phrase and is overlapped by the unison response of many followers. This call-and-response is in loud nasal tones, a progression of quarter and half notes. Such chants alternate with Ketchaklike staccato grunts-pants-shouts. From about one to five in the afternoon the two groups engaged in fierce ritual combat. Each cycle of singing and dancing climaxed when parties of warriors rushed forward from both sides, spears ready for throwing, and, at apparently the last second, did a rapid kick-from-the-knee step instead of throwing their weapons. The weapons became props in a performance of aggression displaced, if not into friendship, at least into a non-deadly confrontation.

The assaults of the invaders were repeated dozens of times; a lush and valuable peanut field was trampled to muck; each assault was met by determined counterattack. But foot by foot the invaders penetrated to the heart of the camp ground—to the pile of meat and the altar of jaw bones and flowers. All the meat previously laid out in rows was now piled three feet deep—a hugh heap of legs, snouts, ribs and flanks all tangled together. Three live white goats were tethered to a pole at the edge of the meat pile. Once the invaders reached the meat they merged with their hosts in one large, whooping, chanting, dancing doughnut of warriors. Around and around the meat they danced, for nearly an hour. I was pinned up against a tree, between the armed dancers and the meat. Then, suddenly, the dancing stopped and orators plunged into the meat, pulling a leg, or a flank, or a side of ribs, and shouted-sung-declaimed things like:

> This pig I give you in payment for the pig you gave my
> father three years ago! Your pig was scrawny, no fat on it

at all, but my pig is huge, with lots of fat, much good
meat—much better than the one my father got! And my
whole family, especially my brothers, will remember that
we are giving you today better than what we got, so that
you owe us, and will help us if we need you beside us in a
fight!

Sometimes the speechifying rises to song; sometimes insults are
hurled back and forth. The fun in the orating, and the joking, stands
on a very serious foundation: the participants do not forget that not so
long ago they were blood enemies. After more than an hour of orating,
the meat is distributed. Sleds are made to carry it shoulder high and
whole families, with much singing, leave with their share of meat.

The performance at Kurumugl consists of displaying the meat,
ritual combat, the merging of the two groups into one, orating and
carrying the meat away. Preparations for this performance are both
immediate, the day before at the camp (and at the visitors' residence),
and long-range: raising the pigs, acquiring costumes and ornaments.
After the performance comes the cleanup, the travel home, the distribution of the meat, feasting and stories about the *sing-sing*. By
means of the performance the basic relationship—one might say the
fundamental relationship—between the invading and the host groups
is inverted.

ACTUALITY 1	→	TRANSFORMANCE	→	ACTUALITY 2
Group A is debtor				Group B is debtor
to Group B				to Group A

As in all rites of passage something has happened during the performance; *the performance both symbolizes and actualizes the change in
status*. The dancing at Kurumugl is the process by which change
happens and it is the only process (other than war) recognized by all
the parties assembled at Kurumugl. Giving and taking the meat not
only symbolizes the changed relationship between Group A and B, it
is the change itself. This convergence of symbolic and actual event is
missing from aesthetic theatre. We have sought for it by trying to make
the performer "responsible" or "visible" in and for his performance—
either through psychodramatic techniques or other psychological
means. This use of psychology is a reflection of our preoccupation with
the individual. Where performances have been sociologically or politically motivated—such as happenings and guerrilla theatre—the authenticating techniques have included emphasis on the event in and
for itself, the development of group consciousness and appeals to the
public at large. But a fundamental contradiction undermines these
efforts. At Kurumugl enough actual wealth and people could be assembled in one place so that what was done in the performance focused actual economic, political and social power. In our society only a
charade of power is displayed at theatrical performances. When this is
recognized, authenticating theatres preoccupy themselves with sym-

bolic activities, feeling helpless in the face of the hollowness of the authenticating tasks they set up for themselves. So-called real events are revealed as metaphors. In a society as large and wealthy as ours only aesthetic theatre is possible. Or authenticating theatres must seek a basis other than economics; or fully ally themselves with established authority. None of these options is as easy as it sounds.

At Kurumugl the change between Group A and B is not simply the occasion for a celebratory performance (as a birthday party celebrates but does not effect a change in age). The performance effects what it celebrates. It opens up enough time in the right place for the exchange to be made: it is liminal: a fluid mid-point between two fixed structures. Only for a brief time do the two groups merge into one dancing circle; during this liminal time/place *communitas* is possible—that leveling of all differences in an ecstasy that so often characterizes performing.[19] Then, and only then, the exchange takes place.

war parties	transformed into	dancing groups
human victims		pig meat
battle dress		costumes
combat		dancing
debtors		creditors
creditors		debtors
two groups		one group

The transformations above the line convert actualities into aesthetic realities. Those below the line effect a change from one actuality into another. It is only because the transformations above the line happen that those below the line can take place in peace. All the transformations—aesthetic as well as actual—are temporary: the meat will be eaten, the costumes doffed, the dance ended; the single group will divide again according to known divisions; today's debtors will be next year's creditors, etc. The celebration at Kurumugl managed a complicated and potentially dangerous exchange with a minimum of danger and a maximum of pleasure. The mode of achieving "real results"—paying debts, incurring new obligations—was performing; the dancing does not celebrate achieving results, it does not precede or follow the exchange, it is the means of making the transformations; the performance is effective.

The Tsembaga, Arunta and Kurumugl performances are ecological rituals. Whatever enjoyment the participants take in the dancing, and however carefully they prepare themselves for dancing, the dances are danced to achieve results. In religious rituals results are achieved by appealing to a transcendent Other (who puts in an appearance either in person or by surrogate). In ecological rituals the other group, or the status to be achieved, or some other clearly human arrangement is the object of the performance. An ecological ritual

with no results to show "below the line" would soon cease. The "above
the line" transformations change aggressive actions into harmless
and pleasure-giving performances (in the cases cited). One is struck
by the analogy to certain biological adaptations among animals.[20]

In the New Guinea Highlands, at first under the pressure of the
colonial police, later under its own momentum, warfare is transformed into dancing. As above-the-line activities grow in importance,
entertainment as such takes over from efficacy as the reason for the
performance. It is not only that creditors and debtors need to exchange roles, but also that people want to show off; it is not only to get
results that the dances are staged, but also because people like dancing for its own sake. Efficacy and entertainment are opposed to each
other, but they form a binary system, a continuum.

EFFICACY $\longleftarrow$ $\longrightarrow$ ENTERTAINMENT	
(Ritual)	(Theatre)
results	fun
link to an absent Other	only for those here
abolishes time, symbolic time	emphasizes now
brings Other here	audience is the Other
performer possessed, in trance	performer knows what he's doing
audience participates	audience watches
audience believes	audience appreciates
criticism is forbidden	criticism is encouraged
collective creativity	individual creativity

The basic opposition is between efficacy and entertainment, not between ritual and theatre. Whether one calls a specific performance
ritual or theatre depends on the degree to which the performance
tends toward efficacy or entertainment. No performance is pure efficacy or pure entertainment. The matter is complicated because one
can look at specific performances from several vantages; changing
perspective changes classification. For example, a Broadway musical
is entertainment if one concentrates on what happens onstage and in
the house. But if the point of view expands—to include rehearsals,
backstage life before, during and after the show, the function of the
roles in the careers of each performer, the money invested by backers,
the arrival of the audience, their social status, how they paid for their
tickets (as individuals, expense accounts, theatre parties, etc.) and
how this indicates the use they're making of the performance (as
entertainment, to advance their careers, to support a charity, etc.)—
then the Broadway musical is more than entertainment; it reveals
many ritual elements.

Recently, more performances have been emphasizing the rehearsal
and backstage procedures. At first this was as simple as showing the
lighting instruments and using a half-curtain, as Brecht did. But
within the last fifteen years the process of mounting the performance,
the workshops that lead up to the performance, the means by which

an audience is brought into the space and led from the space and many other previously automatic procedures, have become the subjects of theatrical manipulations. These procedures have to do with the theatre-in-itself and they are, as regards the theatre, efficacious: that is, these procedures are what makes a theatre into a theatre regardless of themes, plot or the usual "elements of drama." The attention paid to the procedures of making theatre are, I think, attempts at ritualizing performance, of finding in the theatre itself authenticating acts. In a period when authenticity is increasingly rare in public life the performer has been asked to surrender his traditional masks and be himself; or at least to show how the masks are put on and taken off. Instead of mirroring his times the performer is asked to remedy them. The professions taken as models for theatre are medicine and the church. No wonder shamanism is popular among theatre people: shamanism is that branch of doctoring that is religious, and that kind of religion that is full of ironies and tricks.[21]

At present efficacy is ascending to a dominant position over entertainment. It is my belief that theatre history can be given an overall shape as a development along a core which is a *braided structure* constantly interrelating efficacy and entertainment. At each period in each culture one or the other is dominant—one is ascending while the other is descending. Naturally, these changes are part of changes in the overall social structure; yet performance is not a passive mirror of these social changes but a part of the complicated feedback process that brings about change. At all times a dialectical tension exists between efficacious and entertainment tendencies. For Western theatre, at least, I think it can be shown that when the braid is tight—that is, when efficacy and entertainment are both present in nearly equal degrees—theatre flourishes. During these brief historical moments the theatre answers needs that are both ritualistic and pleasure-giving. Fifth-century Athenian theatre, Elizabethan theatre, and possibly the theatre of the late 19th century and/or of our own times show the kind of convergence I'm talking about. When efficacy dominates, performances are universalistic, allegorical, ritualized, tied to a stable established order; this kind of theatre persists for a relatively long time. When entertainment dominates, performances are class-oriented, individualized, show business, constantly adjusted to suit the tastes of a fickle audience. The two most recent convergences—the rise of entertainment before the Elizabethan period and the rise of efficacy during the modern period—are necessarily opposites of each other. The model that I offer is of course a simplification. I present it as a help in conceptualizing my view of the progression of theatre history, which I think has its own logic and internal force. The late medieval period was dominated by efficacious performances: church services, court ceremonies, moralities, pageants. In the early Renaissance these began to decline and popular entertainments, always present, gained, finally becoming dominant in the form of the public theatres of the Elizabethan period. The private and court theatres developed alongside the public theatres. The private theatres were for the upper classes. Although some professionals worked in both public and private theatres, and some spectators attended both, these entertainments were fundamentally opposed to each other. The conflicts between the public and private theatres never worked themselves out because all the theatres were closed in 1642. When theatres reopened at the Restoration the Elizabethan public theatre was gone and all the theatres resembled the private theatres and masques, the property of the upper classes. During the 18th and 19th centuries this aristocratic theatre developed into the bourgeois theatre, as that class rose to displace the aristocracy. The dominant efficacious mode of the medieval centuries went underground to re-emerge in the guise of social and political drama during the last third of the 19th century. This new naturalistic theatre opposed the commercialism and pomposity of the boulevards and allied itself to scientific theatrical styles and techniques. The avant-garde identified itself both with Bohemianism—the outcasts of bourgeois society—and science, the source of power. Avant-garde artists used terms like "experimental" and "research" to characterize their work, which took place in "laboratories." Efficacy lies at the ideological heart of all aspects of this new theatre.

Efficacy/Entertainment Braid:
Fifteenth to Twenty-First Centuries
in the English and American Theatres

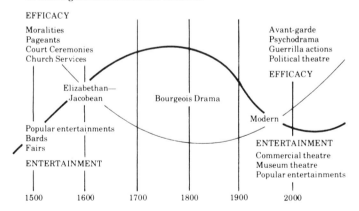

In the 20th century the entertainment theatre, threatened with extinction, broke into two parts: an increasingly outmoded commercial theatre typified by Broadway and a subsidized community museum typified by the regional theatres. The FACT meeting at

Princeton[23] was an attempt by commercial interests to ally themselves with the regional theatres. Although such an alliance is inevitable, it's most likely that the regional theatres will absorb the commercial theatres. Whatever the outcome, the entertainment theatres
remain fundamentally opposed by the avant-garde—which has itself,
by mid-20th century, expanded to include direct political action,
psycho-therapy and other manifestly efficacious kinds of performances. It is my opinion that efficacious theatres are on the upswing
and will dominate the theatrical world within the next 20 years.

Up to here I've said this: (1) in some social settings ritual performances are part of ecosystems and mediate political relations, group
hierarchy and economics; (2) in other settings ritual performances
begin to take on qualities of show business; (3) there is a dialectical-
dyadic continuum linking efficacy to entertainment—both are present
in all performances, but in each performance one or the other is dominant; (4) in different societies, at different times, either efficacy or
entertainment dominates, the two being in a braided relationship to
each other.
O. B. Hardison quotes Honorius of Autun's 12th-century view of
the Mass as evidence that people at the time saw this ceremony as
drama:

> It is known that those who recited tragedies in theatres
> presented the actions of opponents by gestures before the
> people. In the same way our tragic author [i.e., the
> celebrant] represents by his gestures in the theater of the
> Church before the Christian people the struggle of Christ
> and teaches to them the victory of his redemption.
> [Honorius then compares each movement of the Mass to an
> equivalent movement of tragic drama.] . . . When the
> sacrifice has been completed, peace and Communion are
> given by the celebrant to the people. . . . Then, by the *Ite,
> missa est,* they are ordered to return to their homes with
> rejoicing. They shout *Deo gratias* and return home
> rejoicing.[24]

What is extraordinary about Honorius' description is that it is a
medieval view, not a backwards glance by a modernist. Honorius'
Mass is more familiar to those who have attended avant-garde performances than to those whose experience is limited to orthodox
theatre. The 12th-century Mass employed many avant-garde
techniques: it was allegorical, it used audience participation, it
treated time teleologically, it extended the scope of the performance
from the church to the roadways to the homes. But for all this I still
think it is fair to call this Mass a ritual rather than theatre. My
opinion is founded on the almost totally efficacious nature of the Mass.

As Hardison says, "The service ... has a very important aesthetic dimension, but it is essentially not a matter of appreciation but of passionate affirmation."[25] The Mass was a closed circle which included only the congregation and the officiants; there was literally and figuratively no room for appreciators. The Mass was an obligatory action entered into either joyfully or sullenly, through which members of the congregation signaled to each other and to the hierarchy their continued participation in the congregation. What I say of the 12th-century Mass, Rappaport has said of the Tsembaga:

> While the scope of the social unity is frequently not made explicit, it would seem that in some studies it is what Durkheim called a "church," that is, "a society whose members are united by the fact that they think in the same way in regard to the sacred world and its relations with the profane world, and by the fact that they translate these common ideas into common practices." ... Such units, composed of aggregates of individuals who regard their collective well-being to be dependent upon a common body of ritual performances, might be called "congregations."[26]

Because of its all-inclusive hold on its congregation the Mass was not theatre in the classical or modern sense. Theatre comes into existence when a separation occurs between audience and performers. The paradigmatic theatrical situation is a group of performers soliciting an audience who may or may not respond by attending. The audience is free to attend or stay away—and if they stay away it is the theatre that suffers, not its would-be audience. In ritual, staying away means rejecting the congregation—or being rejected by it, as in excommunication, ostracism or exile. If only a few stay away, it is those who are absent who suffer; if many stay away, the congregation is in danger of schism or extinction. To put it another way: ritual is an event upon which its participants depend; theatre is an event which depends on its participants. The process is not cut-and-dry. But evidence of the transformational steps by which theatre emerges from ritual—by which an efficacious event in which the participants depend on the performance is transformed into an entertainment in which the entertainers depend on an audience—is not locked in ancient or medieval documents. The transformation of ritual into theatre is occurring today.

Asaro is a village about seventy miles east of Kurumugl. There the famous dance of the Mudmen is performed as a tourist entertainment three times a week. It was not always so. The villagers originally performed only when they felt threatened by attack. Before dawn village men went to a local creek, rubbed their bodies with white mud (the color of death) and constructed grotesque masks of wood frames covered by mud and vegetation. Emerging from the creek at dawn, possessed by the spirits of the dead, the dancers moved in an eerie,

slow, crouching step. Sometimes they went to the village of their
enemies and frightened them, thus preventing attack; sometimes
they danced in their own village. The dances took less than ten minutes; preparations took most of the previous night. (This ratio of preparation to performance is not unusual; it is present even in modern
Western theatre in the rehearsal-performance ratio.) The dance of the
Mudmen was performed occasionally, when needed. After pacification
by Australian authorities there was less need for the Mudmen. However, in the mid-sixties a photographer from the *National Geographic
Magazine* paid the villagers to stage the dance for him. These photos
became world famous—and it was not long before tourists demanded
to see the Mudmen. (Even the name "Mudmen" is an invention for
tourists; I don't know the original name of the ceremony.) Because
Asaro is near the Mount Hagan-Goroka road it was easy to arrange
for minibuses to bring spectators to the village. Tourists pay up to $20
each to see the short dances; of this sum the Asaroans get 10%. Because the 10-minute dance is not a long enough show by Western
standards, the dancing has been augmented by a display of bow-and-
arrow marksmanship, a photo session and a "market." But Asaro is
not (yet) a craft village, and the few necklaces and string bags I saw
for sale were pathetic—the day I was there no one bought anything.

The people of Asaro don't know what their dance is any more.
Surely it's not to frighten enemies—it attracts tourists. It has no
relationship to the spirits of the dead who appear only before dawn,
and the tourists come a little after midday. The social fabric of Asaro
has been torn to shreds, but the changes required of the Mudmen
dance are a result of the deeper disruptions of Highlands life and only
in a minor way a cause of these disruptions. In fact, despite the exploi-
tation of the village by the tourist agencies, the meager sums paid the
Asaroans are needed desperately during a period when the barter
economy has fallen apart. I expect future changes in the dance will
make it longer, more visually complicated, possibly adding musical
accompaniment; the craft skills of the villagers will improve, or they
will import stuff to sell; their percentage of the take will rise. In short,
the dance will approach those Western standards of entertainment
represented by the tastes of the audience, and the benefits will rise
accordingly. Presently, the Asaroans perform a traditional ritual
emptied of its efficacy but not yet regarded as a theatrical entertainment.

Joan MacIntosh and I arrived before the tourists and stayed after
they left. The villagers looked at us curiously—we were taking pictures of the tourists as well as of the dancers. After the other whites
left, a man came up to us and in pidgin asked us to come with him. We
walked four miles along a ridge until we got to Kenetisarobe. There
we met Asuwe Yamuruhu, the headman. He wanted us to go to
Goroka and tell the tourists about his dancers; he wanted tourists to

come and watch a show which, he assured us, was much better than the Mudmen. It began to rain very hard as we squatted in the entrance to a round hut—around us, in the rain, a few villagers watched. We agreed on a price—$4 a person—and a time, the next afternoon; not only would we see dances but we could tape-record songs too.

The next afternoon we arrived with two friends, paid our $16, and saw a dance consisting of very slow steps, as if the dancers were moving through deep mud, their fingers splayed and their faces masked or tied into grotesque shapes. (Peter Thoady, headmaster of the Goroka Teacher's College, told us that the distortion of the faces probably was in imitation of yaws, a disfiguring disease common in the area.) The dancers moved in a half-crouch and occasionally shouted phrases and expletives. The Grassmen of Kenetisarobe were very like the Mudmen of Asaro. After the dancing we spent about an hour recording music, talking and smoking.

The Kenetisarobe dance was adapted from ceremonial farces of the region. Asuwe staged them for us—he knew that Asaro was making money from its dance, and the Kenetisarobe show was modeled on the Asaro formula: slow dance, grotesque masks, plenty of opportunity for photographs and a follow-up after the dance. What the people of Asaro did with a minimum of self-awareness, Asuwe did with a keen sense of theatre business. Examples of the same pattern abound. In Bali tourist versions of Barong and Ketchak are everywhere—along the Denpasar to Ubud road signs advertising these performances are as frequent as movie marquees in America. Signs, in English, often read: "Traditional Ketchak—Holy Monkey Dance Theatre—Tonight at 8," or "Barong—Each Wednesday at 8 on the Temple Steps." The Balinese, with characteristic sophistication, make separate tourist shows and keep authentic performances secret—and, more important, far from the main road. Tourists want to drive to their entertainments; they want a dependable schedule; and they want a way to leave conveniently if they choose to go early. Most authentic performances—of Ketchak and of other actual ritual performances—are accessible only on foot, through rather thick jungle and only with the permission of the village giving the performance. During my two weeks in Bali I saw two such performances. We stumbled on a Ketchak while walking through the monkey forest near Ubud—we followed some women carrying offerings of food. Once we entered Tigal we stayed there for ten hours before the Ketchak began a little after 9 P.M. At Tenganan we saw the final two days of the annual Abuang. Some of the ceremony was public and about fifty tourists joined the villagers to enjoy the afternoon dancing. These people were asked to leave by 5 P.M. We were quietly told to remain in the town office. Then, after dark, we were taken to different compounds in the village for different aspects of the ceremony. We were also allowed to listen to special gamelon music played before dawn. We weren't allowed to photograph, and only a limited amount of tape recording was allowed. The daytime ceremonies definitely had the feel of an entertainment: outsiders came in, shops were open and doing a brisk business, the dances were carefully choreographed to the gamelon music. At night the operation was different: each aspect of the ceremony was privatized and done not with an eye to its prettiness but to its correctness; time gaps between elements were longer and more irregular; many discussions concerning how to do certain things were held, and this delayed the ceremonies. The subject matter of the Abuang—if I can use that phrase—is the presentation of all the unmarried males to all the unmarried females. The daytime dances showed everyone off; the nighttime ceremonies concerned actual betrothal.

Surely the tourist trade has influenced so-called "genuine" performances in Bali and elsewhere. I have no contempt for these changes. Changes in conventions, themes, methods and styles occur because of opportunism, audience pressures, professionalism (itself often a new concept) and new technology. Tourism has been really important and worldwide only since the advent of cheap air travel. Theatre historians will regard tourism as of as much importance to 20th-century theatre as the exchange between England and the Continent was in the 16th and 17th centuries. Theatre people imitate popular imported modes, and the locals respond to the demands of rich visitors—or local audiences demand changes because they've absorbed the tastes of alien cultures. From one point of view these changes are corruptions—a clamor is raised to establish cultural zoos in which the original versions of age-old rituals can be preserved. But even traditional performances vary greatly from generation to generation—an oral tradition is flexible, able to absorb many personal variations within set parameters. And the cultural-zoo approach is itself the most pernicious aspect of tourism. I hate the genocide that has eradicated such cultures as that of the Australian Aborigines. But I see nothing wrong with what's happening in Bali and New Guinea, where two systems of theatre exist. The relationship between these is not a simple division between tourist and authentic. More studies are needed on the exchange between what's left of traditional performances and emerging tourist shows. And at what moment does a tourist show become itself an authentic theatrical art?

Tourism is a two-way street: travelers bring back experiences, expectations, and, if the tourists are practitioners, techniques, scenes and even entire forms. The birth ritual of *Dionysus in 69* was adapted from the Asmat of West Irian; several sequences in the Living Theatre's *Mysteries* and *Paradise Now* were taken from yoga and Indian theatre; Phillip Glass's music draws on gamelon and Indian raga; Imamu Baraka's writing is deeply influenced by African modes of storytelling and drama. The list could be extended, and to all the arts. Many innovators since World War II (a great war for travel) have been decisively influenced by work from cultures other than their own; this means, for Western artists, Asia, Africa and Oceania. The impact of communal-collective forms on contemporary Western theatre is like that of classical forms on the Renaissance. The diffferences, however, are also important: in the Renaissance all that remained of classical culture were architectural ruins, old texts and relics of the plastic arts. This material was frequently fragmented and corrupt. Also, Renaissance scholars looked with universal respect, even awe, at what they found of classical Greece and Rome. Today's cross-cultural feed is mainly in the area of performances; the shows have been seen intact; the originators of the performances are former colonial peoples, or peoples who were considered inferior by populations around the north Atlantic basin. In other words, it is logical that today's influences should be felt first in the avant-garde.

A very clear and provable Asian influence on contemporary Western theatre is seen in Grotowski's work, particularly its "poor theatre" phase, from around 1964 to around 1971. This period includes several versions of *Akropolis, The Constant Prince* and the first versions of *Apocalypsis Cum Figuris*. The foundation of this work is the psychophysical/plastique exercises which Grotowski and Ryszard Cieslak taught in many of their workshops in Poland and abroad. Ever since I learned some of these exercises in 1967, I felt they were influenced not only by yoga, which Grotowski acknowledges, but by the south Indian dance-theatre form, Kathakali. In 1972, while visiting the Kathakali Kalamandalam in Kerala, I asked about Grotowski's visits to the school. No one remembered him, but Eugenio Barba was remembered, and in the school's visitors' book I found the following entry:

29 September 1963

The Secretary
Kalamandalam
Cheruthuruthy

Dear Sir:

I had not the occasion, last night at the performance, to thank you for all the kind help you have given me during my stay here. To you, and to the Superintendant, and to all the boys who were so willing to be of service, I would like to express my gratitude and sincerest thanks.

My visit to Kalamandalam has greatly helped me in my studies and the research material I have collected will surely be of the greatest assistance to those people working at the Theatre Laboratory in Poland.

Many thanks once again,

    Yours sincerely,
    Eugenio Barba [signed]

Barba brought Kathakali exercises to Grotowski in Poland—they form the core of the plastique and psychophysical exercises. When Barba founded his Odin Teatret he used these exercises—as modified by the Polish Lab—as the basis of his own work. Grotowski has visited India on several occasions, the first in 1956-57, when he also traveled to China and Japan.

Peter Brook's three-month trip in 1972-73 with a troupe of 30 persons through Algeria, Mali, Niger, Dahomey and Nigeria is another version of the "trading partner" idea. Brook, even more consciously and fully than Grotowski-through-Barba, went to Africa to trade techniques, perform, observe performances. In Brook's words:

> Once we sat in Agades in a small hut all afternoon, singing. We and the African group sang, and suddenly we found that we were hitting exactly the same language of sound. Well, we understood theirs and they understood ours, and something quite electrifying happened because, out of all sorts of different songs, one suddenly came upon this common area.
>
> Another experience of that same sort occurred one night when we were camping in a forest. We thought there was no one around for miles, but as always, suddenly, children appeared from nowhere and beckoned. We were just sitting and doing some improvised song, and the children asked us to come down to their village, only a couple of miles away, because there was going to be some singing and dancing later in the night and everyone would be very pleased if we could come.
>
> So we said "sure." We walked down through the forest, found this village and found that, indeed, there was a ceremony going on. Somebody had just died and it was a funeral ceremony. We were made very welcome and we sat there, in total darkness under the trees, just seeing these moving shadows dancing and singing. And after a couple of hours they suddenly said to us: the boys say that this is what you do, too. Now you must sing for us.
>
> So we had to improvise a song for them. And this was perhaps one of the best works of the entire journey. Because the song that was produced for the occasion was extraordinarily moving, right and satisfying, and made a real coming together of the people and ourselves. It is impossible to say what produced it, because it was produced as much by the group that was working together in a certain way, with all the work that has gone into that, and as much by all the conditions of the moment that bore their influence: the place, the night, the feeling for the other people, so that we were actually making something for them in exchange for what they had offered us.[27]

Throughout Asia, MacIntosh and I found this same "exchange policy."

We were invited to stay at Tenganan because the people knew we performed, and at the main public performance the chief insisted that I do a dance.[28] At Karamui in New Guinea—far from any road (we flew in)—we were shown funeral ceremonies (a villager, with much laughter, played the role of the corpse), but we were expected to sing songs in exchange. In the Sepik River village of Kamanabit the headman insisted that MacIntosh be awakened and brought to his house to sing even though she was exhausted from a day's travel; his demand came after I'd been listening to village women singing.

The kind of influence through observation and trading reflected in Barba's letter, Brook's trip and my own experiences is different from Artaud's reaction to Balinese theatre. Artaud was influenced, but the Balinese didn't care; there was no exchange. In the more recent examples work was consciously traded, professionals sought to expand their knowledge.

Whatever the ritual functions of Kathakali within the context of Kerala village life, the Kalamandalam is a professional training school and its troupe performs for pay in India and overseas. Foreigners come to study at the Kalamandalam (while I was there about five Westerners were studying). This training does not eventuate in the establishment of Kathakali troupes outside India—rather the work is integrated into existing styles. It remains to be seen how the presence of outsiders at the Kalamandalam, and the frequent tours of the troupe, affect the work in Kerala. The situation with Brook is different. The African villagers were in the midst of a religious ritual (a funeral ceremony) but they were also eager to share their entertainment (trading songs) to use their ritual as an item of trade. That the exchange was mutually moving is no surprise—entertainment and ritual co-exist comfortably.

Touring ritual performances around the world—and thereby converting them into entertainments—is nothing new: the Romans were fond of importing exotic entertainments, the more authentic the better. Every colonial or conquering power has done the same. In 1972, at the Brooklyn Academy of Music the following show took place (I quote from the program):

THE BROOKLYN ACADEMY OF MUSIC
in association with
Mel Howard Productions, Inc.
and
Ninon Tallon-Karlweis
in cooperation with
The Turkish-Ministry of Tourism and Information

Present
THE WHIRLING DERVISHES OF TURKEY.
(THE PROGRAM IS A RELIGIOUS CEREMONY. YOU ARE
KINDLY REQUESTED TO REFRAIN FROM APPLAUSE.)

The audience had to be told that what they paid money to see as an entertainment retained enough of its ritual basis to require a change in conventional theatrical behavior. The performance was simple and moving—I suppose a fairly accurate presentation of the dervish ritual. I know that several theatre groups in New York were influenced by it. Both Robert Wilson's Byrd Hoffman group and The Performance Group have used whirling.

In October, 1973, the Shingon Buddhist monks came to the Brooklyn Academy of Music with "ceremonies, music and epics of ancient Japan." The dervishes whirled on a stage facing the 2,000-seat opera house. The monks performed in a room designed for Brook's appearance after his African trip—a space 75' × 40', with a height of about 30'. The audience numbered around two hundred, seated on cushions scattered on the floor, and on bleachers. As at Asaro and Kenetisarobe the Buddhist rituals were not long enough to constitute an entertainment by Western standards. So the program was augmented by performers of Japanese contemporary music and a recitation of Japanese war tales from the 12th to 14th centuries. Only after the intermission did the monks perform their temple service. The program described in detail what the monks were doing, what it meant and how the ceremony is used in Japan. Thus the audience was treated as if it were attending Grand Opera, where the libretto is summarized, or a new kind of sport in which the rules, equipment and structure are explained. It seemed to me that the monks, like the dervishes, were deeply into what they were doing. They were "in character"—and it was impossible to distinguish what they were doing from what Stanislavski required of actors. I was convinced: these dervishes were Dervishes, these monks were Monks. A defined interface between spectators and performers existed; on one side was authenticity, efficacy and ritual, on the other side was entertainment and theatre.

Any ritual can be lifted from its original setting and performed as theatre—just as any everyday event can be.[29] This is possible because context, not fundamental structure, distinguishes ritual, entertainment and ordinary life from each other. The differences among them arise from the agreement (conscious or unexpressed) between performers and spectators. Entertainment/theatre emerges from ritual out of a complex consisting of an audience separate from the performers, the development of professional performers and economic needs imposing a situation in which performances are made to please the audience rather than according to a fixed code or dogma. It is also possible for ritual to arise out of theatre by reversing the process just described. This move from theatre to ritual marks Grotowski's work and that of the Living Theatre. But the rituals created were unstable because they were not attached to actual social structures outside theatre. Also, the difference between ritual, theatre and ordinary life depends on the degree spectators and performers attend to efficacy, pleasure or routine; and how symbolic meaning and effect are infused and attached to performed events. In all entertainment there is some efficacy and in all ritual there is some theatre.[30]

The entire binary "efficacy/ritual—entertainment/theatre" is performance: performance includes the impulse to be serious and to entertain; to collect meanings and to pass the time; to display symbolic behavior that actualizes "there and then" and to exist only "here and now"; to be oneself and to play at being others; to be in a trance and to be conscious; to get results and to fool around; to focus the action on and for a select group sharing a hermetic language and to broadcast to the largest possible audiences of strangers who buy tickets.

At this moment The Performance Group is working on Brecht's *Mother Courage and Her Children*. Most of our rehearsals have been open—when weather permits, the big overhead front garage door of our theatre has been raised and people off the street, students and friends have come in to watch us work. Every rehearsal has had from five to forty people watching. The rehearsals have a feeling of stop and go, with nothing special planned to accommodate the spectators. Yet their presence makes a deep difference: work on the play now includes a public social core; and the work is about showing-a-way-of-working. This theme will be worked into the formal performances. The space for *Courage*—designed by Jerry N. Rojo and James Clayburgh, collaborating with all the other members of the Group—expresses the interplay between Brecht's drama and the larger performance in which it takes place. A part of the room has been made into a Green Room wholly visible to the audience. When a performer is not in a scene he or she goes into the Green Room, gets some coffee, reads, relaxes. The rest of the theatre is divided into three main spaces: an empty cube 30' × 30' × 20' (including an open pit 20' × 8' × 7'); a 20' × 20' × 20' cube filled with irregular scaffolding, platforms, and ropes; galleries, walkways and a bridge about 11 feet off the ground. The audience can move freely through the entire space, continually changing perspective and mood. It is possible to see everything from a single vantage, but only if one looks through other structures. Scene Nine takes place outside the theatre in Wooster Street, with the large Garage door open. The door stays open for the final three scenes—in winter this means that the temperature in the theatre plunges.

Our production has one intermission, after Scene Five. During intermission supper is sold, and the performers mix with the audience. During supper the "Song of the Great Capitulation" (Scene Four) is sung, as in a cabaret, without insistence that people pay attention. When the drama resumes after supper I think it is experienced differently because of the hour of mingling, talking and sharing of food and drink.[31] Another shift in the mode of experiencing the play comes when the performance moves outside, and the theatre takes on the feeling of the outside. *Mother Courage* is treated as a drama nested in a larger performance event. The ideas behind The Performance Group's production of *Courage* are common to ritual performances: to control or manipulate the whole world of the performance, not just present the drama at its center. In this way a theatrical event in SoHo, New York City, is nudged a little way from the entertainment end of the continuum towards efficacy. Without diminishing its theatricality, I hope to enhance its ritual aspects.

Orthodox theories say that ritual precedes theatre, just as efficacy and monism ("primitive oneness") precede entertainment. It is a cliché of interpretations of Paleolithic cave art that some kind of "ritual" generated the art—and by ritual is meant a serious, efficacious, result-oriented performance either to insure fertility, to placate the powers who control the hunt, to maintain a balance between male and female or something. These things, or some of them, may be true; but they are not the whole truth: entertainment, passing time in play and fun (not the passive and cut-off feeling of "art for art's sake," but an active involvement with the process of making art) are interwoven with and inseparable from any efficacious aspects of the earliest art. The idea of a primitive oneness is a combination of Edenic fantasy and the Protestant work ethic supported by the projections of early ethnographers too many of whom were missionaries. Accummulating evidence from Paleolithic, early historical, classical, Asian, African and contemporary communal peoples suggest that a complicated social life and rich, symbolic art are co-existent with the human condition. The idea of the "simple primitive"—either noble or savage—has been killed by Lévi-Strauss, La Barre and others. Shamans were artists and performers and doctors and trance-possessed (temporary) psychotics and priests and entertainers. To argue that because several roles are played simultaneously by one person (or class of people), or that because a single performance expresses many contradictory impulses that the art of such people (and their societies) is simple is to look at things upside down.

Industrial societies separate/standardize functions/expressions; communal societies combine many functions/expressions in single often extended complicated events. The experience of urban life is to move from one "pure" event to another—only over time and by means of a synthesis managed by each individual (and many people can't manage it) is there a sense of unity emerging from the multiplicity and pluralism. I personally enjoy this pluralism, but it can go too far and fragment people, not cut them off so much as cut them up. Communal life, on the other hand, includes in each event—even a ceremony as short as the ten-minute Arunta dance—a bundle of meanings/functions/expressions. These are not implicit: each participant knows the connections, and the initiate is taught them. The leader of the dance is also the leader of his band, is also a skilled hunter, is also related to the boys being initiated, etc. And, as I've shown, the dance is nested in a complex of ceremonies where each part is a synecdoche. Much of the post-war avant-garde is an attempt to overcome fragmentation by approaching performance as a part of rather than apart from the community. Sometimes this community is the community of the artists making the work; this has been the pattern in New York, London, Paris and other Western cities. Sometimes—as in the general uprisings of 1968—the art is joined to large political movements. Sometimes, as in black and Chicano theatre, and more recently in other "special interest" theatres, the artists identify with—even help to form—a sense of ethnic, racial or political identity. This community-related avant-garde is not only a phenomenon of the industrialized West, but also of countries that are industrializing or undergoing great changes in social organization. In Eastern Europe, Japan and in the work of people like Rendra in Indonesia, Soyinka in Nigeria, Boal in Brazil and Argentina we see the same process.

This work is not simple atavism, it is not a wild attempt to dismantle industrialism, or to halt its spread. It is an active seeking to find places within industrial societies—even within the industrial process itself—for communities to exist; and to demand a restructuring of the social order in terms of community, collectively and person-to-person interaction, or "meetings," as Grotowski says. The problems of industrialization and fragmentation are clearly not problems of capitalism alone. Experiments of the kind I've been talking about are taking place in socialist states too. These experiments—still relatively scattered and tentative, and always facing a hostile establishment, are showing signs of taking root; they address themselves to the audience not as a collection of money-paying individual strangers, or forced participants in a show of solidarity (as in mass rallies or coercive church-going), but as a community, even as a congregation, as Turner calls them. And the object of such performances is both to entertain—to have fun—and to create *communities*: a sense of collective celebration. This contemporary movement originated in the avant-garde theatre and is moving toward ritual.

Performance doesn't originate in ritual any more than it originates in entertainment. It originates in the binary system: efficacy-entertainment which includes the subset ritual-theatre. From the beginning—logically as well as historically—both terms of the binary are present, are required. At any historical moment there is movement from one pole toward the other. This oscillation is continuous—performance is in an active steady-state.

The whole binary system efficacy/ritual—entertainment/theatre is what I call "performance." Performance originates in impulses to make things happen and to entertain; to collect meanings and to pass the time; to be transformed into another and to be onself; to disappear and to show off; to bring into a celebratory space a transcendent Other who exists then-and-now and later-and-now and to celebrate here-and-now only us who are present; to get things done and to play around; to focus inward on a select initiated group sharing a hermetic language and to broadcast out to the largest possible collection of strangers. These oppositions—and all the others generated by them—comprise performance: it is an active situation, a steady process of transformation. The move from ritual to theatre happens when a participating audience fragments into a collection of people who pay, who come because the show is advertised, who evaluate what they are going to see before they see it; the move from theatre to ritual happens when the audience as a collection of separate people is dissolved into the performance as participants. These opposing tendencies are present in all performances. Brecht, and Meyerhold before him, worked to keep the tension between these extremes working throughout each performance by moving an audience back and forth moment to moment. The deep effect of Brecht's *verfremdung* is to unexpectedly shift modes, styles, rhythms, perspectives; and at the moment of change, when the affective part of a scene abruptly stops, or when a distanced beat suddenly becomes moving—the dramaturgic structure allows the writer/director/performer to make a "statement," to insert an ironic comment, to encourage the spectator to think about what he's seen and/or felt. The structure of the performance is obliterated by its anti-structure and in the liminal moment a direct communication, a deep contact, with the audience is made. Of all the experiments with theatrical structure over the past century this one is most likely to stick. It resonates back to medieval theatre, and to many folk theatres existing now.

I can best summarize by drawing four models, explaining each as I go.

Actuality 1 ←——————— ENCOUNTER/EXCHANGE ———————→ Actuality 2

A meeting takes place at a market or on a battlefield. Goods are traded, money is earned, territory taken, a group routed. The encounter is intended to be entirely efficacious—even though sometimes nothing is traded or battles end in stand-offs. The rituals in this kind of activity are ethological and/or sociological. That is they are based on "fixed-action patterns," and they are intended to regulate human interaction so that what is supposed to happen, or be determined, by the meeting of individuals and/or groups actually happens. The entertainment/theatrical elements in these kinds of meetings are reduced to a minimum, though they are present. The job is to get through the encounter/exchange as efficiently as possible and arrive at Actuality 2. But even this model doesn't show all that really happens. Markets are places of display, joking, gossiping, singing; they often attract mountebanks and other popular entertainments. Battlefields are places to show the colors, parade strength and in general scare your opponent off the field. Guerrilla war and mass combat work against these theatrical qualities. Thus even at this level the ethological and sociological rituals are embroidered with entertainment. There is a tendency toward:

Actuality 1   PERFORMANCE   Actuality 2

This is the case with ecological rituals such as those among the Arunta and Tsembaga. Their performances effect changes both in the status of some people participating (through initiation, marriage and other rites of passage) and in economic matters (pigs, sago, trade items). In fact, how good a performance is can be an important element in determining social status. The Greeks offered prizes to their tragedians; our society offers wealth and fame. Among Aborigines and New Guinea people high status is conferred on the better performers. A shaman among the American Indians or in Siberia is honored for his or her tricks and style.

This process can itself become highly advanced resulting in:

Actuality   By Means of Theatre   Entertainment

This is what happened when the Dervishes or the Monks performed at the Brooklyn Academy. Rituals which have efficacy in a defined setting become entertainments in another setting. *The Yoshi Show,* presented at the Public Theatre in New York in 1975, included a Buddhist monk, a Shinto priest, a martial arts expert and a Tibetan monk performing along with Yoshi, a Japanese actor who had studied extensively with Peter Brook. The show combined elements of different religious ceremonies with theatrical performing. The event was very confusing because it was neither the presentation of a ritual as theatre nor an entertainment. On the other hand this ambiguity gave it a special power, almost as sacrilege because of the clash of different kinds of worship. In shows of this kind money is exchanged for a peek at ritual. And "new rituals" are synthesized for the sake of entertainment.

Another example of this model is its reverse:

Entertainment ◄───────── By Means of Ritual   Actuality

This is what Grotowski is doing. This tendency has been present in his work for the last 10 years. He sets many of his performances in churches, selecting audiences either on an individual basis, or by some means (including very high prices) that limit the number of people making audiences into elites. In *Fire on the Mountain* each *ul* was peopled by invited participants only. And the nature of the work in the *uls* was to bring about a kind of intimacy and quasi-religious solidarity by means of performance exercises, group encounter/ therapy techniques and submission to the will of a strong leader.[32] Grotowski's experiments are like EST in America where groups of people are "broken down" over a weekend's experience of extreme intensity, often an ordeal of shouting, physical work and direct confrontation. Although this subject won't be explored here the means of encounter therapy are very close to traditional initiation rites where the young boy is broken down and re-made in a short period of time through a series of instructions and ordeals.

During the appearance in Philadelphia in 1973 of the Polish Laboratory Theatre the performances of *Apocalypsis cum Figuris* were only the first step in a more elaborate ceremony. During the performances Grotowski literally "tapped" 5 to 10 students and asked them to remain after the performance. These were then invited to go with Grotowski and his company to a retreat in the hills not far from Philadelphia where the students and the performers would meet "on a one-to-one basis." Clearly the performance of *Apocalypsis* was an entry into some other kind of experience, one which can't be called theatre in the usual sense.

In *Paradise Now* the Living Theatre attempted a similar transformation of entertainment into actuality—in their case a political rather than religious actuality. By challenging the audience where they sit, by inviting them onto the stage, by not presenting a drama or even a set of incidents but rather a plan and a series of provocations, the Living undercut orthodox theatre, even avant-gardism. Then, after many spectators left, often the majority—a winnowing similar to Grotowski's but carried out in a different way: where Grotowski selected who was to go with him, the Living allowed the spectators to individually select themselves—the performers led some of the remaining spectators into the streets. An actual political event arose out of the entertainment event by means of a theatrical confrontation. In the streets the performers and spectators were often met by the police. While Grotowski's work eventuates in religious meetings the Living's eventuates in public acts.

The origins of theatre—considered since Aristotle's day to be found in ritual—look different when seen from the perspective of popular entertainment. E. T. Kirby sees theatre beginning in shamanism, certainly a ritual system. But shamanism itself—as Kirby notes—is closely connected to magic acts, acrobatics, puppetry and other popular entertainments. La Barre points out that the Asiatic-American Trickster—a figure that can be traced back to Paleolithic times—is a "mixture of clown, culture hero and demigod." La Barre reminds us of the connections between the Trickster and the Greek origins of theatre:

> The great antiquity of the trickster should be suggested
> first of all by his being much the same in both
> Paleosiberian and American hunting tribes; and again by
> the fact that the more a tribe has been influenced by
> agriculture in America, the less important he becomes in
> the total tribal mythology as compared with his
> pre-eminence among both Siberian and American hunters.
> [. . .] We must not forget the element of *entertainment* in
> Old World shamanism: were tales of the erotic escapades of
> eagle-Zeus once told in the same tone of voice as those of
> Sibero-American Raven? And did not shamanistic rivalry
> develop into both the Dionysian bard-contests of Greek
> drama in the Old World and into *midewewin*
> medicine-shows in the New? As for that, have modern
> medicine-men entirely lost the old shamanic
> self-dramatization?[33]

So wherever we look, and no matter how far back, theatre is a mixture, a braid, of entertainment and ritual. At one moment ritual seems to be the source, at another it is entertainment that claims primacy. They are a twin-system, tumbling over each other, and vitally interconnected.

Even at this more or less quiet moment, 1976, it's clear that the orthodox dramaturgy—the theatre of plays done in fixed settings for a settled audience relating stories as if they were happening to others—is finished. At least this kind of theatre doesn't meet the needs of many people—needs as old as theatre itself, combining ritual and entertainment. These needs also include actual group interaction as a remedy for a runaway technology. I am not reacting against technology—I have not bought a cabin in Vermont yet. But I know an authentic need exists for encounters that are neither just informal person-to-person gatherings like parties nor formal, mediated, programmed routines like office or factory work—or watching television and films, for that matter. Theatre is a middle world where actual group interaction can happen—not only through audience participation but by subtler means of audience inclusion and environmental staging; theatre combines artistic-composed behavior with everyday-spontaneous behavior. Theatre people are moving into areas once solely occupied by religion and politics. Priests and politicians will doubtlessly pick up new techniques from theatre. But whether they will be able to restore public confidence in their professions is questionable. Will theatre then become a big avenue rather than the sideroad it's been for the past 300 years?

Notes

1. In describing the *kaiko* I followed the account in Rappaport (1968). His study is a paradigm of how to examine ritual performances within an ecological context.
2. A fight package is a small bundle containing "the thorny leaves of the males of a rare, unidentified tree growing in the *kamunga,* called the 'fight tree,' and personal material belonging to the enemy, such as hair, fragments of leaves worn over the buttocks, and dirt scraped from the skin," Rappaport (1968), 120. It is said that pressing the packages to the heart and head will give a man courage and improve his chances of killing an enemy. Materials used in fight packages are acquired from neutrals who have relatives among the enemy; fight packages are items of trade. Their use in peaceful dancing shows the relationship between the dancing and combat; in many parts of Asia performance forms have arisen from martial arts.
3. Rappaport (1968), 187.
4. Rappaport (1968), 188.
5. Rappaport (1968), 189.
6. Rappaport (1968), 195-6.
7. Rappaport (1968), 156.
8. Rappaport (1968), 214.
9. Spencer and Gillen (1968). This study has the advantage over later ones that the tribes described were relatively intact, having just been contacted by the invading Europeans. In Australia contact meant extermination both demographically and culturally.
10. This rhythm of relatively long preparations followed by a brief performance, with a series of performances given on a single day, is common in Australia. See also Elkin and Berndt (1950) and Berndt (1964). Although we accept this rhythm in dance and music, it has not

yet found acceptance in theatre. Still dominated by Aristotelian injunctions we act as if a work has to be of a certain length to acquire seriousness.

11. In Oceania it is not unusual—or was not until the eradication of traditional ways—for ritual performances to form the core of a person's life. Van Gennep's classic analysis of rituals into crisis moments preceded and followed by long periods of relative calm is not wholly descriptive of the situation in New Guinea and Australia. Although the performances are peak experiences, preparations for them continuing over months and years dominate the lives of the people. See Williams (1940) and Schechner/ACTUALS: A LOOK INTO PERFORMANCE THEORY. See also Turner (1969) and Turner (1974).

12. See the discussion of "reactualization" and its relation to the Dreamtime in Eliade (1965).

13. An excellent account of the intimate association among events, landmarks and body decorations is given in Gould (1969). See also Roheim (1969).

14. The Highlands consist of a central valley, and many spur valleys, surrounded by mountains rising to 15,000 feet. The whole area is about three hundred miles long and one hundred and fifty miles wide. It is sparsely populated, by less than three million; villages average four hundred inhabitants. Because of the terrain many local groups have little contact with each other—and there is much local warfare and feuding. There are about five hundred languages, most of them mutually unintelligible, and the largest of them spoken by only 130,000 people. English and pidgin are the basic *linguae francae.*

15. By now criticism of the Cambridge Anthropologists' thesis concerning the ritual origins and structure of Greek theatre is well known. See, for example, Dodds (1951).

16. Joan MacIntosh, a performer with The Performance Group and my wife, was my partner on the trip to Asia in 1971-72 which forms the experiential background to this piece.

17. Burns (1972), 132. This way of looking at ordinary experiences as theatre has roots, of course, in literature. But its systematic application has only recently begun. The key observations have been made by Goffman (1959) and (1971).

18. Brustein (1974). According to Brustein news theatre is "any histrionic proceeding that results from a collaboration between newsworthy personalities, vast public, and the visual or print media (television, films, book publishing, magazines and newspapers). News theater, in other words, is any event that confuses news with theater and theater with news." I think Brustein's description is accurate, but that he is wrong when he says that "news" and "theatre" should be kept distinct. Certainly there are areas of independence, but the two are inherently interdependent. Both are public, action-centered, and crisis dominated. Furthermore, as the means of news transmission

abandons print and uses visual media they approximate the means of theatre. The problems stirred up are not solved by bemoaning the inevitable. Only in finding ways of controlling what's happening will a satisfactory process occur. Take one limited, but decisive, area—the ethics of news reporting. I refer to the ways in which reporting shapes people's responses to events. We all know that so-called "objective" reporting is anything but objective. But is it distorted simply through the evil designs of the news managers, or is there at work a deep structure which makes even attempts at objectivity impossible? Drama has long had an ethical purpose which is expressed not only overtly but in dramatic structure. News broadcasting uses the same structures but without consciousness of the ethics inherent in them. And it is axiomatic that an unconscious ethic will automatically reinforce the *status quo*; or, as Brecht put it, to remain neutral is to support the stronger side. The need then is to make the structures of news reporting—especially its dramatic structures—more conscious; this will lead to greater control over what is being said. Whether these new powers will be used to advance the causes of the people or to repress them remains in doubt.

19. For extended discussions of the concepts of liminality and *communitas* see Turner (1969) and (1974).

20. Lorenz (1967) discusses at some length the development of "appeasement ceremonies" in animals. More technical descriptions are offered by Eibl-Eibesfeldt (1970). Lorenz's description of a special kind of ceremony is almost exactly what I saw in New Guinea, and what so many others have described. "Of all the various appeasement ceremonies, with their many different roots, the most important for our theme are those appearing or greeting rites which have arisen from redirected aggression movements. They differ from all the already described appeasement ceremonies in that they do not put aggression under inhibition but divert it from certain members of the species and canalize it in the direction of others. This new orientation of aggressive behavior is one of the most ingenious inventions of evolution, but it is even more than that: wherever redirected rituals of appeasement are observed, the ceremony is bound to the individuality of the participating partners. The aggression of a particular individual is diverted from a second, equally particular individual, while its discharge against all other, anonymous members of the species is not inhibited. Thus discrimination between friend and stranger arises, and for the first time in the world personal bonds between individuals come into being" (pp. 131-2). Or, as the Tsembaga say, "those who come to our *Kaiko* will also come to our fights." It is also important to note that the ceremonies Lorenz focused on were greeting ceremonies; the dances in the Highlands may correctly be called greeting dances.

21. Kirby (1974). Kirby sees shamanism as "The 'great unitarian artwork' that fragmented into a number of performance arts" (p. 6).

See also E. T. Kirby (1973) and Schechner (1973c), the chapter "Shaman."

22. Becker (1963). See especially Emile Zola's "Naturalism in Theatre" and Strindberg's "Naturalism in Theatre."

23. The First American Congress of Theatre met in Princeton June 2-6, 1974. It brought together more than 200 leaders of the American theatre—very heavily weighted towards producers, managers of regional theatres, and professional administrators. Also the conference was weighted toward New York, organized as it was by Alexander H. Cohen, the New York producer. Eleven panels discussed various problems confronting the theatre, but the real action was in the interaction among individuals and interest groups. It seems likely that a second Congress will be held, one which is less New York dominated. However, it does not appear as if theatre artists will be given any more prominence—that is, writers, directors, actors, and designers will still be under-represented in relationship to the overall number of delegates. The fundamental theme of the Congress—and future Congresses as well—is a growing recognition of a contradictory reality: theatre is marginal, economically speaking, but it seems also to have enduring roots in society. Means are therefore necessary to bring the disparate wings of the theatre together for a common rumination of basically economic issues. Whether politics can, or should, be kept out of these meetings is another question. As for aesthetics, forget it.

24. Hardison (1965), 40.

25. Hardison (1965), 77.

26. Rappaport (1968), 1.

27. Brook (1973), 45-6. Brooks's anecdote is a fine example of what I mean by "preparations" rather than rehearsals. Rehearsal is a way of setting an exact sequence of events. Preparations are a constant state of training so that when a situation arises one will be ready to "do something appropriate" to the moment. Preparations are what a good athletic team does. Too often those interested in improvisation feel that it can arise spontaneously, out of the moment. Nothing is further from the truth. What arises spontaneously is the moment itself, the response is selected from a known repertory and joins with the moment to give the impression of total spontaneity. Most performances among communal peoples are not rehearsed, they are prepared.

28. His invitation was based on my reputation on the island. Although I was there for only two weeks I used to play games with children in which I would imitate animals. I did one act that especially amused the children: making my hands into horns I would charge at them as if I were an enraged bull. On several occasions while riding a bus to a remote village some children would spot me and make the horn gesture. At Tenganan the dance I did at the public performance was a variation on the animal game. MacIntosh's singing was appreciated everywhere, and people would actually get very

angry if she refused to sing. In New Guinea especially, almost anything—an object, a relationship, an event, a performance—is made into an item of trade; there are no neutral or valueless events.

29. The late sixties and early seventies saw a number of performances based on this premise. A family in Greenwich Village sold admission to their apartment where spectators watched them in their daily lives. Of course the Loud Family epic on television carried this style of documentary drama to its logical end: the feedback from the weekly series actually affected the lives the Louds lived, and so we watched the family change under the impact of their knowledge that they were being watched. The theoretical foundations of this kind of art lie in Cage's assertion that theatre is actually an attitude on the part of the spectator—to set up a chair in the street and to watch what happens is to transform the streets into a theatre. These ideas are still very much with us in Process Art.

30. The kind of classification I'm indicating for performance is one which is becoming increasingly used in the sciences, and is replacing older forms of classification where one class of events excludes another. "Classifications need not be hierarchic and the clusters may overlap (intersect). The whole idea of hierarchic, nonoverlapping (mutually exclusive) classifications which is so attractive to the human mind is currently undergoing reexamination. From studies in a variety of fields the representation of taxonomic structure as overlapping clusters or as ordinations appears far preferable." Robert R. Sokal, "Classification: Purposes, Principles, Progress, Prospects," *Science,* 27 September 1974, p. 1121. One "locates" a performance by using the coordinates of efficacy and entertainment.

31. In *Commune* there was, one night, an interruption of more than three hours. During that time the spectators and the performers came to know each other in a way much more intimate and actual than is usually possible in a theatre. When the play resumed there was a feeling surrounding the performance that added power to it. The supper sequence in *Mother Courage* is an attempt at building-in the kind of relationship between performers and spectators that accidentally occurred that night at *Commune*. See Schechner (1973c), 49-56.

32. This experiment, now called "Mountain Project," has been revised and is still going on. It is part of Grotowski's "paratheatrical phase" which began in 1969. In the paratheatrical work there are no spectators, the form is not fixed, the process is what emerges from each participant. Members of the Polish Lab working alone or in teams lead this work. Each project has its own title, such as: *Acting Therapy, Vigil, Meditations Aloud, Soundings,* etc. The events take from a few hours to several weeks, and use all kinds of space from rooms to large sections of the countryside (pilgrimages).

33. La Barre (1972), 195-6.

Kinesics and Performance

> Analogic codification constitutes a series of symbols that in
> their proportions and relations are similar to the thing,
> idea or event for which they stand. [. . .] Such a form of
> codification deals with continuous functions, unlike digital
> codification, which deals with discrete step intervals. [. . .]
> The principles of analogic codification as contrasted with
> digital codification have a central importance to students
> of human behavior that is still perhaps insufficiently
> understood. The use of words, whether in speech or
> writing, has certain limitations akin to those of digital
> computers: words remain identifying or typifying symbols
> that lack the impelling immediacy of analogic devices.
> Words or a series of words are emergent phenomena that,
> because of their step characteristics, lack the property of
> efficiently representing continua or changes over time.[1]

All studies of movement in art are studies of analogic phenomena; but
to what degree are studies of movement *in life* also art? Or to extend
Cage's dictum that there is no separation between art and life—to
what degree does life imitate art? This is not a nit-picking or trivial
question. The history of modern art has seen defiguration and
abstraction—both in the graphic and performing arts—and is now
experiencing a refiguration, a return to the concrete. But this "return"
is neither naturalistic nor realistic, although the elements of natural
action constitute the material and iconographic arrangement of the
action.

The Grand Union dances "naturally." In Richard Foreman's

Ontological-Hysteric Theatre, according to Michael Kirby's words, "almost all of the scenes are presented as sequences of static pictures. The actor or actors are motionless, posed in position like mannequins displayed in a store window. Often only one actor at a time adjusts his position or moves to alter the stage picture. The new picture remains for a moment or, perhaps, for quite a while, until some clear movement changes the picture again."[2] Peter Brook tours his experimental group through Africa; Robert Wilson "stages" *Ka Mountain* on several mountains close to Shiraz in Iran. The last show of the Open Theater, *Nightwalk,* is nearly wordless, often in slow motion, but still a clear permutation of "regular" human behavior.

We contrast these evidences with another, more expressionistic, style best typified in the last decade by Ryszard Cieslak's extraordinary contortions and verbalizations in *The Constant Prince* or *Apocalypsis cum Figuris.* Or, to place the contrast in deeper historical perspective, Grotowski's poor theatre is a function of Meyerhold's understanding of the "grotesque" and "stylized"—an abstraction/distortion that attempts to disclose the "inner" person. The work of Foreman, Wilson, Chaikin in his most recent phase, and the impulse that drove Brook to seek "communication" between his group of non-African performers and the peoples of Central Africa—are not abstract. Rather, they are arrangements, or displacements, or reintegrations of what are, in fact, "everyday" gestures in contexts that make the spectator *think differently* about both the gestures and contexts presented. This new work, joined by a preponderance of work in The New Dance is analogical and it is parallel to work in kinesics—a science of human body motion behavior based on analogical analysis of gesture, posture, grouping and constellations of groupings, all of which are presumed to contain understandable communications.

What is new about kinesics is the methodology used to study analogic behavior; and what is consequential for performance is that these methods are already being widely applied, copied, or adapted to performance situations. Feedback is in the process of growing between specialists in kinesics and performers/directors who recognize in this science a parallel as rich as that which at one time existed between optics and painting.

Kinesics is new because, like other disciplines which presume no new assumptions about human behavior but merely a new way of studying what has always been assumed, equipment is available today that was not when Darwin wrote *The Expression of the Emotions in Man and Animals* (1872). We mean photography, and especially the moving picture. Previously there was no bridge between scientific research and discussion, which is digital, and the phenomena being studied, which is analogical. The motion picture is the perfect bridge. Its mode of recording human action can be adjusted to any shutter and frame speed—although 18 or 24 frames per second is what is usually used; these being the speeds at which the discrete frames projected on a screen no longer flicker; thus, human action-in-action can be recorded in an analogic mode. But the action is then analyzed frame-by-frame, in a digital mode. Through analogic recording and digital analysis it is possible to look at human body behavior from two previously mutually incompatible perspectives. The consequences for performing arts have already been substantial—but we believe the future effects will be much deeper and more widespread.

Because in a brief introductory survey such as this, designed to familiarize people in performance with methods that may appear arcane, it is not possible to scan the whole field with any kind of concreteness, we wish only to name a few of the important figures in the development of kinesics, and then concentrate on Ray L. Birdwhistell, an acknowledged founder-leader of kinesics. We select Birdwhistell not merely because of his preeminence but because he has defined a vocabulary and methodology; those who want to do kinesic research of their own can do so on the basis of Birdwhistell's work.

We have already spoken of Darwin's 1872 book that lays the basis for ethology, which is closely related to kinesics because, obviously, animals communicate with each other and with men analogically not digitally. The theories and observations of Tinbergen, Lorenz, Morris and Goodall are relevant to our study here, although ethology goes off in its own, parallel, direction. The strongest link between ethology and kinesics is, in our opinion, Gregory Bateson—a man who has played John Cage's role to the behavioral sciences. Bateson's career spans four decades. His early work on ceremony (*Naven*, 1936) in New Guinea lead to his collaboration with Margaret Mead and their classic study of non-verbal behavior: *Balinese Character: A Photographic Analysis* (1942). Bateson has also influenced the influential Stanford school of behavioral scientists, and has helped define such diverse areas as family therapy and treatment of schizophrenics, the study of communication among dolphins and general communications theory. Another reasonably early worker in the field, which he calls proxemics, is E. T. Hall, an anthropologist. Hall's two best studies for our purposes are *The Silent Language* (1959) and *The Hidden Dimension* (1966). And, then, there is Erving Goffman, a sociologist of wit and perception, who in a long series of books examines the networks of non-verbal behaviors that he believes knits American society together. Almost monthly new studies are added—and the growth of the field is akin to the development of psychoanalytic theories in the period between the two World Wars. Psychoanalysis, using mostly digital methods, explored relationships between fantasy, acting out and "reality." Psychoanalysis is profoundly discursive and individualist. Kinesics is analogic and collective—as such it has more of a bearing on performance which traditionally communicates through images, actions and gestures; even, as in opera, using words-as-sounds rather than discursively. (This operatic use of words is a recurring characteristic of modern experimental performance.) Performance is a collective activity both from the performers' and the spectators' points of view.

Birdwhistell's work is collected in *Kinesics and Context* and a series of other papers, dating from 1952. His writing is technical, even turgid at times. His interest is in the "communicative stream"—the various channels of communication which mutually determine each other. He theorizes that these channels give definition to, and actually control, the social order. This theme is taken up by Birdwhistell's colleague, A. E. Scheflen (1972), and will not concern us here. In fact, content is of little relevance to understanding Birdwhistell. His work is not an elaboration on theses of "body language," whereby certain gestures have certain meanings. Rather his work posits "channels of communication" in which limited sets of gestures acquire unlimited sets of meanings, depending on context. This assertation is not new, and actors have long been trained according to it. What is new is the methodology for scrutinizing it in detail, and the consequences for performance include developing body movement patterns that are at one and the same moment "natural" and "abstract."

Birdwhistell postulates that communication is a continuous process conveyed through a multi-channel system.[3]

> I have posited communication as a multi-channel system
> emergent from and regulative of the influenceable
> multi-sensory activity of living systems. Within such a
> frame of reference, spoken and the body motion languages
> are *infra*-communicational systems which are
> *interdependently merged* with each other and with other
> comparable codes utilizing other channels to become
> communicative.[4]

No one channel can alone convey "meaning." Meaning is in fact the confluence of multi-channeled information. When one channel is separated out, say negatively by subtracting speech as in pantomime, or through a change in speed as when Foreman freezes an action or Wilson presents one in extreme slow motion, a dissociation between "meaning" and "channeling" occurs. This is somewhat like the old dissociation between "content" and "form" but different at the decisive point of communications flow. For what happens while watching Wilson or Foreman is:

> There is plenty of time to become aware of the possibilities
> inherent in the actor. As the eyes move over the static
> composition, they may repeatedly send the same data,
> resulting in several identical messages. [. . .]
> Contemplation may provide intensification through
> redundancy.[5]

Thus, meanings are combined with meanings because any change in the rate, flow, intensity or channel used in communicating not only changes the messages but alters the context.

Body movement is seen as interdependent with linguistics, and with tactile, olfactory, gustatory and proprioceptive systems. Each of these senses receives information, and puts it in context. The matter is complicated by two factors: the context in which channeled information is put is also generated by the very information received—living is feedback and cross-referencing. Secondly, research indicates some universal human gestures, some of these apparently rooted in primate behavior; and these gestures—such as greeting with the open hand, submitting by lowering the eyes—apparently have "meaning." It remains to be seen exactly what this meaning is. It is not identical to emotional codes developed by Delsarte, or by the currently popular books on "body language." What Birdwhistell wisely does is insist on the complexity of the cross-referencing and multi-channeled systems. In his view none of the infra-systems generate contexts (meanings). The patterns that have meaning are culturally, not biologically, determined; learning these patterns begins at birth, or before. The communications systems of face-to-face encounters—and all performance is just that—is incredibly thick. We are just at the beginning of unraveling the many strands: symbolic, expressive and raw.

Thus, performance is in the same self-examining situation as painting was from the time of Monet. Kinesics is a tool equivalent to optics and color theory. The factors being examined in performance are gesture, posture, grouping and constellations of groupings; these are looked at not abstractly but as infra-communications channels. These channels, according to Birdwhistell, are not species-specific, but cultural. There are no universal symbols that indicate physiological or emotional states. (This is where Darwin was wrong.) And motor, sensory and linguistic patterns (codes) are learned, they are not innate. In other words, artists are experimenting with symbols and codes because there are no changeless patterns of these.

Birdwhistell's classic example of this is his analysis of the "smile." The "smile" is formed by the lateral extension of mouth corners and upward pull on the upper lips. Both movements vary in extent, and various combinations are possible (upper teeth exposed, both rows of teeth exposed, etc.). The "smile" itself is cross-referenced by other facial motions such as eyebrow and cheek motions, still more cross-referencing takes place in the shoulders, hips, arms and hands. All of these are cross-referenced by simultaneous or intermittent vocalizations, such as words, laughter or other things. The point is that the primary facial moves could "mean" either "smile" or "grimace," depending on the cross-referencing and social context. Looking at a silent film of one person alone it is not possible to say whether the person is smiling or grimacing. By a process which we will not follow out here Birdwhistell, and others, have identified a number of "universal" gestures which are not universal except in the gross, physical sense.

In seeing exactly how the gesture is liberated from its meaning, the performing artist is able to explore a number of dissociations of gesture from meaning. This can lead to new associations of meaning that are not consciously controlled by the artist—as in the Grand Union's work—or in more controlled new contexts, as in Wilson and Foreman. Richard Schechner, working with Dan Stern and The Performance Group, hopes to conduct a further experiment this fall. In this work, performers will assist in a kinesic analysis of their own behavior as reflected in rehearsals and performances. The "kines" thus isolated will be fed back into rehearsals, re-analyzed and so on. We cannot discuss the outcome of this work because it is still in the early stages of planning. But the hope is to develop two parallel systems—one kinographic and the other narrative. Rather than have these joined unconsciously as in orthodox theatre, they will be consciously, and often ironically, played off against each other as in contrapuntal musical structure.[6]

Initial investigations of kinesic systems disclosed that movement systems were homologous to linguistic systems. Birdwhistell uses linguistics as a model for the annotation of movement, and as the source of his basic vocabulary. A few working definitions will help in our discussion of methodology:

> The *kine* is the smallest kinesic unit—the smallest particle of visually perceptible motion (for example, the eyelid closure in a wink). The *kinemorph* is a set of kines that compose the particular motion isolated for study (for example, the wink itself). *Allokines* are variations of kines that do not change the meaning of the kine within the pattern of a particular kinemorph (for example, closure of the right or left eyelid in a wink—"rightness" and "leftness" are allokinic, one can be substituted for the other). A *kinemorphic construction* is a combination of kinemorphs (for example, a wink plus a head nod).

Determining structurally meaningful units is done by contrast analysis. Birdwhistell shows frames taken from films to an observer. Each series of projections contains variations of one kinemorph that has been abstracted for study. Each projection varies only one component (kine) of the kinemorph. After each projection the investigator records the observer's comments and makes a tentative analysis. What the investigator is looking for is whether or not a change in any one of the component kines changes the meaning of the pattern. Obviously, these changes are culturally determined. What may be significant in one culture may not be in another. Of contrast analysis Birdwhistell says:

> I believe that by this method we are orienting the study of

> body motion in a direction whereby it will ultimately be
> possible to analyze *contextual* meaning empirically, and
> through scientific experimentation, rather than through
> the often misleading devices concerning meaning
> derivation supplied by intuitionist philosophical
> approaches.[7]

Contrast analysis is already widely in use in the theatre, but mostly on an intuitive basis. Kinesics introduces into training, directing and choreography means of being analytic where previously one was limited to intuition. We are not sure if film and video equipment are to become as standard in training and rehearsal situations as work lights, but we believe there is a tendency in this direction.

Again we wish to emphasize that this method is *not* a way of managing "feelings." It is a way of understanding movement. We twice previously have used terms describing movement and stasis, and now we wish to delineate more exactly what we mean by these terms.

> Gesture: the movements of the face and hands.
> Posture: the body, taken as a whole.
> Grouping: two or more people in relation to each other.
> Constellation: two or more groupings in relation to each
> other.

Most kinesic work to date has been done in the areas of gesture and posture. However, although individuals are studied, they are usually studied as one-of-a-couple. The mother-child dyad is a favorite for examination because of what Winnicott calls the "mirror relationship" existing between them. Scheflen has done work on groupings, but there is relatively little work on constellations. Furthermore, most of the work has been done either on "everyday" situations— social gatherings, interviews, work patterns, domestic life—or on pathological behavior, especially the behavior of schizophrenics. We suggest that a fruitful collaboration is possible between performing groups and kinesicists. The performing group is particularly close-knit; rehearsals themselves may be looked at as a means of generating harmony among a group of people who normally might each go their own way. The traditional advantage of "ensemble" performing has been this "harmony." But what is harmony, insofar as it applies to performance? We believe that it may be kinesic congruence, what Scheflen calls "reciprocals." All human interaction (and the behavior of apes and monkeys) shows a high degree of intra-group reciprocation of movement. It is our contention that performing groups show much more than the average; that, in fact, it is the high density of reciprocal gesturing, posturing and grouping that is the basis for what is "felt" as an "ensemble." If this thesis is true, and it can be tested, then new exercises in reciprocal gesturing, posturing and grouping can be developed to directly foster ensemble performing. These exercises will include a number of "mirroring" exercises, but will move beyond them to more subtle exercises.

Very little careful observation has been done concerning constellations. Clearly the director's and choreographer's stock-in-trade is constellations; but most of this work has been achieved intuitively. We
suggest that kinesic contrast analysis is a most powerful tool for
working out over-all patterns of staging.

Much kinesic work is individualized—even though two or more
people are studied the object is to understand individual communication, mainly the one-to-one relationship. However, another area of
kinesics is of more relevance to performance. Birdwhistell defines
"social kinesics" as (1) the integration of common past experiences,
such as is seen at initiation ceremonies or other traditional observances; and (2) the introduction of new information not held in common, such as how a new discovery is "accepted." It is Birdwhistell's
contention that these two processes are achieved more through
kinesic behavior than through verbal behavior. This appears to be
true about traditional ceremonies in which Goffman says people "act
out their realities." But how is it true of, say, scientific knowledge,
which is largely communicated in the technical language of technical
journals? It is our opinion that the conferences, seminars and countless face-to-face meetings, which usually do not introduce any new
information (information not already existing in written form),
achieve a deep ceremonial objective of integrating this new information into the life-stream of the particular sub-culture that is gathered.
Conventions, conferences etc., serve a socially kinetic function that is
absolutely necessary, for the transmission of information insofar as
transmission = acceptance. In this sense, scientific and literary
gatherings are as *strictly ritual* as Australian Aborigine initiation
ceremonies; and these gatherings can, through kinesic analysis, be
examined as the ritual performances they in fact are.

What are the implications of kinesics for theatre? We have outlined
some of the theatrical applications of kinesics. Since Diderot, at least,
a debate has gone on concerning performer training, and the basic
nature of performing itself. Is performing intuitive, or is it analytic?
This question will not be answered definitively, but will exist as a
bipolar oppositional system, constantly alternating from one extreme
to the other. The neo-expressionistic phase of performance, so brilliantly incarnated in Grotowski's theatre, is passing away now; a
more analytic mode is replacing it. Within this analytic mode kinesics
is finding an important place as a tool for rehearsals and as a source of
images for performance. However, we feel that kinesics will endure as
a training and performance tool even when performance shifts back to
more expressionistic modes. This is because whatever the mode there
is a long-standing wish among performers to codify physical expressions. Delsarte, Dalcroze and Meyerhold each designed what they
believed to be "scientific" ways of analyzing and presenting movement. However, by-and-large, these systems, purporting to be analy-

tic, were in truth intuitive. That is, they were based on the assumption that particular gestures had a particular meaning or effect. They did not probe deep enough into the non-symbolic nature of body movement. Birdwhistell's work begins this in-depth probing—by strictly insisting that *all* meaning is contextual and no meaning is inherent in the kinemorph, Birdwhistell opens up an avenue for continued research that we believe will have a permanent effect on performer training and performer styles. This effect will not lead to a single style, or set of styles, such as "biomechanics" does. Because kinesics insists on the non-symbolic nature of body movement, any number of stylists can make use of the information uncovered through kinesic analysis.

Notes

1. Ruesch and Kees (1972), 8.
2. M. Kirby (1973), 10.
3. A survey of current thinking in the field is contained in a special issue of *Scientific American,* Vol. 227, No. 3 (September 1972), devoted to communication.
4. Birdwhistell (1964), 2.
5. M. Kirby (1973), 28.
6. This experiment was not carried out.
7. Birdwhistell (1952), 17.

Towards a
Poetics of Performance

The earliest human societies were hunting and gathering bands. These bands were neither primitive nor poor; the best evidence suggests an abundance of food, small families (birth control was practiced), an established range; the cultural level—at least in terms of painting and sculpting—was very high: the masterpieces of the caves of southwest Europe and the mobile art of Eurasia are testimony enough. Human bands did not live in one spot, neither did they wander aimlessly. Each band had its own circuit: a route through time/space in a specific range. I say "time/space" because the hunting schedule was not gratuitous; it took into account the movement of game in pursuit of its own feeding and mating patterns. In brief, humans occupied an ecological niche that kept bands on the move in a regular, repetitive pattern, following game and adjusting to the seasons.

Repetitous beyond modern calculation: evidence shows that certain decorated caves were in constant use for more than 10,000 years. What kind of use shall be made clear soon. Human bands did not number more than 40 to 70 individuals, and more than one band used adjacent and overlapping ranges. For most of the year bands probably met only occasionally, by chance, or perhaps to exchange information and goods. But indications are that at special times—when game was assembled in one area, when certain edible fruits and nuts were ripe for gathering—a concentration of bands took place. This still happens among the few hunting peoples left, in the Kalahari with the !Kung,

108

at the coroborrees of the Australian Aborigines; the farming and hunting highland tribes in New Guinea stage elaborate "payback" or exchange ceremonies on a regular basis.[1] Pilgrimages, family reunions marked by feasting and the exchange of gifts and theatrical performances are three other variations on the same action.

V. and F. Reynolds report a strikingly similar phenomenon among the chimpanzees of the Budongo Forest in Africa. The Reynolds' account makes me want to root "going out to the theatre" or "ceremonial gathering" in behavior common to humans and certain other species.

> Garner (1896: 59-60) wrote that, according to native hearsay, 'one of the most remarkable habits of the chimpanzee is the *kanjo* as it is called in the native tongue. The word . . . implies more of the idea of 'carnival.' It is believed that more than one family takes part in these festivities.' He went on to describe how the chimpanzees fashion a drum from damp clay and wait for it to dry. Then 'the chimpanzees assemble by night in great numbers and then the carnival begins. One or two will beat violently on this dry clay, while others jump up and down in a wild grotesque manner. Some of them utter long rolling sounds as if trying to sing . . . and the festivities continue in this fashion for hours.' Apart from the question of the drum, the account given above describes quite well what occurred in the Budongo Forest in its extreme form, as we heard it six times, once when we were very close to the chimpanzees. Only twice, however, did this happen at night; the four other times it lasted for a few hours during the daytime.
>
> The 'carnivals' consisted of prolonged noise for periods of hours, whereas ordinary outbursts of calling and drumming lasted a few minutes only. Although it was not possible to know the reason for this unusual behavior, twice it seemed to be associated with the meeting at a common food source of bands that may have been relatively unfamiliar to each other.[2]

The Reynolds aren't sure what the carnivals were for—they think it may signal a move from one food source to another. It does occur when certain edible fruits are ripe. The 19th-century report indicating some kind of entertainment (singing, dancing, drumming) apparently romanticizes and anthropomorphizes the gathering of chimpanzees: a mood of excitement and well-being, the meeting of many animals from different bands who are on friendly terms with each other. This description fits neatly that of human gatherings. But the Reynolds confirm the 19th-century reports:

> Calls were coming from all directions at once and all groups concerned seemed to be moving about rapidly. As we oriented the source of one outburst, another came from another direction. Stamping and fast-running feet were

> heard sometimes behind, sometimes in front and howling
> outbursts and prolonged rolls of drums (as many as 13
> rapid beats) shaking the ground surprised us every few
> yards.[3]

What these carnivals are are prototypes of celebratory, theatrical events. Their qualities are worth noting: (1) a gathering of bands—not individuals—who are neither living with nor total strangers to each other; (2) the sharing of food or, at least, a food source; (3) singing, dancing (rhythmic movement), drumming: entertainment; (4) use of a place that is not "home" for any group as the grounds for the gathering. (In regard to the last point I note that even in our own culture parties held in the home use rooms especially marked out or decorated "for the occasion"; and other rooms are more or less off limits.)

The entertainment aspect of the gathering is of special importance. This kind of behavior Turner describes as "liminal," it characterizes initiation rites and pilgrimages. At celebratory gatherings people are free to engage in behavior and associations that would otherwise be forbidden: in fact, special non-ordinary behavior is not only permitted, it is expected, prepared for, rehearsed.

Where two or more groups meet on a seasonal schedule, where there is abundant food either available or stored and where there is a geographical marker—cave, hill, waterhole, etc.—there is likelihood of a ceremonial center. Of the many differences between human and ape ceremonial centers none is more decisive than the fact that only humans permanently transform the space by "writing" on it or attaching a lore to it. The art in the caves of southwest Europe and the stories of the Aborigines about the landmarks in their range are means of transforming natural spaces into cultural places: ways of making theatres. But every architectural construction or modification is the making of a cultural place—what is special about a theatre?

A theatre is a place whose only or main use is to stage performances. A performance is an event which includes at its center a drama, in the strict sense of Turner's definition. It is my belief that this kind of space, a theatre place, did not arrive late in human cultures (say with the Greeks of the 5th century B.C.) but was there from the beginning: is itself one of the marks which, taken together, characterize our species. The first theatres were ceremonial centers—part of a system of hunting, following food sources according to a seasonal schedule, meeting other human bands, celebrating and marking the celebration by some kind of writing on a space; an integration of geography, calendar, social interaction and the ability of people to transform natural items into cultural items. The first theatres were not merely "natural spaces"—as the Budongo Forest where the chimpanzees stage their carnivals is—but were also, and fundamentally, "cultural places." The transformation of space into place is at the heart of the construction of a theatre; this transforma-

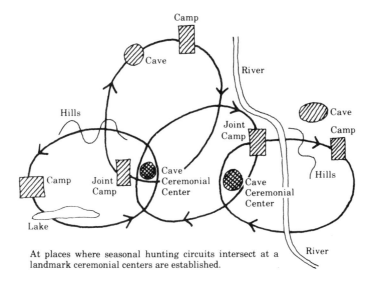

At places where seasonal hunting circuits intersect at a landmark ceremonial centers are established.

tion is accomplished by "writing on space," as the cave art of the Paleolithic period demonstrates so well.[4] This writing need not be visual, it can be oral as with the Aborigines. The Aborigines are a people with few material possessions but possessing a culture rich in kinship systems, rites, myths, songs and dances. With them the transformation of space into place cannot be seen so much as it can be heard. Remembering the Aborigines we must be cautious when assuming an area that has left little visual evidence of high art is necessarily artistically impoverished.

The functions of the ceremonies—or performances—at the ceremonial centers, and the exact procedures, cannot be known precisely. Heelmarks left in the clay in at least one of the caves indicates dancing; authorities generally agree that performances of some kind took place.[5] But more often than not the reconstructions suit the tastes of the reconstructor: fertility rites, initiations, shamanist-curing and so on. My own tastes run towards "ecological rituals" such as outlined by Roy A. Rappaport: performances which regulate economic, political and religious interaction among neighboring groups whose relation with each other alternates between hostility and collaboration. In fact, Rappaport in *Pigs for the Ancestors* discusses war as part of a total ecological system. My own views are close to Rappaport's:

> . . .ritual, particularly in the context of a ritual cycle,
> operates as a regulating mechanism in a system, or set of
> interlocking systems, in which such variables as the area
> of available land, necessary lengths of fallow periods, size

> and composition of both human and pig populations,
> trophic requirements of pigs and people, energy expended
> in various activities, and the frequency of misfortunes are
> included. [. . .] Underlying these hypotheses is the belief
> that much is to be gained by regarding culture, in some of
> its aspects, as part of the means by which animals of the
> human species maintain themselves in their
> environments.[6]

Rappaport is writing of a contemporary New Guinea people; I am trying to reconstruct performances of Paleolithic hunters—I think both bear relevantly on patterns within modern industrial societies. Extrapolating from Rappaport, from the pictorial and other evidence within the caves and from patterns within contemporary theatre I think I can say that the performances at the ceremonial centers occurring where hunting bands met functioned in at least the following ways:

1. To maintain friendly relations.
2. To exchange goods, mates, trophies, techniques.
3. To show and exchange dances, songs, dramas.

Furthermore, I think these performances followed rhythms familiar to us of:

1. Gathering.
2. Performing.
3. Dispersing.

In other words, people came to a special place, did something that can be called theatre and went on their way. Simple and self-apparent as this rhythm may seem it is not the only thing that can happen when two or more groups approach each other. They could avoid each other, meet in combat, pass each other by as travelers do on a road and so on. The pattern of gathering, performing, dispersing is one which I call the basic theatrical pattern.

This pattern occurs "naturally" in urban settings. An accident happens, or is caused to happen (as in guerrilla theatre); a crowd gathers to see what's happened. The crowd makes a circle around the event or, as in the case with accidents, around the aftermath of the event. Talk in the crowd is about what happened, to whom, why; this talk is largely interrogative: like dramas and courtroom trials, which are formal versions of the street accident, the event itself is absorbed into the *action of reconstructing what took place*. In trials this is done verbally; in dramas this is done analogically, by doing again what happened (actually, fictionally, mythically, religiously). The questions asked in the crowd are those which Brecht wanted theatre audiences to ask of dramas.[7] The shape of this kind of street event—a heated center with involved spectators blending out to a cool rim where people come, peer in and move on—is like that of some medieval street theatre.[8] Accidents conform to the basic performance pattern; even after the event is "cleaned up" some "writing" is left on the site: for example, bloodstains, knots of witnesses and the curious and so on. Only slowly does the event evaporate and the crowd disperse. I call such events "eruptions."

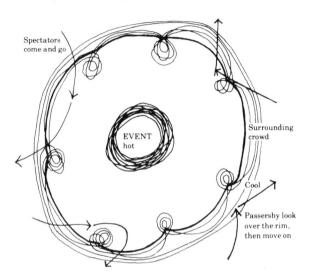

Spectators come and go

EVENT hot

Surrounding crowd

Cool

Passersby look over the rim, then move on

An "eruption," with a heated center, a cool rim, with spectators coming and going. The eruption occurs either *after* an accident or during an event whose development is predictable such as an argument, the construction or demolition of a building and so on.

An eruption is like a theatrical performance because it is *not* the accident itself that gathers and keeps an audience. They are held by a reconstruction or re-enactment of the event. In the case of an argument or, at a much slower pace, the construction of a building watched by sidewalk superintendents, it is the unfolding of an event which can be measured against a predictable scenario that gathers and holds people. Totally unmanageable occurrences—a falling wall, sudden gunfire—scatters people; only after the wall has fallen or the shooting stops does the crowd gather to make the drama.

Eruptions are one kind of "natural"[9] theatre, *"processions"* are another. Together they form the bipolar model of the performances that took place in the ceremonial centers at the intersecting points of Paleolithic hunting bands moving across the terrain on their seasonal treks. In a procession—which is a kind of pilgrimage—the event moves along a prescribed path, spectators gather along the route, and at appointed places the procession halts and performances are played. Parades, funeral corteges, political marches, the Bread & Puppet Theatre are processions.

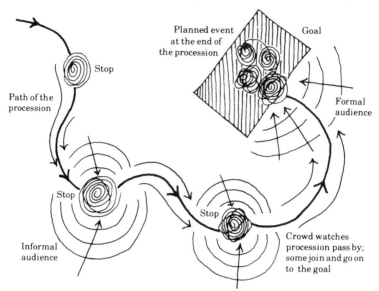

A "procession," with a fixed route and a known goal. At several points along the way the procession stops and performances are played. Spectators watch the procession pass by, some may join and go on to the goal.

Usually a procession moves to a goal: the funeral to the grave, the political march to the speakers' stand, the circus parade to the big-top, the pilgrimage to the shrine. The event performed at the goal of the procession is the opposite of an eruption: it is well planned for, rehearsed, ritualized.

However, eruptions and processions can occur simultaneously, especially when large numbers of people are involved and the leadership of a group is flexible. The meeting of bands of chimpanzees in the Budongo Forest is both eruptive and processional: at a known place in a known circuit the abundance of food, the meeting with strange bands, triggers an eruption of the "carnival." It is my belief that a roughly similar thing happened countless times on the hunting circuits of Paleolithic humans. Out of these hunting circuits developed ritual circuits, meeting places, ceremonial centers and theatres.

The fact that theatres occur at special times in special places is worldwide. It locates theatre in a complex of performance activities which also includes rites of passage, sports and trials (duels, ritual combats, courtroom trials). Theatres are maps of the cultures where they exist. That is, theatre is analogical not only in the "literary" sense—the stories dramas tell, the convention of explicating action by staging it— but also in the architectonic sense. Thus, for example, the Athenian theatre of the 5th Century B.C. has at its center the altar of Dionysus, around this altar the chorus dances physically between the audience and the men who play the dramatic roles; the semicircular tiers of seats—not individuated as in modern theatres but curving communal benches—literally enfolds the drama, containing its *agons* within an Athenian solidarity. Conceptually this pattern of solidarity containing *agon* is repeated in the contest among the poets for the best play. The proscenium theatre of the 18th to 20th centuries in the West also shows a definite sociometric design.

At the center of the Athenian theatre was the open eye of the Altar of Dionysus. Around it danced the Chorus, giving a nest of solidarity for the agonistic actions of the actors. The audience nests both Chorus and actors. But the agon of the contest among poets for the prize surrounds the whole theatrical event. Yet the solidarity of Athens, the polis, provides the ultimate nest for the entire sequence of performances. Each agon is literally held

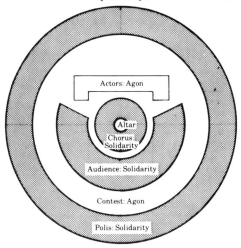

in a nest of solidarity. The outer nest—the polis—is *not* metaphorical: there were definite geographical, ideological and social limits to Athens; and each person knew what it was to be a citizen. The shape of the theatre is a version of the social system which alternated agon and solidarity; which was open about debate and interrogation, but closed about who was or was not a member, a citizen.

The Greek amphitheatre is open, beyond and around it the city can be seen during performances which take place in daylight. It is the city, the *polis,* that is tightly boundaried geographically and ideologically. The proscenium theatre is a tightly boundaried individual building with access from the street strictly controlled. Within the part of the structure where the performance takes place and is viewed much effort is spent in directing attention only on the drama; everything not in the show is hidden or sunk in darkness. The building, like the events within it, is compartmentalized; the time for the audience to look at each other is regulated and is limited to before the show and intermissions.

The proscenium theatre is divided into three precincts. The lobby, "A," actually begins in the street in front of the theatre; the lobby is open to all, patrons and non-patrons. In the lobby the box office offers tickets for sale to those who want to go beyond the lobby into the house. Theatre workers enter the building from another door, the

The City

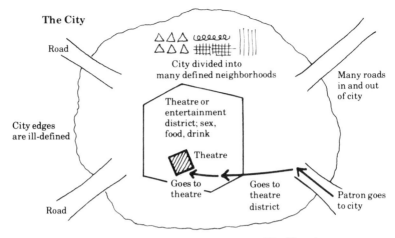

The Theatre

Adjoins other theatres

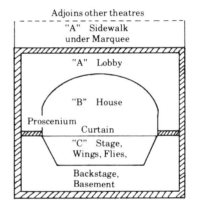

The theatre is not in itself a central structure at the heart of a clearly boundaried *polis*. It is in a threatre district which is one neighborhood in an ill-defined "urban area." Other theatres adjoin or are close to the theatre.

The theatre itself is divided into three areas: lobby, house, stage. Fixed seating aims the audience at the stage. The stage floor is open, often slightly raked so as to tilt the action toward the house. Stage machinery is hidden in wings and flies; quick scene changes are possible.

The lobby, which extends into the street under the theatre marquee is a gathering place for the audience.

stage door, because part of the proscenium style—a version of the industrial practice of separating the production of goods from their marketing— is to conceal all preparations from the patrons.

The house, "B," is divided into different classes of seats, some better than others; however, even the cheap seats are individual. Usually the house is gaudily decorated, displaying cash outlay, even though during the show these decorations can't be seen. The box seats are placed so that patrons sitting there can be seen by other spectators.[10] A curtain covers most of the wall facing the seats. However, even when this temporary barrier is lifted, patrons are not allowed on stage.

The stage, "C," is architecturally separated from the house by the proscenium arch, a unique and dominating feature. The arch is actually a wall interrupted in its center portion so that quite literally the audience is in one room looking into another with the wall separating the two rooms *partially* removed. As the proscenium theatre developed over the 17th through 20th centuries the forestage jutting into the house receded until it vanished eliminating any sharing of space between the stage and the house. The open theatre movement of the 20th century has made the playing space part of the viewing space once again; this has been attempted in many variations—thrust stage, arena, environmental. In the proscenium theatre the part of the stage visible to the audience is a surprisingly small portion of the area behind the proscenium. In the Greek theatre almost every space was visible, as well as the city behind and around the theatre. In the proscenium theatre the wings, flies, dressing rooms, offices and storage bins are all concealed. The stage portion of the building is usually more than half the area of the theatre, but from the house it looks much less spacious than the house, Flies and wings were developed to facilitate quick changes of scenery—visual surprises. Additional storage space was necessary as productions involving bulks of scenery were kept for future productions; dressing rooms became more ornate as costumes and makeup increased in complexity. The "C" space of the proscenium theatre is an efficient engine for quick scene changes and mounting sumptuous effects; this theatre produces "numbers" and *coups de théatre* like a many-coursed meal at an expensive restaurant. Every attempt is made to hide how effects are achieved while displaying how much they cost. Dramas written for the proscenium include one or two intermissions because it's necessary for patrons to see each other, evaluate the product they've purchased, drink, smoke and re-experience the thrill of the rising curtain.

Theatres are located in a theatre district; performances are offered in the interstices of the work week or on general holidays. Being a model of the mercantile process the theatre can't impede that process; appealing to the middle class it is not proper to entice people from their jobs. The theatre district stimulates consumer appetites offering a sequence of shows just as each show offers a sequence of scenes. Competition is fierce among theatres—this competition is for customers not prizes; when prizes are given they are used to attract more customers. Most shows fail (which means they don't attract buyers) but hits run as long as people will pay to see them regardless of their artistic quality. Thus, in all these ways, the proscenium theatre is a model of capitalism in its classic phase. Today, as capitalism evolves into corporatism, new kinds of theatres arise. Cultural centers—art fortresses run not by impressarios but boards of directors—are examples of conglomeratism. Environmental theatres—built in cheap hit-and-run spaces, often in out of the way neighborhoods—exemplify a resistance and alternative to the conglomerate; but environmental theatres exist only in the creases of contemporary society, and off leavings, like cockroaches.

Creases are not marginal—they run through the actual and conceptual center of society, like faults in the earth's crust. Creases are places to hide, but more importantly they signal areas of instability, disturbance and radical change in the social plane. This change is always a "change in direction," that is, not a change only of technique. Throughout the urban environment in places abandoned, or not yet reclaimed, individuals and small groups work. Even in large, apparently smooth operations like corporations and universities creases exist; look for them, quite literally, in "out of the way places." An existing neighborhood is not transformed instantly by the bulldozer (as when building a cultural center whose monuments rest on murdered neighborhoods) but step-by-step through infiltration and renovation. At the time when a balance/tension exists between several classes, income levels, interests and uses—as in New York's Soho district—crease phenomena—experimental art, active bars and cafés, street life, parties which move from living area to living area—peak. But when a threshold of visibility and "stability" is crossed, the neighborhood freezes in a new form, becomes an "attraction" (like the theatre district which draws most of its life from outside its own precinct) and the crease is smoothed out. Then artists—and others who need a crease environment—follow along, or create, a new fault.

The fact that theatre places are scenographic models of sociometric patterns is universal. Pointing out that "most of the traditional theatre performances [of India] are open-air events, organized on the level ground, a platform stage or as a mobile processional spectacle," Suresh Awasthi goes on to say:

> They are presented in fields after the harvest, streets, open
> spaces outside town (often permanently designated for
> performances), fairs, markets and—especially for the
> Ramayana and the Krishna legend shows—temple
> gardens, riverbanks, market squares and courtyards. [...]
> The performances are social events not separated from the
> community activity. The actor is an active member of his
> community. He is also a farmer, a mechanic, a carpenter, a
> fruit vendor, a vegetable hawker. [...] An important factor
> that determines the nature of the scenography in this
> theatre is the nonrealistic and metaphysical treatment of
> time and place.[11]

Traditional Indian theatre is very like Western medieval theatre—and modern avant-garde or experimental theatre. In all cases the performer often has a second or third occupation, but this does not mean that his skills as a performer are amateurish; far from it, a connection to a community may deepen all aspects of his art. The flexible treatment of time and space—the ability of one space to be transformed into many places through the skills of the performer more than through the illusionistic devices of the scenographer—goes

hand-in-hand with a transformational view of character (role dou-
bling, role switching) and a close contact with the audience (the performer both as character and as storyteller, the use of such devices as
the aside and direct address to the audience). The connectedness—a
mobility among spheres of reality rather than social mobility in the
modern sense—is an important quality of traditional performances,
and even the avant-garde (where the life of the bohemian is lived
outside the usual social categories). The totality of theatre is nowhere
better expressed than among the Aborigines:

> The daily life of the Aborigines is rewarding but routine.
> There is a kind of low-key pace to the everyday round of
> living. In their ritual lives, however, the Aborigines attain
> a heightened sense of drama. Sharp images appear and
> colors deepen. The Aborigines are masters of stagecraft
> and achieve remarkable visual and musical effects with
> the limited materials at hand. [. . .] Gradually I
> experienced the central truth of Aboriginal religion: that it
> is not a thing by itself but an inseparable part of a whole
> that encompasses every aspect of daily life, every
> individual and every time—past, present and future. It is
> nothing less than the theme of existence, and as such
> constitutes one of the most sophisticated and unique
> religious and philosophical systems known to man.[12]

We are accustomed to a theatre that locates "the real" in relationships
among individual people; but most of the world theatre takes a
broader, and deeper, view of what's real. Modern Western theatre is
mimetic, reactualizing on stage what has occurred elsewhere. Traditional theatre, and again I include the avant-garde in this category, is
transformational, creating or incarnating in a theatre place what
cannot take place anywhere else. Just as a farm is a field where edible
foods are grown, so a theatre is a place where transformations of time,
place and persons (human and nonhuman) are accomplished.
Aborigine scenography creates a theatre out of a combination of
natural and built elements. Each rock, waterhole, tree and stream is
embedded in a matrix of legend and dramatic action. Thus a particular place is where a ceremony takes place, where a mythic event has
happened in the past, where beings manifest themselves through songs
and dances and where everyday and special actions converge—for
example, a waterhole is a place where people come to drink and where
ceremonies are enacted. Modifications of space transforming it into a
theatre may consist of clearing the space and doing sand or rock
paintings; or a space may become a theatre by being "learned"—a
novice is taught the legends, songs and dances associated with a
space: geography itself is socialized; the uninitiated sees nothing but
an outcropping of rock or a waterhole, while the initiated experiences
a dense theatrical setting. This technique of creating a theatre place

by poetic means is used by Shakespeare and practitioners of guerrilla theatre.

Transformances

Victor Turner analyzes "social dramas" using theatrical terminology to describe disharmonic or crisis situations. These situations—arguments, combats, rites of passage—are inherently dramatic because participants not only do things they try *to show others what they are doing or have done;* actions take on a "performed for an audience" aspect. Erving Goffman takes a more directly scenographic approach in using the theatrical paradigm. He believes all social interaction is staged—people prepare backstage, confront others while wearing masks and playing roles, use the main stage area for the performance of routines and so on.[13] For both Turner and Goffman the basic human plot is the same: someone begins to move to a new place in the social order; this move is accomplished through ritual, or blocked; in either case a crisis arises because any change in status involves a readjustment of the entire scheme; this readjustment is effected ceremonially—that is, by means of theatre.

Turner says that "Social dramas are units of aharmonic or disharmonic process, arising in conflict situations. Typically, they have four main phases of public action. [. . .] These are: 1. *Breach* of regular, norm-governed social relations. [. . .] 2. *Crisis* during which [. . .] there is a tendency for the breach to widen. [. . .] Each public crisis has what I now call liminal characteristics, since it is a threshold between more or less stable phases of the social process, but it is not a sacred limen, hedged around by taboos and thrust away from the centers of public life. On the contrary, it takes up its menacing stance in the forum itself and, as it were, dares the representatives of order to grapple with it. [. . .] 3. *Redressive action* [ranging] from personal advice and informal mediation or arbitration to formal juridical and legal machinery, and, to resolve certain kinds of crisis or legitimate other modes of resolution, to the performance of public ritual. [. . .] Redress, too, has its liminal features, its being 'betwixt and between,' and, as such furnishes a distanced replication and critique of the events leading up to and composing the 'crisis.' This replication may be in the rational idiom of a judicial process, or in the metaphorical and symbolic idiom of a ritual process. [. . .] 4. The final phase [. . .] consists either of the *reintegration* of the disturbed social group or of the social recognition and legitimization of irreparable schism between contesting parties."[14] This way of growing by means of conflict and schism Bateson calls "schismogenesis."[15] It is a major agency of human cultural growth.

Turner's dramatistic approach is interesting on many levels. The replication of the redressive action phase is, of course, a theatrical performance, a formal re-staging of events. The whole four-phase plan, also, is a drama—this scheme can be discerned in any Greek tragedy, Shakespearean play or drama of Ibsen or O'Neill. It is less easy to find in Chekov, Ionesco or Beckett—but it is there; the way it is distorted opens insight into dramatic structure. For example, in *Waiting for Godot* there is breach (the separation from Godot) and crises (waiting, the arrival of the Boy at the end of each act to tell Gogo and Didi that Godot will not come). There is a truncated redressive action: the (negative) doing of nothing, which is all the characters can (not) do. But there's no reintegration. Significantly the play ends with the stage direction "They do not move." Most other dramas, the plays of Shakespeare for example, end with a journey: to get crowned, to go to the grave to dispose of corpses, to go to the authorities to relate what's happened. Life literally "goes on." This movement at the ultimate moment of drama is akin to the *Ita, missa est* which concludes the Mass: it is a dismissal of the audience, a signal within the drama that the theatrical event is coming to a close. The performance continues as the audience disperses, spreading the news (good or bad) of the show. Even a play as non-conventional and non-religious as *Mother Courage and Her Children* follows this nearly universal pattern. The play climaxes in scene 11 with the murder of Kattrin. The next and final scene is Courage's leave-taking of her daughter (lullaby and burial), and the tag (comparable to the final couplets of Shakespearean drama), directed to the audience, reminding them that the everyday world is about to resume, is Courage's shout as she hitches herself to her wagon, "I've got to get back into business. Hey, take me with you!" The last action of the play is Courage marching off, on the move.

Turner says that this Western pattern of breach, crisis, redressive action and reintegration is actually universal. He shows how Ndembu (African) social process conforms to this dramatic paradigm. I could show how Aborigine, Papua-New Guinean and Indian social process conforms. What is just as interesting is that the theatre of every culture I know about also conforms. This suggests a universal dramatic structure parallel to social process: drama is that art whose subject, structure and action is social process.

I want to go two steps beyond what may be, after all, just an elaborate tautology. First, the basic performance structure underlies, literally contains, the dramatic structure.

Breach-Crisis-Redressive Action-Reintegration
GATHERING	PERFORMING	DISPERSING

The bottom line is solidarity, not conflict; the action is transformation. Conflict is made possible (in the theatre, and perhaps in society too) by the building of a nest out of the agreement to gather at a specific time and place, and to disperse once the performance is over. Especially the extreme forms of violence that characterize drama are contained in this nest built from an agreed-on social procedure. In all cultures people "go to" the theatre: they make special times and places for it; and there are special observances, practices, rituals that lead into the performance and away from it. Not only getting to the theatre, but entering the exact precinct where the show is to be performed involves ceremony: ticket-taking, passing through gates, entering in controllable groups, finding a place from which to watch. Ending the show and going away also involves ceremony: applause or some ratification of the conclusion of the formal performance, a wiping away of the reality of the show and a re-establishment of the reality of everyday life. The performers even more intensely than the audience prepare for the performance and then participate in "cooling-off" procedures after the show is over. In many cultures this cooling-off involves ritual to retire props or costumes. The closing of a sacred ark is as important as its opening.

Too little study has been made of the liminal approaches and leavings of performance—how the audience gets to, and into, the performance place, and how they go from that place; and in what ways this gathering/dispersing is related to the preparations/cooling-off aspects of the performers' work. The coming and going of both audience and performers guarantees (in Goffman's usage) the existence of the "theatrical frame" so that events can be experienced as *actual re-actualizations:* in other words, the reality of performance is in the performing; a spectator need not intervene in the theatre to prevent murder as he might feel compelled to do in ordinary life—this is because the violence on stage is actually a performance. That doesn't make it "less real" but "different real." Theatre, to be effective, must maintain its double presence, as *a here and now performance of there and then events.* The gap between "here and now" and "there and then" allows for an audience to contemplate the action, and to entertain alternatives, for drama is the art of enacting only one of a range of virtual alternatives. It is a luxury usually unaffordable in ordinary life; and very educational. *Oedipus* would be much different if there were a plague afflicting the town where the drama was being played and the audience believed the plague would end if the murderer of their former leader—a murderer they knew is concealed in their midst—was found and brought to judgment here and now. Some people want performance to achieve this level of authenticity. But when drama approaches this limit it changes fundamentally: either the events enacted are symbolic—as in the knocking out of an incisor tooth, circumcision or scarring—or they are transformed entirely as at rock concerts where music played by (temporary) folk heroes leads to euphoric hysteria. Or the theatrical frame is imposed so strongly as to permit the enactment of "aesthetic dramas" only: shows whose actions, though extreme, as in the staging of *Oedipus* with his poked-out eyes, are recognized by everyone, including the performers, as a "playing with" rather than a "real doing of." This "playing with" is not inauthentic—it results in changes happening to both performers and spectators.

People who want to make "everything real" including killing animals, the "art" of self-mutilation, or "snuff films" where people are actually murdered[16] are deceiving themselves if they feel they are approaching a deeper or more essential reality. All of these actions—like the Roman gladitorial games or Aztec human sacrifices—are as symbolic and make-believe as anything on stage. What happens is that living beings are reified into symbolic agents. Such reification is monstrous, I condemn it without exception. It is no justification to point out that modern warfare does the same, killing "things" at a distance. Nor will these blood performances act as a cathartic: violence mimetically replicated, or actualized, stimulates more violence. It also deadens peoples' abilities to intervene outside the theatre when they see violence being done.

Second, Turner locates the essential drama in conflict and conflict resolution. I locate it in *transformation*—in using theatre as a way to experiment with, act out and ratify change. Transformations in theatre occur in three different places, and at three different levels: (1) in the drama, that is, in the story[17]; (2) in the performers whose special task it is to temporarily undergo a *rearrangement* of their body/mind; (3) in the audience where changes may either be temporary (entertainment) or permanent (ritual).[18] All over the world performances are accompanied by eating and drinking. In New Guinea, Australia and Africa feasting is at the very center of theatre; even in modern Western theatre a show without something to eat or drink at intermission or just before or after the theatre is most unusual. This action recalls not only the chimpanzee carnivals but the hunting circuit; it suggests that theatre stimulates appetites, and is an oral/visceral art.[19] And, as Levi-Strauss has shown, the basic transformation from raw to cooked is a paradigm of culture-making: the transformation from natural into human.[20] At its deepest level this is what theatre is "about," the ability to frame and control, to change from raw to cooked, the most problematic (violent, dangerous, sexual, taboo) items of human interaction.

Theatre includes mechanisms for transformation at all levels. At the level of the staging there are costumes and masks, exercises and incantations, incense and music: all designed to "make believe" in the literal sense—to help the performer make into another person, or being, at another time in another place and to manifest this presence here and now so that time and place are doubled. At the level of the audience a change in mood and/or consciousness is effected; this change is either temporary or permanent. And, in some kinds of performances—rites of passage, for example—a permanent change of status of the participants is achieved. But all of these changes are in the service of social homeostasis. Changes within a system are accomplished in order to maintain the balance of the whole system. It is necessary to change girls into women (in an initiation rite) because somewhere else within the system women are being changed into dead people (in funeral rites); a vacancy exists that must be filled. It is less easy to see how this works in an aesthetic drama. say a performance of *Long Day's Journey into Night.*

The key difference between social and aesthetic dramas is the permanence of the transformations effected. Some kinds of social dramas such as feuds, trials and wars effect permanent change. In other kinds of performances which share qualities both of social and aesthetic drama—rites of passage, political ceremonies—changes in status are permanent (or at least cannot be undone except through more ritual) while changes in the body are either temporary, the wearing of some costume, or not severe: piercing an ear or septum, circumcision. The ordeals which are features of initiation rites, though extreme, are temporary. But the idea of these body alterations and ordeals is to signal and/or enforce a permanent change in the participants. In aesthetic drama no permanent body change is effected. A gap is intentionally opened between what happens to the figures in the story and what happens to the performers playing that story. To play a person in love, or someone who murders or is murdered (to use common examples from Western theatre) or to be transformed into a god, or to go into a trance (to use common examples from non-Western theatre) involves fundamental, if temporary, transformations of being, not mere appearances.

Aesthetic drama works a transformation on the audience who is separate from the performers. This separation is a chief evidence of the existence of aesthetic drama. In social drama all present are participants, though some are more decisively involved than others. In aesthetic drama everyone in the theatre is a participant in the *performance* while only those playing roles in the drama are participants in the *dramatic event* nested within the performance event. This performance event is fundamentally social, and it is at the level of performance that aesthetic and social drama converges. The function of aesthetic drama is *to do for the consciousness of the audience what social drama does for its participants:* to provide a place for, and a means of, transformation. Rituals carry participants across limins transforming them into different persons. For example a young man is a "bachelor" and through the ceremony of marriage he becomes a "husband." His status during that ceremony, but only then, is that of "groom." Groom is the liminal role he plays as a way of transformation from bachelor into husband. Aesthetic drama compels a transformation of the spectators' view of the world by rubbing their senses against enactments of extreme events, much more extreme than they would usually witness. The nesting pattern makes it possible for the spectator to reflect on these events rather than flee from them or intervene in them. That reflection is the liminal time during which the transformation of consciousness takes place.

The situation for the actor in aesthetic drama is complicated because the drama is repeated many times and each time the actor is supposed to start from nearly the same place. In other words, although spectators come and go, and they are encouraged to change, techniques are developed to prepare the actor for and bring him down from the experience of playing relatively unchanged—no more changed than any ordinary career changes a person. Metaphorically speaking, the actor is a circular printing press who, in rolling over makes an impression on his audience; but he is not ready to roll over again until he is back in his original position; for each performance there is a new audience on whom an impression is to be made. The actor makes a journey that ends where it began, while the audience is "moved" to a new place. In aesthetic drama techniques have been developed to transform the actor into the role and other techniques are used to bring him back to his ordinary self. In some ritual theatre the officiators are very like actors in aesthetic drama: the shaman working a cure must effect change in his patient, and often does this by transforming himself into another being; but at the end of his performance the shaman must return to his ordinary existence. It is this ability to "get into" and "get back from" that makes the shaman a continually useful person, not one who can be used once only. Thus there are at least three categories of performance: (1) aesthetic where the audience changes consciousness while the performer "rolls over," (2) ritual drama where the object of the ceremony is transformed while the officiating performer "rolls over," (3) social drama where all involved change.

The ambiguity of theatre since 1960 regarding whether or not an event is "really happening" is an outcome of the blurring of the boundaries between these categories of performance. So much of experience can now be theatricalized by editing bits of events for showing "news" that people feel nothing strange about a complementary actualization of art. When people watch extreme events knowing these are (1) actually happening and (2) edited to make them even more dramatic and to make them fit into a "showtime" format, but also knowing (3) that as observers they are stripped of all possibility of intervention—that is, they are turned into an audience in the formal sense—the reaction is paralysis and despair. Emotional feedback is not even possible for the media are not used as two-way communications systems as live theatre is. Another reaction is making art more "real," introducing into aesthetics the interventions and feedback eliminated from ordinary life.

Thus it is increasingly common in theatre to witness actual encounters among people, the staging of religious retreats and meetings (as Grotowski is now doing) and involving the audience directly in the story. These are attempts to regain some balance between information—which today overwhelms people—and action, which seems more and more difficult to effect. Terrorism, as opposed to ordinary street violence which is a function of economic deprivation, is a way of getting the attention of society, of making a show; it signals a basic dysfunction of the communication process. The actualization of art—the existence of theatre which combines the social and aesthetic—is traditional in many parts of the world: avant-garde and political theatre find already prepared paths. I once strongly encouraged these breaches of categories.

I try now in my work with The Performance Group, and in my teaching, to locate the actuality of performances in the immediate theatrical event recognized as such. I emphasize the gathering and dispersing aspects of performance. Upon entering the theatre spectators are greeted, either by me or other Group members. They see the performance being prepared—actors getting into costume, musicians tuning up, technical equipment checked, etc. Intermissions, and less formal breaks in the narration such as scene shifts, are underlined. In *Mother Courage* a full meal was served during intermission—during this break in the narration the performance was carried on by other means, by mingling performers and audience, by encouraging spectators to use parts of the space otherwise, and at other times, reserved for the performers. I try to establish non-storytelling time as an integral part of the whole performance scheme, while clearly separating this time from the drama. When the drama is over I speak to spectators as they are leaving. I direct many of them back to the performers so that the experience ends not with a dramatic moment, or even the curtain call, but with discussions, greetings and leave-takings.

The history of intermissions in the Western theatre is an interesting example of the importance of the underlying social event as a nest for the dramatic event. When performances were staged outdoors (medieval, Elizabethan) the spectators could all see each other in daylight. The court performances of masques and dramas were so lit that spectators could see each other as well as the actors. This kind of general illumination, and a mixing of focus including spectators as well as actors, continued throughout the 17th and the 18th centuries. But as scene changes began to necessitate complicated machinery which producers wanted to mask from the audience the front curtain was introduced and the forestage was eliminated in steps. Also changed lighting, especially in the 19th century with the introduction first of gas and then of electricity, widened the gap between stage and house until the stage was brightly lit and the house dark. In this situation naturalism arose, with its slice-of-life and peeping-Tom staging. But along with these conventions came the intermission: a formal period when the house was illuminated and the spectators, either remaining in the house or, trouping to lounges and restaurants, had the opportunity to see each other. The intermission served the purpose, that was not necessary either in outdoor or fully lit theatres, of giving the spectators a chance to see themselves; this is a way of confirming the fulfillment of the "gathering," the getting together of a *group,* or the formation of a group by virtue of having gotten together. Performances such as Grotowski's which keep the audience in the dark and with no intermission generate anxiety and contradict the social impulses of theatre. I do not criticize such performances, but note that they run against the grain of the Western tradition; in the deepest sense they are unconventional.

The techniques I use to show that "a story is being played for you, all around you, needing your active support" actualize the "performance nest" wherein the drama happens. Performers in The Performance Group are trained to display their double identities: as themselves and as the characters they are playing. By keeping these both out front the spectator sees the performer *choosing to act* in a certain way. Even "being in character" is seen as a choice not an inevitability. Thus the spectator, too, is encouraged to choose how to receive each action. There is no fixed seating, several actions go on simultaneously—spectators can shift focus from one aspect of the performance to another; and by no means are these aspects all concerned with the drama: a spectator can focus on a performer changing costume (that is, becoming another character), the technical crew, other spectators, etc. Instead of working for a unanimity of reaction, as in sentimental drama, I strive for a diversity of opportunities. These encourage spectators to react intellectually and ideologically as well as emotionally. What is "really happening" is a gathering of spectators of different ages, sexes, classes and ideologies watching a group of performers tell a story by theatrical means. Within this context the Group explores the most radical theatrical means we can handle: participation, environmental staging, multi-focus, etc. These are combined with the traditional theatrical means of our culture: narration and characterization.

What Performers Do: The Ecstasy/Trance Wheel

Looking at performing in a world-wide scan two kinds of process are identifiable. A performer is either "subtracted," achieving transparency, eliminating "from the creative process the resistances and ob-

stacles caused by one's own organism;"[21] or he is "added to," becoming
more or other than he is when not performing, he is "doubled," to use
Artaud's word. The first technique, that of the shaman, is ecstasy; the
second, that of the Balinese dancer, is trance. In the West we have
terms for these two kinds of acting: the actor in ecstasy is Cieslak in
The Constant Prince, Grotowski's "holy actor"; the actor in trance
possessed by another, is Stanislavski as Vershinin, the "character
actor."

To be in trance is not to be out of control or unconscious. The
Balinese say that if a trance dancer hurts himself that shows that the
trance was not genuine. In some kinds of trance the possessed and the
possessor are both visible. Jane Belo describes a Balinese horse dance
where

> the player would start out riding the hobbyhorse, being, so
> to speak, the horseman. But in his trance activity he would
> soon become identified with the horse—he would prance,
> gallop about, stamp and kick as a horse—or perhaps it
> would be fairer to say that he would be the horse and rider
> in one. For though he would sit on the hobbyhorse, his legs
> had to serve from the beginning as the legs of the beast.[22]

This is the centaur; and it is an example of the performer's double
identity. When, in Western theatre, we speak of an actor "portraying
a role," using a metaphor from painting where the artist studies a
subject and produces an image of that subject, we slide away from the
main fact of theatrical performance: that the "portrayal" is a transformation of the performer's body/mind; the "canvas" or "material" is
the performer. Interviewing Balinese performers of *sanghyangs,* village trance performances, Belo probed the way trance possession happens:

> GM: What is your feeling when you are first smoked?[23]
>
> DARJA: Somehow or other suddenly I lose consciousness.
> The people singing I hear. If people call out, calling me
> "Tjittah!" [a pig call] like that, I hear it too. If people talk
> of other things, I don't hear it.
>
> GM: When you are a *sanghyang* pig, and people insult you,
> do you hear it?
>
> DARJA: I hear it. If anyone insults me I am furious.
>
> GM: When you finish playing, how do you feel, tired or
> not?
>
> DARJA: When it's just over, I don't feel tired yet. But the
> next day or the day after that, my body is sick.
>
> [. . .]
>
> GM: When you become a *sanghyang* snake, what is the
> feeling like, and where do you feel your body to be?

DARMA: When I'm a *sanghyang* snake, suddenly my
thoughts are delicious. Thus, my feelings being delicious
suddenly I see something like forest, woods, with many
many trees. When my body is like that, as a snake, my
feeling is of going through the woods, and I am pleased.

[. . .]

GM: And if you're a *sanghyang* puppy, what does your body
feel like? Where do you feel yourself to be?

DARJA: I just feel like a puppy. I feel happy to run along the
ground. I am very pleased, just like a puppy running on the
ground. As long as I can run on the ground, I'm happy.

GM: And if you're a *sanghyang* potato, where do you feel
yourself to be, and like what?.

DARMA: I feel I am in the garden, like a potato planted in the
garden.

[. . .]

GM: And if you're a *sanghyang* broom, what's it like, and
where do you feel?

DARMA: Like sweeping filth in the middle of the ground.
Like sweeping filth in the street, in the village. I feel I am
being carried off by the broom, led on to sweep.[24]

Belo notes that "a considerable crowd had to be present to insure
that the trancer did not get out of hand." She tells of the time when a
man playing a pig escaped from the courtyard. He was not caught
until the next morning. "He had by that time ravaged the gardens,
trampled and eaten the plants, which was not good for the village. He
had also, being a pig, eaten large quantities of excreta he had found in
the roadways, which was not good for him."[25]

Belo finds these accounts "surprisingly satisfactory," and I do too.
They show that trance performing is a kind of character acting: being
possessed by another = becoming another. Eliade says that shamans,
too, are often possessed by animals.

During seances among the Yakut, the Yukagir, the
Chukchee, the Goldi, the Eskimo and others, wild animal
cries and bird calls are heard. Castagné describes the
Kirgiz-Tarter *baqca* running around the tent, springing,
roaring, leaping; he 'barks like a dog, sniffs at the
audience, lows like an ox, bellows, cries, bleats like a lamb,
grunts like a pig, whinnies, coos, imitating with
remarkable accuracy the cries of animals, the songs of
birds, the sound of their flight and so on, all of which
greatly impresses his audience.' The 'descent of the spirits'
often takes place in this fashion.[26]

And La Barre says that this kind of performing arose very early in
human history, associated with hunting:

> Mimetic ritual—part symbolic gesture in the telling, play
> or practice, and part boast-become-magic, compelling that
> wish to come true—must have appeared early. [. . .] The
> puzzling character of the Asiatic-American "Trickster" as
> a mixture of clown, culture hero and demigod, comes only
> from the procrustean attempt to force our categories on the
> clear and consistent aboriginal date. [. . .] The trickster [is]
> the animal form or familiar of the shaman himself. The
> great antiquity of the trickster should be suggested first of
> all by his being much the same in both Paeleosiberian and
> American hunting tribes. [. . .] We must not forget the
> element of *entertainment* in Old World shamanism: were
> tales of the erotic escapades of eagle-Zeus once told in the
> same tone of voice as those of Sibero-American Raven? And
> did not shamanistic rivalry develop into both the
> Dionysian bard-contests of Greek drama in the Old World
> and into midewewin *medicine-shows* in the New?[27]

Balinese trance, shamanic possession, the Trickster are not examples of acting in the Stanislavski tradition. But neither are they essentially different. Stanislavski developed exercises—sense memory, emotional recall, playing the through-line of action, etc.—so that actors could "get inside of" and act "as if" they were other people. Stanislavski's approach is humanist and psychological, but still a version of the ancient technique of performing by becoming or being possessed by another.

Belo says that the pleasure of the "trance experience is connected with the surrendering of the self-impulse. [. . .] Being a pig, a toad, a snake, or a creepy spirit are all enactments of the feeling of lowness in a very literal, childish and direct manner." She thinks this "urge to be low" is one of the foundations of trance.[28] To be low is to take the physical perspective of a child; to be filthy—playing with excrement and mud—is a regression to infantile behavior. It opens a channel to farce—and farce is probably more ancient than tragedy.[29] Finally, to be low is to escape from rigid mores—being low is a way to be free.

But these phenomena are only half of the dialectic of performing. The other half is ecstasy: a soaring away from the body, an emptying of the body. Eliade:

> The shamanic costume tends to give the shaman a new,
> magical body in animal form. The three chief types are
> that of the bird, the reindeer (stag) and the bear—but
> especially the bird. [. . .] Feathers are mentioned more or
> less everywhere in the descriptions of shamanic costumes.
> More significantly, the very structure of the costumes
> seeks to imitate as faithfully as possible the shape of a bird.
> [. . .] Siberian, Eskimo and North American shamans fly.
> All over the world the same magical power is credited to
> sorcerers and medicine men. [. . .] An adequate analysis of

the symbolism of magical flight would lead us too far. We
will simply observe that two important mythical motifs
have contributed to give it its present structure: the
mythical image of the soul in the form of a bird and the
idea of birds as psychopomps.[30]

An example of this kind of performing is the Aborigine "dreamtime"
songs and dances. A person, often in sleep but sometimes while
awake, is transported to the original "timeless mythical past during
which totemic beings traveled from place to place across the desert
performing creative acts."[31] Some of these beings are natural species
such as kangaroo and emu; but some are special beings like Wati
Kutjars (the Two Men) and Wanampi (the Water Snake). "Although
they lived in the past, the dreamtime beings are still thought of as
being alive and exerting influence over present-day people."[32] Performances are passed on down the generations. When new material is
added it is learned by "dreaming": a man participates with the mythical beings in their ceremonies, then he teaches his comrades what he
has learned. Aborigine performances are staged with extreme care,
especially regarding scenography, body decorations and execution of
song and dance routines. This care is not a matter of beauty in our
sense—smoothness, efficiency; but of making sure that all the prescribed steps are taken in proper order. Propriety is more important
than artistry. If the material is new every care is taken that it is
learned exactly and passed on intact.

During his "poor theatre" phase (1960-68) Grotowski followed a
procedure close to that of the Aborigines. But instead of seeking material in the dreamtime (archeology, history), Grotowski's performers
sought it in their own experiences.

> In our opinion, the conditions essential to the art of acting
> are the following, and should be made the object of a
> methodical investigation:
> (a) To stimulate a process of self-revelation, going back
> as far as the subconscious, yet canalizing this stimulus
> in order to obtain the required reaction.
> (b) To be able to articulate this process, discipline it and
> convert it into signs. In concrete terms, this means to
> construct a score whose notes are tiny elements of
> contact, reactions to the stimuli of the outside world:
> what we call "give and take."
> (c) To eliminate from the creative process the resistances
> and obstacles caused by one's own organism, both
> psychical and physical (the two forming a whole).[33]

Using this method Grotowski composed "gesticulatory ideograms"
comparable to the signs of medieval European theatre, Peking Opera
and other fixed forms. But Grotowski's ideograms were "immediate
and spontaneous [. . .] a living form possessing its own logic."[34] This

was because his actors were transparent: they were able to let impulses pass through them so that their gestures were at one and the same time intimate and impersonal. Grotowski, his scenographers and the performers of *Akropolis, The Constant Prince* and *Apocalypsis cum Figuris* (first version) achieved a total ikonography of body, voice, group composition and architecture. The totality was so complete that Western audiences felt uncomfortable: even Oriental performances as tightly structured as Nō or Kathakali allow open spaces for audience inattention. The productions of the Polish Laboratory Theatre were totally without "noise." Such clarity of signal evoked as much anxiety as it did pleasure.

No performing is "pure" ecstasy or trance. Always there is a shifting, dialectical tension between the two.

The ecstatic flight of the shaman leaves the body empty and transparent: absolutely vulnerable. Cieslak travels by means of subtraction towards ecstasy when he plays the Prince in *The Constant Prince*. The trance dancers of Bali are possessed or "taken over" by whomever or whatever possesses them. Olivier travels by means of addition towards possession; he systematically converts the "as if" of his Hamlet into a "becoming of" Hamlet. Those techniques of performer training which begin with a movement toward ecstasy—psychophysical exercises, yoga, etc.—help the performer "follow impulses," that is, yield and become transparent. In this state a performer may suddenly "drop into" his role because the vulnerability of ecstasy can be suddenly transformed into the totality of trance possession.

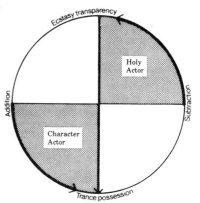

Rehearsal Procedures

Every aspect of gathering/performing/dispersing needs careful examination both from the point of view of the performers and of the spectators. In expanding our knowledge beyond drama to performing and beyond performing to the whole performance process much will be learned not only about art-making (for theatre, as Alexander Alland pointed out to me, is the only art where the creative process is by necessity visible) but also about social life because theatre is both intentionally and nonconsciously a paradigm of culture and culture-making. In this concluding section I will look only briefly at one small aspect of this large problem: what rehearsal is. I think I will be able to show that *the essential ritual action of theatre takes place during rehearsals.*

At the 1957 Macy Foundation Conference on Group Processes Ray Birdwhistell explained the following model:

> We have been running trajectories on dancing and other acts described as graceful behavior.

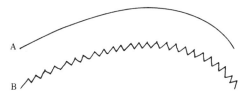

> Note B and A as trajectories of an arm or leg or body. A is a smooth curve; B is the zigzag line. The sizes of these zigzags are unimportant. It is the shape of the movement with which I am concerned. A and B express the same trajectory. However, ultimately trajectory A shows minimal variation or adjustment within the scope of the trajectory. In A there is a minimum of messages being reacted to in process. This is "grace." In B multiple messages are being introduced into the system and there is the zigzag. The things we call graceful are always multi-message acts in which the secondary messages are minimized, and there the role of the whole is maximized.[35]

Lorenz pointed out that:

> with the elimination of the noise in the movement, when the movement becomes graceful, it becomes more unambiguous as a signal. [. . .] That is exactly the situation in which the communicating system of expression movements is, because the receptor part of the system, whether IRM [Innate Release Mechanisms] or learned Gestalt, has its limitations with regard to pregnancy. The more pregnant and simple the movement is, the easier it is to take up unambiguously by receptor. Therefore, there is a strong selection pressure working in the direction of making all signal movements, these releasing movements, more and more graceful, and that is also what reminds us of a dance.[36]

Grace = simplification = increasing the signal efficiency of a movement = a dance.

Some artworks, even performances, are notoriously complex. The *Ramayama*, the *Bible*, the *Odyssey*, the plays of Shakespeare, the spectacles of Robert Wilson—are these less graceful (that is, less artistic) than the plays of Beckett or the paintings of Mondrian? Clearly a single, normative standard for "evaluating art" abolishes any cultural, historical or evolutionary perspective. The difficulty is solved by relocating the question of simplification (grace) from a comparison of the finished work in its exhibition phase to the work in the process of being made in its selection-of-what's-done-as-against-all-other-possibilities phase. It is not a matter of comparing the work to other works, or to the world. Important and revealing as such comparisons are they yield nothing concerning the issue Birdwhistell raises. One must fold the work back in on itself, comparing its completed state to the process of inventing it, to its own internal procedures during that time when it was not yet ready for showing. Although all arts have this phase only performance requires it to be public, that is, acted out among the performers as rehearsal. Comparing a work to its own process of creation applies to multi-authored works such as the Homeric epics, the *Bible* and medieval cathedrals and all other projects that extend beyond a single person's attention or life-span. In these cases the process of making the work has an extra step, that of arriving at a "finished form" that cannot be known with certainty beforehand. This solidification may take many generations and be ratified historically in structures which, under different circumstances, may have turned out differently. For example, Notre Dame of Paris has only one "finished" tower; but how "wrong" it would be to finish the "incomplete" structure. As an ideal cathedral the building lacks a tower; as Notre Dame it is complete *only* as it now stands. In all cases the process of solidification, completion, historical ratification is a process of rehearsal: how a work is re-worked until it crosses a threshold of "acceptability" after which it can be "shown."

The theatre is unique in that it is always undergoing the rehearsal process. Even the most traditional works with apparently fixed forms are rehearsed, that is, changed to accord with immediate circumstances. These changes, tectonic when a dogma is fixed in writing as the Catholic Mass is, move slowly—but then suddenly readjust themselves around a fault in the ritual. In this way the Vatican Council II legislated the saying of the Mass in the vernacular. With aesthetic drama there is a delight taken in the reinterpretations of the classics; but there are also unspoken limits—if a theatre group goes beyond these it is not praised for being inventive but attacked for "violating" the material. Such was the reaction against The Performance Group for our productions of *Dionysus in 69* (Euripides' *The Bacchae*) and *Makbeth* (Shakespeare's *Macbeth*). But even in doing a brand new play a tension arises between the author's intentions and what finally happens on the stage. Sometimes, as in the famous disputes between Chekhov and Stanislavski, Williams and Kazan, the tension reaches a breaking point.

But what exactly is the "rehearsal process"? At the Macy Conference W. Gray Walter commented on Birdwhistell's model:

> Grace may be the result of efficiency in a goal-directed
> movement. In the case of an artificial animal or guided
> weapon, the early guided weapons and some modern ones,
> when they are searching and are not goal-directed, have a

> trajectory with a messy curve like B. They perform a
> hunting movement, which looks quite random and is
> certainly not very graceful. It is jerky and disjointed,
> incoherent, often a series of cycloid loops. But the moment
> the goal or target is perceived, the trajectory becomes a
> graceful parabola or hyperbola. So, the appearance of a
> goal will transform a graceless and exploratory mode of
> behavior (which may have a high information potential in
> it, in the sense that it is looking in many directions) into
> one which has only one bit of information, if the target is
> there, but looks smooth and pretty.[37]

Early rehearsals, or workshops, are jerky and disjointed, often incoherent. The work is indeed a hunt, actions with "high information potential," but very little goal-orientation. Even in working on texted material this kind of "looking around" marks early rehearsals: actors try a variety of interpretations, designers bring in many sketches and models most of which are rejected, the director doesn't really know what he wants. And especially if the project is to develop its own text and actions the basic question of the early work is an anxiety-laden, "What are we doing?" If, by a certain time, a target is not visible (not only a production date but a vision of what is to be produced), the project falters, then fails. A director may maintain confidence by imposing order in the guise of set exercises; but he may do this too soon and cut off chances of discovering new actions. A balance is needed. Comparable processes occur in traditional societies. John Emigh writes about a rehearsal of a funeral ceremony on the Sepik River:

> As the rehearsal proceeded an old man would stop the
> singing from time to time to make suggestions on style or
> phrasing or, just as often, just as much a part of the event
> being rehearsed, he would comment on the meaning of the
> song words, on the details of the story. The rehearsal was
> at once remarkably informal and absolutely effective. A
> middle-aged woman with an extraordinary, searing voice
> seemed to be in control of the singing. She would start and
> stop at whim, repeating phrases, checking points with the
> old man, pausing to hear his explanations. [. . .] As the
> rehearsal proceeded, men and women would occasionally
> drift by. The assembled singers and drum beaters and
> witnesses practiced the movements of the dance to
> accompany the mother's lament.[38]

We are used to rehearsals for weddings, funerals and other religious and civic ceremonies. In all cases rehearsal is a way of selecting from the possible actions those actions to be performed, of simplifying these to make them as clear as possible in regard both to the matrix from which they have been taken and the audience to which they are meant to communicate. Along with this primary task the secondary work of rehearsal is to have each performer perform his part with maximum clarity. Farce is interesting because it turns clarity on its head. Charlie Chaplin staggering drunkenly across the street is acting "messy" but with consummate skill—just as a clown performs a graceless pratfall gracefully. The signal sent reads "graceless" but this signal is sent clearly—i.e., gracefully. Audiences admire the ease with which great farceurs play at being clumsy. The same may be said about dissumulation of all kinds so popular in theatre: lies, disguises, double plots, ironies. In every case the performer's problem is to be clear about the lie, to be convincing in both aspects of the situation so that an audience can see around the action and perceive it and its opposite simultaneously.

Comparable to rehearsal, but not exactly identical to it, is preparation. The Aborigines spend many hours preparing for a ten-minute dance. They carefully lay out all the implements of the dance, they paint their bodies, they prepare the dancing area. Before each performance members of The Performance Group take up to two hours warming up their voices, doing psychophysical exercises, dance steps and yoga, reviewing difficult bits from the show, etc. The Moscow Art Theatre was famous for its preparation period immediately before an actor went onto the stage. Every performer I know goes through a routine before performing. These preparations literally "compose" the person and the group: they are a kinesic recapitulation of the rehearsal process; they allow for a settling into the special tasks at hand, a concentration by means of shrinking the world to the dimensions of the theatre.

Both rehearsal and preparation employ the same means: repetition, simplification, exaggeration, rhythmic action, the transformation of "natural sequences" of behavior into "composed sequences." These means comprise the ritual process as understood by ethologists. Thus it is in rehearsals/preparations that I detect the fundamental ritual of theatre.

I find nothing disturbing about relating the finest achievements of human art—indeed, the very process of making art: the ritual action of rehearsal and preparation—to animal behavior because I detect no break between animal and human behavior. And especially in the realm of artistic-ritual behavior I find continuities and analogies. Activities thicken—get more complicated, dense, symbolic, contradictory and multivocal—along a continuum of expanding consciousness. The human achievement—shared by a few primates and aquatic mammals but not elaborated by them—is the ability to make decisions based on virtual as well as actual alternatives. These virtual alternatives take on a life of their own. Theatre is the art of actualizing them, and rehearsal is the means of developing their individual shapes and rhythms. By turning possibilities into action, into performances, whole worlds otherwise not lived are born. Theatre doesn't arrive suddenly and stay fixed either in its cultural or individual manifestations. It is insinuated along a web of associations spun from play, games, hunting, slaughter and distribution of meat, ceremonial centers, trials, rites of passage and storytelling. Rehearsals and recollections—preplay and afterplay—converge in the theatrical event.

Notes

1. See Schechner/FROM RITUAL TO THEATRE AND BACK.
2. Devore (1965), 408-9.
3. Devore (1965), 409.
4. See Marshack (1972). Also Giedion (1962). And La Barre (1972).
5. Ucko and Rosenfeld (1967). This book is a summary of scholarly thought on the subject. They say: "The relative frequencies of animals, the absence of representations of vegetation and also the evidence reviewed in the previous pages, which shows that many representations were intended to be viewed, suggest that 'theatre' may well be behind some of the parietal representations" (p. 229). Although there are many disputes in the field of cave art, all authorities agree that performances of some kind (rites, increase ceremonies, theatre) took place in the caves. The antiquity, one could almost say the primacy, of performance is clear.
6. Rappaport (1968), 4-5.
7. See, particularly, "The Street Scene" in Willett (1964), 121-9.
8. In England medieval cycle plays were staged on wagons which moved from site to site re-enacting their plays. The wagon was used as a staging area, a backdrop and a dressing room. The audience gathered around as the play moved from the wagon to the street, employing both the raised space of the wagon and the flat space of the street. Spectators stood in the street and looked from the windows surrounding the narrow roadway. Playing of plays began at dawn and ran throughout the day; there must've been much coming and going among the audience. This mixing of social and aesthetic continued into the Renaissance.
9. I use the word natural to mean the kind of theatre that happens in everyday life; there is no need to stage or create it: when an accident or dispute occurs people will watch it: when something sumptuous visually passes by people will turn to look at it pass, whether it be an ocean liner going downriver or a head of state motorcading up a street. There's no accounting for taste.
10. Box seats themselves developed from the earlier practice of allowing special people to sit on the stage itself. When this became disruptive—or, rather, when the disruptions were no longer tolerable—boxes came into fashion. It is interesting how in environmental theatre the presence of everyone, or anyone, on stage—or in

the same area as where the players play—is a democratization of the presence onstage of some of the audience, the rich and/or privileged. It extends to everyone a once restricted privilege.
11. Awasthi (1974), 36-8. Indian traditional theatre, like European medieval theatre, is often processional.
12. Gould (1969), 103-4. See also Kirby (1972), 5-21.
13. Goffman (1969).
14. Turner (1974), 37-41.
15. Discussion of the dynamics of schismogenesis in Bateson (1965), 171-97.
16. As of this writing I have just heard of an ultimate violent theatre: the pornographic "snuff film." In these movies a person is hired to make a porn film but at the moment of climax the person is killed: the camera records the shock and agony of the murdered and the actions of the murderers. The film is then exhibited for high admissions to private parties. Sometimes, it is said, a person agrees to be killed in the film, usually for much money. The comparison of snuff porn to the Roman gladitorial games is obvious; and the decadence of these shows is equally clear. As for the cathartic effect of viewing violent activities, studies reported by Eibl-Eibesfeldt (1970), 329, 331-2, indicate that the cathartic effect of witnessing violence is short-lived. "In the long run, the possibility of discharging aggressive impulses constitutes a kind of training for aggression. The animal becomes more aggressive" (p. 329). The subject is complicated but, as for me, I draw the line against "reality games" that include physical injury.
17. Drama is about the *changes* that happen to the characters. Take any drama and compare who, where, and what any character is at the beginning and at the end, and also see what the scenes are about: always they are about changes, from life to death, from not in love to in love (or out again), from rich to poor or vice-versa, etc.
18. See Schechner/FROM RITUAL TO THEATRE AND BACK.
19. Kaplan (1968), 105-116.
20. Levi-Strauss (1969b). His complicated, and seminal, work elaborates the "two contrasts—nature/culture, raw/cooked" (p. 338). In terms of theatre the "cooked action" is not simply an imitation of problematic behavior; it is an entirely new, but analogically related or metaphoric re-enactment, state, or sequence of behavior. The rites of passage apply to classes of behavior that have to be socialized as well as to individuals who need to be transported from one status to another.
21. Grotowski (1968), 128.
22. Belo (1960), 213.
23. A trance dancer is "smoked" by inhaling the fumes of incense which is burned under his nose. As far as I can determine the smoke itself is not psychotropic; it does not "cause" the trance—it is a deci-

sive moment in the process of achieving trance. When only part of the body is to go into trance—as when the hand becomes a broom—only that part is smoked. The smoking procedure is not confined to Bali—I saw it in Sri Lanka too. GM is Goesti Madé Soemeng, a Balinese member of Belo's research team.

24. Belo (1960), 222.

25. Belo (1960), 202.

26. Eliade (1970), 97. Eliade says of the shaman's transformation: "It is the shaman who *turns himself* into an animal, just as he achieves a similar result by putting on an animal mask" (p. 93).

27. La Barre (1972), 195-6.

28. Belo (1960), 223. "The feeling of lowness, which Darma described as delightful, fits in with the whole constellation of ideas about being mounted, being sat on, and so forth, wherein the pleasurable quality of the trance experience is connected with the surrendering of the self-impulses. This is one aspect of the trance state which seems to have reverberations in the trance vocabulary in whatever country these phenomena appear—and the aspect which is perhaps the hardest for non-trancers to grasp." This "surrendering of the self-impulses" in trance is a surrendering to a definite other: an animal, spirit, person, etc. In ecstasy it is a pure giving up, as in Zen meditation.

29. Although I do not have time to expound here, the short episodes of farce, the swift, violent action, and surprising reversals offer internal evidence for its antiquity; and the fact that every culture has farce performances while only relatively few have tragedies (in the strict, formal sense of, say, Greek tragedy or Japanese Nō) indicates that the universal form is more ancient.

30. Eliade (1970), 156, 477-9.

31. Gould (1969), 106.

32. Gould (1969).

33. Grotowski (1968), 128.

34. Grotowski (1968), 142.

35. Lorenz (1959), 201-2.

36. Lorenz (1959), 202-3.

37. Lorenz (1959), 202.

38. John Emigh in a letter distributed to several of his friends. Emigh observed the rehearsal in 1974.

Selective Inattention

Relationship between Social and Aesthetic Drama

Victor Turner (1974) locates four actions as the nubs of social drama: (1) breach, (2) crisis, (3) redressive action and (4) reintegration. A breach is a situation that schisms a social unit—family, workgroup, village, community, nation, etc. A crisis is a precipitating event that can't be overlooked, must be dealt with, or else the social unit will come undone. Redressive action is what is done to overcome the crisis—the crisis itself having stemmed from the breach. Reintegration is the elimination of the original breach that mothered the crisis; reintegration comes in two ways, either by healing the breach or by schismogenesis (see Bateson, 1958).

Apply Turner's model to an actual social situation, say the November, 1975, dismissal of cabinet members by President Gerald Ford. The breach is the fact that Ford as an appointed rather than elected President carried with him a number of Nixon people on his cabinet. Thus Ford was forced to defend policies he might not agree with and to carry the stigma of a disgraced Administration. At the same time Ford wished to seek the Presidency on his own. The crisis comes from severe embarrassment to the "security community" through revelations of planned assassinations of foreign heads of state, phone-tapping of Americans and a widespread secret police apparatus whose operation pinnacled under Nixon. Other items added to the crisis: the disagreement between Ford and Rockefeller over aid to New York City, the growing feeling nationally that Ford is stupid and indecisive; and, perhaps (though there is no direct evidence), Ford's

140

feeling that he was not the master of his own Administration. The redressive action, as described in the *New York Times* of Monday, November 3, was typically dramatic:

> President Ford has dismissed Secretary of Defense James R. Schlesinger and William E. Colby, Director of Central Intelligence, in a major shuffling of his top national security posts. Administration officials said that the President had also asked Secretary of State Henry A. Kissinger to relinquish his post as national security adviser in the White House, but to stay on as head of the State Department. White House officials said that Mr. Schlesinger would probably be replaced by the White House chief of staff, Donald H. Rumsfeld, and that Mr. Colby's likely successor would be George Bush, the present head of the American liaison office in China.

This redressive action did not end the crisis, but led to further surprising developments—as is often the case ("one thing leads to another"). Rockefeller told Ford that he would not in any case be a candidate for the Vice Presidency in 1976. And, in the Washington scheme of things, this apparent resignation by the Vice President is probably a firing by the President—the reversal of roles being a common face-saving device in American politics. Finally, the Secretary of Commerce resigned and was replaced by the one person in the Nixon Administration whose reputation was untarnished, even more, enhanced: Elliott Richardson, the man who—when his Watergate prosecutor, Archibald Cox, was fired—resigned as Attorney General. The reintegration phase of this social drama will take some time, as Ford establishes "his own" government in preparation for the 1976 elections.

The characteristic structure of this 4-phase operation is that the breach exists for a long time, the corrective action is sudden and almost unpredictable because a precipitating event is usually not a crisis in itself but a "straw that breaks the camel's back." Once the action is over analysts can look back and "see what happened" detecting an orderly development of events that follow Turner's scheme. The scheme looks like:

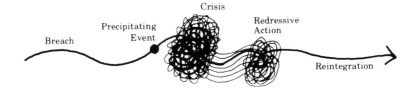

Crisis

Precipitating Event

Redressive Action

Breach

Reintegration

The visible drama is in the crisis and redressive action. From the hindsight of reintegration we reconstruct the whole sequence. This is where social drama and aesthetic drama coincide.

Apply Turner's model to an actual drama, say Shakespeare's *Romeo and Juliet*. The breach is the long-standing feud between Montagues and Capulets. Thus wherever members of the two families meet there is certain to be a fight; the streets of Verona are dangerous. The precipitating event is Romeo's crashing of the Capulet party, his sighting of Juliet, their love at first sight. Romeo recognizes the danger at once—having kissed her, then finding out who she is, he exclaims: "Is she a Capulet?/O dear account! my life is my foe's debt." And Juliet too knows of the crisis: "My only love sprung from my only hate!"

Most of the rest of the play is taken up by the crisis and the redressive action. The crisis is the growing love affair—with each gesture of affection there is a corresponding increase in the danger of discovery and disaster. The redressive action is the answer to the question: how are they to find each other safely in a city where they must only hate each other? Friar Laurence's plan to get them out of Verona is a classic strategy of redressive action. Bateson would call it schismogenesis—the founding of a new social unit in a new place in order to avoid or end conflict. Laurence knows that when Juliet is presumed dead her suit with Paris is ended; after she is buried with the other Capulets Romeo can find her in the tomb and carry her to Mantua where there is nothing to keep a Montague from marrying a Capulet. Throughout the redressive action phase the tension is maintained between the lovers' passion for each other and their parents' hatred. The action of the play is strung like wires on a suspension bridge between these two opposite but identical poles: love and hate; the connecting power is passion, which flows with equal force into both love and hate. Everyone in the play must take sides: Laurence with the lovers, the Nurse with the parents. The redressive action ends in tragedy through a lack of communication. Dramatically three deaths occur, not two: Juliet's, (she isn't really dead but Romeo thinks so); Romeo's (he kills himself—sign of passion—instead of waiting a few minutes until Juliet wakes up); Juliet's (she acts as Romeo did, but in her case there is genuine cause). A this point the tragedy teeters on farce—think what Charles Ludlam would do with the death scene in the tomb.

As in all tragedy (and some farce, the genre closest to tragedy) redressive action doesn't make life comfortable for the heroes who end up dead, maimed and/or exiled: separated from the community—but also sacrificed for the final reintegration of the community. Discovering their beloved children dead Montague and Capulet agree to end their feud, and Verona is made whole again: "A glooming peace this morning with it brings." It is a depressing drama indeed that does nothing to knit up the unraveled social order; that kind of drama we know from Beckett; and other absurd writers who end their plays as they begin, keeping everyone going in Sisyphean circles. These dramas are redressive action, even the breach and crisis are forgotten.

What comparisons can I make between Ford's cabinet shakeup and the tragedy of *Romeo and Juliet*? The hidden structure of one is the visible structure of the other. In Ford's action is a story—an aesthetic component, a scenario—that the President is, both consciously and at a nonconscious level, arranging the release of information and the sequence of events to suit a sense of drama that in turn will portray him as a character of determination, self-will, strength, purpose and independence: all qualities expected of a President by the American people (alas). Ford's social drama did not work out as he had planned it, and its failure was clearly a failure experienced in theatrical terms. Again, from the *New York Times:*

> The strategy behind Vice President Rockefeller's
> withdrawal, the dismissal of Defense Secretary James R.
> Schlesinger and other possible moves yet to come is to put a
> distinct Ford imprimatur on his Administration's domestic
> and foreign policies, Administration sources said today.
> The first move was to be the announcement of Mr.
> Rockefeller's decision not to be Mr. Ford's running mate.
> [. . .] The second move—the removal of Mr. Schlesinger
> [and the others] had been scheduled to be announced this
> Wednesday. [. . .] But this carefully planned scenario went
> awry yesterday when the dismissals and switches were
> leaked prematurely to the press. In the absence of the
> Rockefeller announcement, the officials said, the leaks
> gave off highly undesirable and conflicting signals.
> (November 4, 1975)

Thus the President and his stage managers had a script in mind, but newsmen operate competitively to ventilate as many leaks as possible: thus the change which was designed to show a deft handling of affairs of state became a somewhat confused shakeup. If the President's "image" suffers, as it probably will, his theatrical ineptitude will have repercussions on his career. It has always been this way in politics, from the village level on up.   ·

Underneath Romeo and Juliet's sentimental love story is a political struggle that Shakespeare weaves into the play—he makes each of the lovers a child of the rulers of Verona's factions thereby guaranteeing that their fates have the profoundest effects on the fight between Montague and Capulet. In doing this Shakespeare plays to Renaissance sensibilities of class and order: for if the lovers were commoners their plight would be as moving (as in *West Side Story*) but its repercussions more limited. The lover's story is richer for being played out against and within the war of their parents. All tragedies, and maybe all dramas, have under their personal and idiosyncratic surfaces deep social, substructures that control the sequence of events.

At another level there is cross-feed. Ford takes techniques from the theatre: how to release the news, how to manipulate the public's reactions, how to disarm his enemies; even how to make up his face, wear his costume, deliver his sentences. This is not a new preoccupation of political leaders. Nor is it restricted to the Louis XIVs of the world: Lenin, a chief of a New Guinea village and George Meany practice stagecraft. Shakespeare, like the Greeks, is a master of situating his dramas of persons in the field of state events. It is this wide field that Brecht understands and uses but which the psychological naturalists and absurdists avoid or reject. This field is not an abstract legendary community—my objection to some of the Open Theater's work and that of the Bread and Puppet Theatre at times is that it mythologizes and generalizes political power which is always and everywhere specific and concrete, dripping with local customs. The field is always the *polis*, full of castes, classes, cross-interests, rivalries and struggle; this not only in Western drama and society, but everywhere. Nor is it true that certain eras have more social structure than others: systems change, they don't disappear. The *communitas* that Turner sees at the opposite of structure is temporary, liminal, a special sequence that is carefully hedged. One of the beautiful ironies of theatre is that it is a *communitas* made in the gestalt of structure, a liminal event refracting the tensions of social order and disorder.

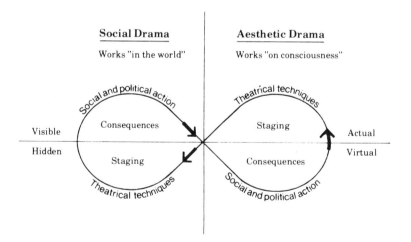

The politician, activist, militant, terrorist uses techniques of the theatre (staging) to support his social action; the social action is consequential—that is, it is designed to effect change in the social order or to maintain stability in an order threatened by change. The theatre person uses the consequential actions of social life as the underlying themes or frames of his art. The theatre is designed to effect change in perception, viewpoint, attitude: in other words, to make the spectator react to the world of social drama in a new way. There is a flow to the relationship between social and aesthetic drama and specific enactments (shows) may "journey" from one sphere into the other, but only in the direction indicated.

The Integral vs. the Accidental Audience

The best way to understand the relationship between ritual theatre—such as initiation rites, marriage ceremonies, funerals, etc.—and aesthetic theatre is to consider the roles the audience plays. The audience is not an either/or lump; and changes in an audience occur during performances as well as from one performance to another. For example, when The Performance Group played Sam Shepard's *The Tooth of Crime* at Amherst College in a barn used for horse shows a male spectator responded to a soliloquy delivered by Spalding Gray playing Hoss. At first Gray responded to the man as Hoss, "in character." But it soon was evident that the man wanted to go on for an undetermined time. Everytime Gray/Hoss began speaking the man began too; instead of a dialogue there was a blur of two voices. Gray then dropped his characterization and spoke from the role of performer: "Look, I want to go on with the play, but I can't if you keep interrupting me. If you've got anything you want to say say it, and when you're finished I'll go on." The man demurred, "Go on, go on, I got nothing to say." But as soon as Gray/Hoss began the man started too. Then the audience began to jump in against the man. "Shut up! Let the actor act!" A person leaned over to me and said, "The guy's stoned," as if a chemical explanation would somehow make things ok. But as soon as some in the audience tried to quiet the man, others began shouting too: "Let him say what he wants! Don't shut him up!" The interchange in the audience went on until a clear sense developed that most of the people wanted to see the play. The heckler must've sensed this too, because when Gray/Hoss resumed he was not interrupted.

The Group's production of *Tooth* was open enough to accept the interruption and debate, but not enough to carry on the play and the interruption at the same time. On the other hand, The Living Theatre's *Paradise Now* was designed to break down into audience-performer and audience-audience interactions. In the case of *The Tooth of Crime* Gray's only strategy was passive: he refused to go on until the man stopped. Gray enlisted the audience that finally mobilized itself *on the side of the play as a play*. In the case of *Paradise Now* the audience was mobilized *on the side of the play as a lead-in to direct action*. In both cases the obvious was activated: a performance is licensed by its audience which can, at any time, re-ratify or withdraw that license.

This license is significantly different for "accidental" and "integral" audiences. An accidental audience is a group of people who, individually or in small clusters, go to theatre—the performances are publically advertised and open to all. On opening nights of commercial shows the attendance of the critics and friends constitute an integral rather than accidental audience. An integral audience is one where people come because they have to or because the event is of special significance: the relatives of the bride and groom at a wedding; the tribe assembled for initiation rites; dignitaries on the podium for an inauguration, etc. Avant-garde performers who send out mailings or by word of mouth gather people who've attended previous performances are in the process of creating an integral audience for their work, a supportive audience. Every "artistic community" develops an integral audience: people who know each other, are involved with each other, support each other. Audiences can be mixed—most public events focus on a show witnessed by an integral audience; but this audience is itself part of the spectacle for the general public. With film and TV even the "general public" becomes part of the performance for those watching it via media. In short, an accidental audience comes "to see the show" while an integral audience is "necessary to accomplish the work of the show." Or, to put it another way, the accidental audience attends from pleasure, the integral audience from ritual need. The presence of an integral audience is the surest evidence that the performance is a ritual drama.

There aren't any hard boundaries between these classes of performances; but their relationship can be expressed schematically:

Integral	*Accidental*
Invited audience	Commercial productions
Opening night	publicly advertised
Audience of those "in the know"	All public performance events

Ritual	*Aesthetic*
Audience at wedding, funeral, etc.	Tourists watching a ceremony
Inaugurations, signing of treaties, state matters	Imported rituals performed at commercial theatres

There's movement between these categories. A commercial production begins as an integral audience event but lives the rest of its existence with accidental audiences—except when theatre parties or benefits buy up the whole house. Rituals once thought to be inaccessible are now rented out on location or imported to world capitals to be exhibited in public theatres. Select mailing lists and word-of-mouth performances are popular in New York now: a kind of secret society of those in the know. There is a definite movement where theatre fills a niche abandoned by religion: solidarity, mutual supportive belief, gathering in the catacombs, etc. Even within the same performance an audience can change from accidental to integral. At the end of *Over Here!*, a light Broadway musical, the two Andrews Sisters came onto the stage and gave an encore of some favorite oldies. The audience immediately picked up on the apparent "special performance" and the theatre was aglow. (Even I was taken in: I later inquired whether the Sisters did this every night, or only the night I was there. Every night.)

Interestingly, the behavior of people as spectators differs greatly depending on whether these individuals comprise an integral or accidental audience—and this difference is not what one would expect. By and large, *the accidental audience pays closer attention than does an integral audience.* On the surface this is due to two reasons: (1) the accidental audience chooses to attend, has most usually paid to attend; (2) they attend as individuals or in small clusters so that large crowd action is unlikely—each spectator is a stranger among strangers. There are deeper reasons for their attentiveness and for the inattention of an integral audience; these will be discussed later. An integral audience often knows what's going on—not paying attention to it all is a way of showing off that knowledge. Sometimes, as during the reading of the Torah prior to the Bar Mitzvah boy's performance, the featured event is heightened by ignoring the preliminaries. The same thing happens for preliminary bouts preceding a championship boxing match. Often the duration of time of performances is so long that it isn't possible to pay attention throughout; ritual performances have a program to fulfill and cannot be fit in between supper and the 11 o'clock news. Performances for accidental audiences are designed to fit convenient time-slots; ritual performances allow their audience to demonstrate their devotion by pilgrimages, duration and/or ordeals.

Selective Inattention: Ritualizing Aesthetic Drama

For the December, 1973, performances of Robert Wilson's *The Life and Times of Joseph Stalin* at the Brooklyn Academy of Music's opera house, the Le Perq space—a room of about 150 feet by 80 feet—was set up with tables, chairs, refreshments: a place where people went not only during the six 15-minute intermissions but also during many of the acts of Wilson's seven-act opera. The opera began at 7 pm and ran more than 12 hours. I remember coming back to Manhattan at about 8:30 am, stopping at Dave's Corner at Broadway and Canal and having an early morning egg cream: a re-entry ritual into New York ordinary life. Each of *Stalin's* seven acts had been performed before, either as part of Wilson's earlier work or as independent pieces. Thus the 12-hour performance in the opera house was a retrospective. Most of the people in the audience had seen at least some of Wilson's work before (this is an assumption I can't prove, but think true): they assembled for *Stalin* to re-experience the work, to try an all-night performance, to meet again with old friends: to use the performance of *Stalin* not only as a thing in itself (accidental audience) but as a ritual experience (integral audience).

The behavior in the Le Perq space was not the same throughout the night. During the first three acts the space was generally empty except for intermission. But increasingly as the night went on people came to the space and stayed there speaking to friends, taking a break from the performance, to loop out of the opera, later to re-enter. About half the audience left the BAM before the performance was over; but those who remained, like repeated siftings of flour, were finer and finer examples of Wilson fans: the audience sorted itself out until those of us who stayed for the whole opera shared not only the experience of Wilson's work but the experience of experiencing it. The opera was advertised and tickets sold publicly. But the accidental audience was winnowed into an integral audience by the long hours, the Le Perq space and the fact that the performance was a retrospective.

A loop developed between the Le Perq space and the opera house. The house was a place of silence, attention on the performance, and—as the night went on—a more and more spatially scattered audience, until at the end less than one half of the 2200 seats were occupied. At first the Le Perq space was used only during intermission. But as the evening went on the tables and chairs were rearranged according to the size of the parties using them, and the space was used continuously until, at around dawn, there were about half as many people in Le Perq as in the opera house. Special people claimed, or were accorded, special places—for example, the little crowd around Allen Ginsberg's table.

What happened during *Stalin* was unusual for orthodox American theatre but common in many parts of the world. People selected for themselves what parts of Wilson's opera to pay attention to, and what parts to absent themselves from. When they went into the Le Perq space to rest, socialize, have a refreshment, prepare for a return to the opera house or whatever the spectators were not ignoring the performance, they were adding a dimension to it. The social end of the loop was as important to *Stalin* as the aesthetic end. In Madras, in 1971, I was impressed by the behavior of the audience at a concert. People came and went, stood outside the hall, re-entered when a musician they wanted to hear played. The festival lasted more than a week, and in each phase—individual concerts, individual performances within concerts, individual passages within performances, individual moments within passages—attention and inattention alternated. There was no necessity to maintain, or appear to maintain, a single focus high-tension attention. But at the same time the use of selective inattention led not to a feeling of laxness or "I don't care," but to a greater discipline on the part of the audience. As I wrote in my notebook at the time:

> Just now the flute and violin are trading and talking and
> mirroring musical phrases. I've heard this before with
> voice and violin. But this is the most *profound* I've ever

heard it—there is here an *essential dialogue*. Also the
audience's close attention and applause makes me think I
am in Athens at the great drama festivals and contests.
This audience is *sitting in judgment*—but that judgment is
based on its knowledge and love of the music—and
somehow the judgment supports the musicians—the way
the sharp, but willingly adoring eye of the sports spectator
supports the athlete. Only these musicians can do what
they're doing—but only this audience can do what it can
do: IMMEDIATELY REWARD THE PERFORMER. No
amount of delayed praise or end of the show applause can
approach the now support of an audience that is really with
it, and not jealous, not 'let me do that too,' not worshipful
—but genuinely appreciative. The lights stay on here so
the audience can see each other, and feel together, and so
the musicians can see the audience.

Also this kind of appreciation takes knowledge of what the
performer is trying to do—a real sense of the task at hand:
the audience can't do it, but they know what's to be done.
We've yet to educate our theatre audiences sufficiently—so
they can really demand excellence, and not just 'an
experience.' Again, this is a function of a tradition—for an
educated audience, and I don't mean academically
educated, arises in the midst of a living tradition which
people experience from birth. A *living* tradition is one with
roots and branches among the people. It can be studied at
school but kept alive only in the streets.

Here the music is everywhere: at weddings, in the shouts of
the vegetable sellers in the streets, in side alleys where
kids bang homemade drums and at hundreds of concerts
happening formally and informally all the time.

It's different than a rock concert. The audience here is not
swept away. They are not after ecstasy or oblivion or
something *other than the music*. The music is not a means,
it is the thing itself. They remain in contact with it, in
touch with the musicians. Spectators keep their critical
faculties intact. This doesn't mean they aren't moved—but
they're *moved into the music not beyond it*.

The audience isn't quiet. I mean they not only accompany
the music, they talk to each other—not loudly, but there's
always a buzz. Also the tsk-tsk, the ooos, the slapping of
hands on the thighs keeping the rhythms, the bursts of
applause (always selective, that is, always just a portion of
the audience), the low talking. Somehow the collective
effect of all this is not distracting—it is natural, business-
like: like eating hot dogs at a ball game. (December 2,
1971)

In DRAMA, SCRIPT, THEATRE AND PERFORMANCE I described
the rhythms of an all-night performance of a Thovil ceremony in Sri

Lanka. The audience there comes and goes, and there are several hours when the performance all but stops, and only a few spectators listen to the music or watch occasional dances. In Australia, Papua-New Guinea, Africa, American Indian villages this same pattern exists. It is not necessarily tied to long performances or performances of cycles, although it is most easily suited to these kinds of episodic events, or loosely tied bundles of events.

In the American theatre not only Wilson but Peter Schumann, Douglas Dunn, other "new dancers" and, in a modest way, The Performance Group have experimented with selective inattention. The parades and outdoor spectacles of the Bread and Puppet Theatre necessarily encourage selective inattention. As a procession goes by a spectator either follows it or not, and during large-scale performances such as *Domestic Ressurection* (1970) it isn't possible to follow all the events. More than that, the outdoor setting (a meadow in Vermont), the crowd shifting from place to place, the people in the audience that I knew—going to Vermont to see the piece was a pilgrimage—meant that greetings, short conversations and a distanced *looking at* rather than *being swept away by* was the way I watched the show. Even when a boat was made from a great sail and streamers of cloth, and I, along with many other spectators, accepted the invitation to walk inside the boat, as passengers escaping the great flood, I felt involved and separate, celebratory and critical simultaneously.

Douglas Dunn's *101* (1974) was a unique experience for me as a spectator. Dunn built in his loft, a space about 25' wide, 75' long and 12' high a maze/honeycomb of loading sleds gleaned from the streets of SoHo. This resulted in a wooden structure that completely filled his loft, wall to wall, ceiling to floor. The performance was sparsely attended—Dunn announced he would be "on" from two to six Wednesday through Sunday afternoons, October 2 through 13. People dropped in one or two at a time. Once in the loft, and after signing a guest book (putting me on Dunn's mailing list) and donating a couple of dollars, I was left alone in the honeycomb. I wandered through, thinking my own thoughts, and then (I don't know why) I looked up and saw a body lying on a sled near the ceiling. I was shocked, scared. I climbed up and saw Dunn. He wore a touch of eye makeup, was dressed all in white and he lay absolutely still. From the corner of his mouth was drawn, very realistically, a trickle of blood. I leaned close to his face and felt his breath: it was reassuring—though I knew he was alive, it was good to have my knowledge confirmed. I wanted to touch him but thought this would violate some convention, so I did nothing but contemplate him. Then I went to a corner of the loft, at ceiling level (on a plane with Dunn) and dozed. A few other spectators arrived and left. I napped and sometimes lay half-awake for nearly two hours, as afternoon gave way to evening. Then the woman at the desk came to the entrance of the performing space and said that the performance was ending. I climbed down and left the honeycomb. I stayed in the kitchen and when Dunn came out about 20 minutes later and we talked for a few minutes. Talking to him was important, reassuring—as was walking home alone. I felt contemplative, rested.

Dunn told me that sometimes spectators tugged at him, pinched him, tried to make him move or scream. I remembered what Judith Malina and Julian Beck told me about the body-pile scene from *Mysteries:*

> MALINA: In Europe, it was more common to be treated aggressively. I have been kicked, stomped, tickled, had my fingers bent back and my hair set on fire.
> SCHECHNER: My God, why, do you think—
> BECK: To get her to move.
> MALINA: To get me to move.
> BECK: To get the corpse not to be a real corpse.
> MALINA: Only in America have we been comforted. Isn't it strange?
> SCHECHNER: Well, in America you are, for better or worse, an American; in Europe you are, for better or worse, an American.[1]

In retrospect I think Beck's metaphysical interpretation was more correct than my political one: people are uncomfortable even in the presence of simulated death. With Dunn's *101* the relationship to him in his honeycomb (or ought I to say catacomb) was ambiguous: Dunn was still but not "actively dead," as the Living was in the plague scene of *Mysteries.* Spectators could choose their own relationship to Dunn, his performance, the space.

In The Performance Group's production of Brecht's *Mother Courage and Her Children* a reverse selective inattention was tried. Here I encouraged the performers to drop their characterizations when they were not involved in a scene—to move from the realm of the story to that of the audience: to simply sit and watch, or relax (read, talk quietly, prepare for their next scene) in a small area fully in view of the audience which we called the Green Room (though it really wasn't one). I took the idea, I think, from work the Open Theater and other groups did in the 1960s where performers not in a scene sat to the side, usually in a quiet, almost formal manner, and then rose to join the scene—something like athletes on the bench. I wanted to use this idea but in a traditionally theatrical way; thus the Green Room. Up to a point the experiment worked. The audience saw performers neither playing roles nor pretending to pay attention to the play. For example, when Mother Courage leaves the performing area in Scene 3 to go shopping, Swiss Cheese takes the cash box, runs away with it, and is arrested. Joan MacIntosh (Courage) and Stephen Borst (Chaplain) are in the Green Room. Clearly they aren't continuing the story offstage—they are not seen, for example, pantomiming buying things at the market. They're just sitting down, as Joan and Steve, while a few feet away Spalding Gray (Swiss Cheese) and Leeny Sack (Kattrin) are performing the story of the cash box. It seems to me that just as a spectator can drop in and out of a drama so the performers can drop in and out of character. The challenge is to arrange, not so much the time for this to happen—the drama will fix that—but the place for it, and in what way it's to be observed. In *Mother Courage* what happened was that the audience's ability to see into the Green Room set up a pressure for still another, authentically private space: performers would drift out of the Green Room to a space behind the light board that spectators couldn't see into—there the performers would talk, smoke and prepare for their next entries. Only some performers, and only some of the time, used the public Green Room.

During the performance a performer could find himself in three different situations: (1) In the midst of a scene which needs tension to carry the narrative; for example, that part of Scene 3 where Courage, using Yvette as an intermediary, is bargaining for the life of Swiss Cheese. (2) As an observer of the scene, but doing work indirectly related to the narrative action of the scene; for example, while Courage is haggling in Scene 3 the Chaplain and Kattrin are setting up tables, cups, trays and flatware for the supper that will be served to the audience after the scene is over—this supper is both part of the story (Courage is preparing to sell lunch to the troops) and part of the performance event (The Performance Group is preparing to sell supper to the audience). While working, Borst and Sack concentrate on their tasks quietly and with as little tension as possible except for those moments that explicitly call for participation in the drama of the scene such as when the Chaplain drops a cup and Courage yells at him. (3) As performers in the space but not in the scene. During the same scene James Clayburgh hauls Swiss Cheese up into the air using the pulley system he designed as one of the Group's environmentalists. Once Clayburgh finishes his work he remains visually in the scene but he isn't "in character," he doesn't "do" anything except watch the action: a kind of intermediary between the spontaneous attentiveness of a spectator and the planned participation of a performer.

This relaxed inattention on the part of the performers allows for a subtle penetration of their everyday lives into the dramatic reality of the performance. Some critics consider this mixture a serious breach of convention. I insist on it for several reasons: it is like the readiness of athletes not only on the sideline but before a play; it shows the double person of the performer, the "myself" and the "him-of-the-character"; it serves as a bridge between the audience and the performers. Some spectators are disturbed by the "lack of energy" of this kind of performing. But when an engaged action occurs the energy resources, not having been squandered, can be spent more powerfully. Some spectators find themselves falling into parallel rhythms of focused attention and selective inattention. As their attention "wanders" people begin picking up on events and images that would otherwise escape notice, or be merely blurred side-visions: movements of spectators, gestures of performers not at the center of the scene, overall arrangement and dynamics of space. Without freezing the performance it can be contemplated; the spectator can choose to be in or out and can move attention around on a sliding scale of involvement. Within a context of selective inattention patterns-of-the-whole are visible that otherwise would be burned out of consciousness by a too tense concentration. It is this manifestation of what Ehrenzweig calls the "primary process" that interests me. Spectators become the artists along with the performers.

> How often have we not observed how an artist suddenly stops in his tracks without apparent reason, steps back from his canvas and looks at it with a curiously vacant stare? What happens is that the conscious gestalt is prevented from crystallizing. Nothing seems to come into his mind. Perhaps one or another detail lights up for a moment only to sink back into the emptiness. During this absence of mind an unconscious scanning seems to go on. Suddenly as from nowhere some offending detail hitherto ignored will come into view. It had somehow upset the balance of the picture, but had gone undetected. With relief the painter will end his apparent inactivity. He returns to his canvas and carries out the necessary retouching. This "full" emptiness of unconscious scanning occurs in many other examples of creative work.[2]

I disagree with Ehrenzweig only in his insistence on correcting the "offending detail." In theatre, at least, these disruptions and disturbances, these variations, are what gives special interest to a performance; what makes it possible—almost by a process analogous to evolution by natural selection working from accidental genetic changes—for a performance to grow over a period of time. Ehrenzweig recognizes these changes:

> A performer may readily change the inarticulate micro-elements of his interpretation from performance to performance. But this instability does make them arbitrary. Any change forces the performer to recast his interpretation of the whole work on the spur of the moment. This total integration can only be controlled by the empty stare of unconscious scanning which alone is capable of overcoming the fragmentation in art's surface structure.[3]

Finally, Ehrenzweig offers a comprehensive explanation for the presence of these disruptions in modern art—disruptions that occur not only in theatre but in the cubist "distortions" of the human figure, in

music that is atonal and dissonant, even in philosophical systems that
stress the absurd.

> The psychoanalytic concept of creative sublimation implies
> that the highest achievement should be linked very
> directly with what is lowest and most primitive in
> ourselves. Our pleasure in music, according to Freud, is
> nourished by an infantile enjoyment of the flatus. [. . .] The
> dynamic tension between the extreme poles of sublimation
> is often bridged by an arc of tenuous fragility. A schizoid
> dissociation of the ego is never far when distant ego
> functions are yoked together in testing creative tasks.
> Such ego dissociations need not always be taken as a
> pathological symptom; they could be due to a temporary
> snapping of the highly tensed links within the creative
> mechanism. We have seen how again and again creative
> imagery is cut off from its matrix in the deep unconscious
> and turned into conscious mannerism and cliché. It may
> well be, then, that the frequent dissociation of sensibilities
> in modern art and the recurrent need for disrupting its
> mannerisms and clichés is not so much pathological as the
> price to be paid for the enormous tension created by its
> conjunction of distant ego functions. The close cooperation
> between precisely focused reasoning and almost totally
> undifferentiated intuition has, to my mind made our time
> so abundantly creative, both in art and science.[4]

Ehrenzweig's ideas link to mine at two points: (1) the notion that
performance is exteriorized fantasy, discussed in ETHOLOGY AND
THEATRE; (2) the coexistence of both poles within the same
performance—selective inattention as individual or collective unconscious scanning.

Related to selective inattention is the question of "presence." What
gives to some performers a special allure, and why do audiences confer
this status and seek out those who have it? It isn't only a Western
phenomenon, this idea of being a star; and it isn't always, or even
mostly, related to the skills of the performer. While watching the
Thovil ceremony in Sri Lanka one of the dancers was a very old man
who, I was told, was the village's most powerful "devil dancer," a kind
of exorcism. This old man executed a few steps and chanted. His
dancing and singing were poor by Western standards of energy, preci-
sion, invention, duration. But he commanded the complete attention
of the previously noisy, socializing crowd. His presence, not his professional skills, carried power: he was an agent, a funnel, a conduit for
power and it was that power, showing meagerly through him, as a
tiny light at the end of a long tunnel, that held the audience. Also, as
someone told me, there was the recollection of the old man's youth
during which he had danced some furious dances, as another young
man would do later the same night. So the crowd's attention was also

due to respect. The same may be said concerning any of the world's political or religious stars. Some may have powerful figures and great oratory. But others, say a pope as old as Paul is today, command respect by virtue of their position: even if feeble-voiced, trembling and off-key a pope presiding at a Mass brings to the performance the authority of his office not merely his skills as a performer. Or Mao appearing briefly in public, stooped with age, barely able to raise his hand: still he is an emblem of the revolution and a pinnacle of its power.

This is star presence—a person whose very presence transcends whatever activity she may be absorbed in. In the case of the devil dancer, the pope and Mao the role transcends the performer; in the case of the movie star the person transcends the role—so no matter what movie she is in Marilyn Monroe is Marilyn and Clark Gable is Gable. The fact that these stars are dead adds to their allure: their performances are finished, as a painting by a dead painter is finished, and can be studied as a completed trajectory. Thus their performances converge on their lives, the two are one, and the mere presence of a star in a film is enough to confer on that film importance.

There are two kinds of presence: the kind where an office, as an emblem or conduit of power, confers on whoever holds it a star quality; and the kind where through publicity, manipulation of the public or some hard-to-define-but-visible quality in the person a presence is felt even though there is no office behind it, as in the movie star. These apparently opposite examples of presence are in fact very closely connected. There are two roads to power—through work, and through being called (elevated by accident). The official path is progressive, step by step, from priest to bishop, to cardinal, to pope; or from party worker, to cell leader, to commissar, to chairman. The magic path is by being "discovered" in Schwab's drugstore. Of course we know the path to stardom is strewn with tasks. But the myth is that of apotheosis. The two paths to power are in fact united through the continuous and conscious manipulation of the public. And in the sense that something is "behind" the star, whether pope or Monroe.

This relates to selective inattention in an interesting way. Presence becomes a kind of absence, a lack of anything complicated to do. In a certain way the star must practice doing very little, actually falling out of character insofar as this character interferes with a direct communication of personality to the spectator. Thus the absence of the star from any specific role is what creates star-quality. I think this is true of official stars as well as movie stars. Mao is seen at a distance, waving; or a picture is released of a President signing a bill, or shaking hands: the actual work these people do, if it exists at all by the time they have ascended to their ultimate positions, is hidden from the public. The revelations of the Nixon tapes, and a revelation that was comforting actually, was that Presidents curse, fumble, speak as humans do; that their policies are forged through prejudice and argument. This is something Genet understands better than any other dramatist. His plays are examinations of the gaps and links between the gestures/costumes of power and the personalities of those who put on these accoutrements. The emblematic, and very simple, appearance of stars encourages the public to project onto them every kind of expectation and fantasy. The stars are in fact blank screens. Ehrenzweig's primary process is not the property of the artist or scientist alone; the general public often shares in it.

In today's performances I see two divergent tendencies. One is the short, intense, you-must-pay-attention kind of work characteristic of Richard Foreman's *Sophia-Wisdom* series; also the kind of work Grotowski did from 1959 through 1968 (the "poor theatre" phase). These intense pieces need a silent, attentive, hard-working audience. But now another kind of theatre is emerging—longer, episodic, loosely constructed. These pieces might appear to be like Piscator and Brecht's epic theatre but actually they are more like the ceremonies and celebrations of non-Western theatre and performances in the West that attract integral audiences. Spectators come and go, pay attention or don't, select what parts of the performance to follow. These habits may be further trained by television—because the sets are often on but not looked at continuously; or by the radio and phonograph which also encourage selective inattention. In work such as Dunn's *101* the action is minimal and the work essentially meditative rather than dramatic. The use of selective inattention encourages a kind of alpha-rhythm performance that evokes deep relaxation rather than tension. Or, as in the episodic pearls-on-a-string pageants of Wilson, a long-wave rhythm stimulates dropping in, dropping out: a different kind of meditation. The experiment I made with performer inattention in *Courage* only partially succeeded. We in the West still have neither an educated audience nor performers and directors confident enough of their work—that is, well enough trained in both doing and in not doing things to drop in and out of a performance with ease and skill. Perhaps we will learn that the full scope of performing, like living, involves not only the push of doing but the release of undoing, the meditation of non-doing.

Notes

1. Malina and Beck (1969), 34.
2. Ehrenzweig (1970), 38.
3. Ehrenzweig (1970), 44.
4. Ehrenzweig (1970), 142-3.

Ethology and Theatre

Darwin first proposed a continuity of behavior from animals to people in his *Expression of the Emotions in Man and Animals* (1872). For a long time his speculations lay fallow, but they are now being followed up. We want to know how much of "body language" is genetically fixed and how much learned. The underlying assumption is that an inclusive web includes both human and animal behavior. Is there also a cultural web? How are human religions, customs and arts extensions, elaborations and transformations of animal cultures? I want to explore this question as it pertains to theatre. But I propose that the theatrical paradigm is a key to understanding larger plans of human social interaction.

Theatrical performances are ritualized versions of gestures and sounds. These may be exaggerated/transformed as in Kabuki, Kathakali, ballet or the dances of Australian Aborigines. Or they may be replications of ordinary behavior as in cinema verité and naturalistic theatre. Or they may be unique behaviors developed for use only during special ceremonies as in ritual combats or initiation rites which are neither mythic nor mimetic. Theatre trades on universally recognized moments—such as can be frozen by a still camera; and on sequences of behavior—such as seeing, greeting with raised eyebrows and embracing another, or freezing with fright or shock—that tell recognizable "stories." I think all kinds of theatre—that on show in theatre buildings, that of rites of passage, that accompanying official displays of power and that happening on a microsocial level in daily routines—are part of a single system of scripts, scenarios, disguises, displays, dances, impersonations and scenes. Studies of this system have been made by people whose knowledge of theatre is from the outside. My experience, and therefore my perspective, is from the inside, as a theatre director.

Both "fun" and "rehearsal" seem to be part of the performance sequences of the great apes. In his studies of the mountain gorilla of central Africa Schaller says the functions of the chest-beating sequence include the discharge of excitement and showing off. Young males "occasionally displayed with great abandon, then sat quietly, and looked all around as if to judge the effectiveness of the behavior."[1] The chest-beating display also repels intruders and maintains group hierarchy. It thereby combines efficacy and entertainment; but so does "professional theatre" with its aspects of money-making, ambition, fame and high art. The function of reducing excitement among the gorillas is parallel to the cathartic function of theatre proposed by Aristotle and Artaud, a therapeutic tradition of performance. Schaller notes that "the primary causation of the chest-beating sequence appears to be the build-up of tension (excitement) above a certain threshold. After the display, the level of excitement temporarily drops below the threshold, and the animals behave calmly until a new accummulation of tension erupts in display.[2] The build-up of tension does not lead to fighting but to display; potential disruption is transformed into entertainment. This outcome is very much like human theatrical performances. There too violence is present in both themes and gestures; but the process of theatricalization renders this violence less harmful than it would be if actualized "in life," and the resulting performance is entertaining.

The chest-beating sequence, and other displays among primates, use drumming and dancing: making rhythms and moving to self-made rhythms. These displays occur among individuals and among groups; they are often accompanied by hooting and other vocalizations; they create and modify moods. Among the many functions of these displays fun appears to be the connecting link. I won't define fun, that will come out step by step. But I do say that fun is private entertainment; entertainment is shared fun. Both are related to showing off, playing around, exploring and pretending (becoming bigger, smaller, other, different). Fun happens when the energy released by an action is more than the anxiety, fear or effort spent either on making the action or overcoming the obstacles inhibiting it.

To perform acts that are otherwise forbidden—punished, taboo, unthought of—is a way of "making fun." In human cultures these acts are often violent and sexual, almost always displaying friends and relatives (not strangers) in forbidden combinations. This is as true of the obscene proto-dramas of Kogu in New Guinea as it is of Aristophanes; of the insulting song-duels of the Tiv in Nigeria as it is of the Alaskan or Greenland Eskimos. And where there is no chance of cultural diffusion we are facing deep structures of human social, aesthetic and biological organization. Rehearsals—whether these be the exploratory repetition of actions of the modern theatre, or the formal preparations of ceremonies that precede many rituals—are a special time of fun. During rehearsals performers experiment with the interface between what is private and what is public. The fun is in trying out what may never be shown, a strictly theatrical version of doing the forbidden.

If not rehearsals then at least practice and perfection through repetition occurs among apes. Lawick-Goodall describes the display of Mike, a male chimpanzee of the Gombe Stream Reserve in Tanzania. (These chimps are not tamed or trained animals; the significance of studies like Schaller's and Lawick-Goodall's is that they were made among wild animals.)

> All at once Mike calmly walked over to our tent and took hold of an empty kerosene can by the handle. Then he picked up a second can and, walking upright, returned to the place where he had been sitting. Armed with his two cans Mike continued to stare toward the other males. After a few minutes he began to rock from side to side. At first the movement was almost imperceptible, but Hugo and I were watching him closely. Gradually he rocked more vigorously, his hair slowly began to stand erect, and then, softly at first, he started a series of pant-hoots. As he called, Mike got to his feet and suddenly he was off, charging toward the group of males, hitting the two cans ahead of him. The cans, together with Mike's crescendo of hooting, made the most appalling racket: no wonder the erstwhile peaceful males rushed out of the way. Mike and his cans vanished down a track, and after a few moments there was silence. [. . .] After a short interval that low-pitched hooting began again, followed almost immediately by the appearance of the two rackety cans with Mike closely behind them. Straight for the other males he charged, and once more they fled. This time, even before the group could reassemble, Mike set off again; but he made straight for Goliath [alpha male]—and even he hastened out of his way like all the others. Then Mike stopped and sat, all his hair on end, breathing hard.[3]

Obviously Mike was challenging Goliath's alpha rank; and not long after this display Mike replaced Goliath. But the challenge—like so many encounters between animals concerning dominance, territory, food and mates—came not as a direct attack or life-and-death fight but contained within ritual, as a theatrical event. Just as "making fun" can be an indirect attack on the authorities, so Mike's charge driving the kerosene cans ahead of him was an indirect attack on Goliath's dominant rank.

Mike's performance can be analyzed two ways. Either the sequence was a performance during which Mike worked himself up step by step in front of the whole band until finally he confronted Goliath in a chimp version of the game of chicken; or the showing-off and charge at the low-ranking males were rehearsals, try-outs, preparations for the main event, the challenge to Goliath. Of these two constructions I prefer the first because there's no need to attribute to Mike the sophistication necessary for the rehearsal hypothesis. But also in theatre I have often seen similar "unconscious" discoveries—where improvisations, or simply "fooling around," during or between work periods in rehearsals have uncovered images/actions later used in performance. The activity of doing things, repeating where necessary, changing, improvising and including even mistakes into the performance, is common in today's theatre. Robert Wilson tape records workshops and rehearsals, and video-tapes when possible, in order to retain fragments or patterns that are repeated and built on. Movements in "post-modern dance" are invented through improvisations and repetition: the emotional core of a work is not known in advance and "expressed," it is uncovered through action. This is the way Grotowski worked during his "poor theatre" phase, the way Peter Brook developed his version of *The Tempest* and *Ceremony of the Birds*. The Open Theater developed its work from *The Serpent* through *Nightwalk* using this method of discovery. I used it in all my work with The Performance Group, and it is the core of the images of *Commune*.

Rehearsals in contemporary theatre are not what they were in Max Reinhardt's day when the director came to rehearsals with all the actions inscribed in his *regiebuch*. Rehearsals are centers of psychophysical, sociological and personal research; the only known thing is a provisional certainty that a performance will happen somewhere during, not after, the process, and that an audience will enter the space to watch or interact with the performers. This kind of work throws a new burden on the performers. They are intermediaries, masters of ceremony, inventors; they must show themselves even as they interpret their roles. And the idea of interpretation takes on new complications since scripts are often radically restructured. All this has been implicit in Western theatre since the end of the 19th century. Stanislavski was the first to put the training of the performer at the top of the theatrical agenda. But why? Because Western theatre has become increasingly ritualized during the last 80 years, moving into areas of human interaction once reserved for religion; and as society is cyberneticized, contact between people programmed, theatre gains importance as an activity occupying a niche between relatively unstructured activity, say a party, and totally formalized or mediated exchanges. Theatre is semi-formal, narrative, personal, direct and fun.

Its methods encourage audience participation on many levels. This aspect of theatre has heavily influenced sports and religious ceremony both of which have become more theatricalized in recent years. On the other hand, movies, despite their apparent immediacy, are a flat medium, ineluctable and non-participatory. Environmental theatre—implicit in the "fourth wall" of Antoine and Stanislavski, explicit since Meyerhold's productions of the early 1920s—needs performers trained in semiotics. What is natural/automatic in other animals is cultural/learned in humans. Training in semiotics is traditionally available in the societies I studied in India, Java, Bali and New Guinea; and in parts of Africa and the Americas. But in the industrialized nations new "ideograms" have to be invented or discovered for each production. As Grotowski says:

> It is not, however, a question of seeking fixed ideograms as,
> for example, in the Peking Opera in which, in order to
> portray a particular flower, the actor makes a specific
> unchangeable gesture inherited from centuries of
> tradition. New ideograms must constantly be sought and
> their composition appear immediate and spontaneous. [. . .]
> The final result is a living form possessing its own logic.[4]

The first results of this method were stiff, mechanical: the biomechanics of Meyerhold; then the carefully arranged, though natural-appearing compositions of Brecht (available for study in his model books). Grotowski developed exercises that helped actors "confront" a text and discover a meeting place between their own body-impulses and the logic of the story. The same confrontation was worked by the Open Theater. The framed, pictorial exactness of Foreman's work is different; there is nothing spontaneous about it: Foreman consciously emphasizes its thought-out-before quality. But in Wilson's super-slow imagery where a move can be predicted and its trajectory followed, and where—as in *A Letter For Queen Victoria*— certain actions were repeated enough times to force a looking at different aspects of the moves; and in the "post-modern" dances of Dunn, Forti, Joanas, Paxton and others;[5] in the theatre work of Allan Kaprow ordinary human actions are isolated, displaced, stopped, slowed or accelerated, repeated: all ritualizations ethologically speaking. The movie camera—particularly the ability to stop action, examine gestures frame by frame, to go forward and backward, to repeat, to study compositions as they condense and evaporate— has deeply reshaped theatrical performance. The theoretical basis for these examinations exist in the work of Eibl-Eibesfeldt, Birdwhistell, Goffman, Hall and others."[6] This kind of ritualization is not of social organization (which exists, and is important) but of microsocial body moves: glances, head tilts, hand gestures, shoulder lurches, pelvic thrusts, etc. To be alive is to dance.

Mike's [the chimpanzee] performance—returning to the ritual of social organization—isn't unique among animals. But he probably didn't have a strategy in mind when he began. His challenge of Goliath arose from the process of doing his performance. Similar discoveries are made by performers all the time. At the January 11,1976, performance of Brecht's *Mother Courage and Her Children*—at least the 80th performance of that play by The Performance Group— Spalding Gray as Swiss Cheese let out four terrified screams as he was hauled into the air during Scene 3: the screams of a two-year-old boy. After the performance Gray and I talked; I realized for the first time that his Swiss Cheese is just a big baby, that this baby believes his mother is omnipotent and that he will never be separated from her. When the sergeant brings Swiss Cheese in under arrest Swiss Cheese knows his mother will fix things up. As he is hauled into the air he has a revelation: his mother is powerless. His screams are a combination of disappointment, rage and terror; at 35 he suffers his first attack of separation anxiety. It took all those performances before Gray discovered, through his body, what Swiss Cheese undergoes. The screams "complete" his character even as they indict his mother who never prepared him to live, or die, in an adult's world. Probably Mike began his performance as unknowing of its end, or its significance, as Gray did his. Maybe Mike only felt a tension vis-à-vis Goliath and took action to relieve it. This tension was there in his body whether or not Mike could conceive of its presence. Each step of the performance both relieved the tension and built new tension, until the final direct charge at Goliath. This kind of performance is one where the actions are discovered during rehearsals; rehearsals are not designed to express what's known but to discover through action what's to be done. Rehearsals, even performances, can be full of surprises; these are not improvisations but variations.

In DRAMA, SCRIPT, THEATRE AND PERFORMANCE I cite Lawick-Goodall's description of the "rain dance" of the Gombe Stream Reserve chimpanzees. This performance is both a prototype and a parallel to human theatre. The spectacle Lawick-Goodall saw, and other observations made in the wild, confirm the fundamental nature of the performer-spectator dyad, even of the protagonist-antagonist-spectator triad. The dyad is the basic performance relationship, the triad the basic dramatic relationship. What a senile Western aesthetics has done is try to freeze who should play what role in this arrangement; among animals and many human societies the roles shift during performance: this moment's observer may be the next moment's protagonist, and this moment's antagonist may be the next's spectator. But can I say with any assurance that the young males and females sitting in the trees observing the mature males rushing with branches down the hillside in the midst of the thunderstorm (the performance Lawick-Goodall saw) are spectators, and are the mature males performers? The display can't be explained parsimoniously any other way. And, as I have tried to show elsewhere, play and pleasure have "survival value." I don't want to make play into a kind of work, but take steps in the opposite direction: work is a specialized form of play.

Lorenz connects animal and human performances in this way:

> The formation of traditional rites must have been begun
> with the first dawning of human culture, just as at a much
> lower level phylogenetic rite formation was a prerequisite
> for the origin of osical organization in higher animals. [. . .]
> In both cases, a behavior pattern by means of which a
> species in the one case, a cultured society in the other,
> deals with certain environmental conditions, acquires an
> entirely new function, that of communication. The primary
> function may still be performed, but it often recedes more
> and more into the background and may disappear
> completely so that a typical change of function is achieved.
> Out of communication two new equally important
> functions may arise, both of which still contain some
> measure of communicative effects. The first of these is the
> channeling of aggression into innocuous outlets, the second
> is the formation of a bond between two or more individuals.
> In both cases, the selection pressure of the new function
> has wrought analogous changes on the form of the primal,
> nonritualized behavior. It quite obviously lessens the
> chance of ambiguity in the communication that a long
> series of independently variable patterns should be welded
> into one obligatory sequence. [. . .] The display of animals
> during threat and courtship furnishes an abundance of
> examples, and so does the culturally developed ceremonial
> of man. [. . .] Rhythmical repetition of the same movement
> is so characteristic of very many rituals, both instinctive
> and cultural, that it is hardly necessary to describe
> examples. [. . .] This 'mimic exaggeration' results in a
> ceremony which is, indeed, closely akin to a symbol and
> which produces that theatrical effect that first struck Sir
> Julian Huxley as he watched his Great Crested Grebes.
> [. . .] There is hardly a doubt that all human art primarily
> developed in the service of rituals and that the autonomy of
> 'art for art's sake' was achieved only by another, secondary
> step of cultural progress.[7]

I doubt whether there ever was such a thing as "art for art's sake." Implicit in Lorenz's assertions is the idea that theatre is a model of, or an experimentally controlled simulation of, human interactions; it is more than that too: it is a reflection or meditation on these interactions, freed as they are by theatrical convention from being actualized "in society." Instead, theatrical actions are segregated "in the theatre" where they at the same time become clearer, exaggerated, metaphorized and simulated. The interactions which are "practiced" in theatre are those which are problematical in society, usually interactions of a sexual, violent or taboo kind. This is not merely a characteristic of the Western theatre, but of theatre everywhere. In my view drama is not a model of all human action, not even most of it measured by time spent, but only the problematical, taboo, difficult, liminal and dangerous. And the theatrical actions that accompany the drama are rhythmic, repetitive, exaggerated; the body adornments are often spectacular: everything is ritualized in the ethological sense. Drama arises where clarity of signal is needed most: it is where the risk is greatest and the stakes highest that communication needs the most careful management, where redundancy is an advantage. Drama connects two basic actions: (1) misunderstanding, a break in communication, a confusion of messages, irony; (2) violence—especially political and sexual violence, often associated in drama—rebellion against authority and decency.

The second point in Lorenz's statement is the connection between aggression and aggregation. He suggests that the underlying effect of releasing aggressive behavior within a ritual pattern is not to separate individuals but to bond them. I have seen this confirmed in New Guinea. Also in workshops and rehearsals where the release of hostile feelings, and especially their channeling into exercises (local rituals), invariably leads to the formation of strong bonds among group members. Thus on two levels simultaneously—the level of drama and the level of theatre—aggression and groupness support each other if the aggression is expressed in ritual. The dramatic event at the core of the performance is itself a ritualized way of presenting to the assembled community, the audience, aggressive material: dramas (both farces and tragedies, often combinations of both) deal with the hurts or potential breaking points within the society attending as spectators. It is no accident that Shakespeare's plays return again and again to the questions of personal versus state interests on the part of kings; or that 19th-20th-century naturalism focused on the disparity between individual needs, mainly sexual and creative, and the grinding routine of the economic order of things. It has been my experience that the more violent the actions dealt with in performance—the more physical the work, the more risky the taboos revealed or violated—the stronger the bonds formed among the group making the performance. If one of theatre's functions is to model interactions resulting from the release of repressed material, another is how to make groups that can control, through ritualization, this explosive material. In this way theatre is a cutting edge of advances in knowledge even as it provides methods of social control.

Lorenz concentrates on the finished artwork, and he doesn't differentiate between theatre and the other arts, namely painting and literature. Literature is a late development, painting goes back at least to Paleolithic times and must be considered coexistent with theatre. But this early painting, in my opinion, was more of an "action painting," closely associated with performances, and done as a kind of performance, than it was a painting done for viewing. Certainly it is difficult to view work done deep in unlit caves; and much of the cave work is superimposed one image over many things, sometimes thousands layed on top of each other. This suggests that the act of making the images was more important than looking at the images when complete. If Lorenz were more familiar with theatre he would see that rehearsal is the connection between animal ritualization and human art. I discuss this connection in more detail in my essay, TOWARDS A POETICS OF PERFORMANCE.

Animals, including humans, exist within the same ecological web, but not all animals are alike: analogies built on similarities must be examined cautiously. I wouldn't call the "dance" of a male cichlid defending his territory against other males and at the same time enticing a female to his nest a dance in the human sense; nor would I call the patterned flight of bees a dance in the human sense. Where everything is genetically determined, where no genuine culture or learning takes place, where no improvisation or variation is possible, we lack the basis for calling these activities art. Of course people may imitate these patterns and make dances modeled on them: such imitation is an example of cultural learning. Also most animal performances lack the performance tools—specially prepared places, props, costumes, conscious impersonations, etc.—of human theatre. But by the time we get to Mike's performance with the kerosene cans we are at the threshold of human theatre. It only remained for Mike to do his act with another chimpanzee playing Goliath while Goliath looked on, and to repeat that performance several times before different spectators. Mike combined fixed elements characteristic of his species— swaying, pant-hooting, drumming, charging—with improvised elements and props: the kerosene cans, charging out of sight allowing for a temporary respite and the building of suspense, a steady rise in the action climaxing with the confrontation with Goliath. The cichild "releases" the same behavior everytime it's stimulated properly. Mike interacts in ways that are only generally predictable (he will display, he will probably challenge Goliath); he composes his own scenario as he goes along combining fixed and found ingredients. Aside from its nonrepeatability and the lack of an audience Mike's display is authentic dance-theatre. I say this without assuming a "psychology" for Mike—his performance is not an "expression of feelings"—but an action which is the feelings.

Schaller points out that people attending mass sports display as great apes do:

> Various aspects of the chest-beating display sequence are

> present in the gibbon, orang-utan, chimpanzee and man,
> although the specificity is sometimes lacking. [. . .] Man
> behaves remarkably like a chimpanzee or a gorilla in
> conflicting situations. Sporting events are ideal locations
> for watching the behavior of man when he is generally
> excited and emotionally off-guard. A spectator at a
> sporting event perceives actions which excite him. Yet he
> cannot participate in them directly, nor does he want to
> cease observing them. The tension thus produced finds
> release in chanting, clapping of hands, stamping of feet,
> jumping up and down, throwing of objects. This behavior is
> sometimes guided into a pattern by the efforts of
> cheerleaders who, by repeating similar sounds over and
> over again, channel the displays into a violent,
> synchronized climax. The intermittent nature of such
> behavior, the transfer of excitement from one individual to
> the next and other similarities with the displays of gorillas
> are readily apparent.[8]

Our century is not alone in giving evidence that such displays can be manipulated by demagogues. Many "mood displays" are seen in people: throwing things when angry, kicking the wall, jumping up and down with enthusiasm or joy, clapping or stamping the feet to get attention or show strong feeling and so on. These displays change character when they are ritualized into mass actions such as spectator sports, political rallies, parades; then individual displays grow rigid, exaggerated, rhythmically coordinated, repetitive—their emphasis shifts from the free expression of feeling to an evocation and channeling of aggression for the benefit of the sponsor: the team, corporation, politician or state.

Before discussing the re-emergence in our day of "phatic theatre," performances based on evoking mood displays, I want to say a few words about the extremes of expression present in mass spectacles and their opposite: therapy situations where individuals learn again, or for the first time, how to let their feelings "out." Therapy groups are quasi-theatrical congregations offering a channel for the expression of otherwise repressed or suppressed feelings. Theatre has both fed from and been a feeder of therapy. Groups theatrical and therapeutic are extended pseudo-families where repressed intra-family feelings (especially violent or other taboo feelings) are let out. The displays I've seen in workshops and in group therapy are versions of what's no longer, or never was, permitted in general society. The displays are framed and controlled, artfully presented as part of theatrical training or therapeutic "sessions." These displays are most artfully managed in theatre where they are rehearsed and scored, but somewhat artful too in therapy where the therapist monitors and coaches the patients, and where patients frequently present "numbers," performances they have recited before. In fact, the idea of abreaction is to encourage the patient to repeat in a therapuetic setting what he did unconsciously or without control in another, earlier setting.

A most radical integration of therapy into theatre is the work of Robert Wilson. His work also draws heavily on non-Western performance styles, especially trance dancing, selective inattention, and extended performances times/places. Wilson's approach to therapy is very like what Australian Aborigines do. Wilson doesn't try to convince the patient—who is the protagonist not in the narrative but in a kinesthetic sense—to "adjust" to the ordinary world, the world which the protagonist has to some degree rejected or been rejected by. Instead, Wilson brings other performers into the protagonist's world, creating a nest for the protagonist.

> In his therapy workshops, Wilson provides movement exercises for participants and at the same time he learns from them—from their particular ways of expression, communication and sensibility. His observations are applied to his theatre workshops and performances. From the early stages, his performances have been influenced to a great extent by his work with exceptional children. During workshops for *The King of Spain* (1969), Wilson began to work with an almost totally deaf boy, Raymond Andrews. [. . .] 'Raymond, with his special sensibility and unusual ways of communication, provided a rich alternative and inspiration for the work. In spite of his near total deafness and virtually no vocabulary, he immediately became a jovial, out-going, convivial and even communicative member of the group. For instance, the movement sections—he is more lively in them and often more imaginative in demonstrating an ability to be exceedingly and exceptionally sensitive to the feelings of others. Only he "perceives" (and transmits) this through kinetic, or kinesthetic awareness rather than through discursive, or verbal dialogue. In these children, I sensed not only a deep, special talent but channels usually unknown for establishing lines of communication. Because of a bodily maladjustment in a certain sense, there was an extended range of feeling or, even, sensibility that, once uncovered, meant an expression of awareness and communication.' (Production Notes on *The King of Spain* in *New American Plays*, 1970.)[9]

It was Andrews' world that Wilson's group created so fully in *Deafman Glance*. Wilson nested Andrews in a world of Andrews' own making. Instead of adjusting the patient to the world—insisting actually if not verbally that the patient's experience of the world is wrong or abnormal—Wilson creates a complete theatrical world arranged in harmony to the perceptions of the patient-protagonist. This is close to the arrangement of dances and ceremonies according to the "dreamtime" of the Aborigines—the Aborigine dreams of certain steps and rhythms and then teaches these to his fellows upon awakening. In Wilson's theatre the patient-protagonist often reciprocates by granting a degree of validity to the ordinary world and channels of communication are opened. By saying to the deaf or autistic child (and Wilson picks people whose problem is that of communication) "do your world" Wilson makes possible an exchange in which the patient says, ultimately, "ok, now do your world." A favorite exercise of Wilson's in rehearsal is the game of follow-the-leader. Or Wilson may ask people to pick up on the rhythms and movements of others. He does many mirror exercises—but not in a mechanical way: the mirrors coincide and improvise, move with each other and take off from each other.

I'm uncomfortable using the word "patient" as a label for Raymond Andrews or Christopher Knowles, Wilson's latest collaborator, a brain-damaged teenager who worked on *The Life and Times of Joseph Stalin* and *The $ Value of Man*. Patient carries with it a stigma of limited personhood; it is by granting full personhood—or even the enhanced status of protagonist—that Wilson creates the environment out of which his extraordinary art grows. When working with Knowles on *Stalin* other performers were asked to follow him, imitate him, play with him: in this nest of experiences other people began to come out and show idiosyncratic elements of their persons; paradoxically, these deeply private worlds were also "universal," recognizable versions of other experiences: in Wilson's work the private and the species-wide converge. In breaking away from the idea of a normative, single world-view, Wilson opens the possibilities of multiple-worlds coexisting and interacting in the same performance space. Maybe this is only a late 20th-century version of our utopian projections. It certainly has a pluralistic political ring to it. But maybe too it creates on stage the interplay between genetically fixed (universal) patterns and culturally invented ones. In any case, Wilson's method has three steps: (1) creating a nest for the protagonist, making him feel that his world-view is authentic, genuine and worth sharing; (2) creating multiple world-views by some, many or all the other performer-participants; (3) integrating these multiple world-views into the vision of the protagonist and the director, Wilson himself.

Spectators say that Wilson's work is comforting, even healing. I think this is because Wilson unfolds his images very slowly, evoking alpha-rhythms. Also because his performances are vast, truly epic world-visions, and thereby all-encompassing, reassuring. While traditional Western art since the Renaissance has been obsessively single-minded, monoscopic and intensive, Wilson's work is many-minded, multiscopic and extensive. Wilson's methods, and their results, are very like certain shamanistic performances, which also are based on therapy, on healing, on opening new channels of communication. I've pointed out already how the Aborigines construct ceremonies from what a shaman "sees" either while asleep or alone in the bush. He returns to his people and shows them what he's seen—a dance, a narrative, a song. The others participate with him in enacting the new ceremony. To "see" while sleeping is different but not less real than seeing while awake. Performances among Eskimos and some Amerindian peoples are made from what one person has experienced during a vision-quest or while hallucinating on psychotropic drugs extracted from plants. These experiences are treated with special respect because they hinge together two spheres of reality. A shaman is a professional connecting link between disparate but interacting spheres. One of the ways a person knows he is going to become a shaman is when he experiences visions that can be translated into performances. Isaac Tens, a shaman of the Pacific Northwest, tells how he was called:

> Thirty years after my birth was the time. [. . .] My heart
> started to beat fast, & I began to tremble, just as had
> happened before, when the shamans were trying to fix me
> up. My flesh seemed to be boiling, & I could hear su------.
> My body was quivering. While I remained in this state, I
> began to sing. A chant was coming out of me without my
> being able to do anything to stop it. Many things appeared
> to me presently: huge birds & other animals. . . . These
> were visible only to me, not to the others in my house. Such
> visions happen when a man is about to become a shaman;
> they occur of their own accord. The songs force themselves
> out complete without any attempt to compose them. But I
> learned & memorized those songs by repeating them.[10]

See Eliade (1970) and Lévi-Strauss (1963) for other versions of how the call comes. The one unifying factor is that the shaman develops, or has revealed to him all at once, a routine: a performance.

Earlier I mentioned "phatic theatre," a kind of performance in which the establishing of a group mood is the most important thing. La Barre defines "phatic communication in man as in apes" as "the establishment of similar subjective states in a group of animals— which is why the shaman's message need not be notably rational cognitively, and very often is not."[11] La Barre sees language developing from phatic cries, especially as humans became hunters:

> The greater complexity of hunting as compared with fruit
> eating, and the swiftly changing contingencies of the hunt,
> also evidently favored a change from closed, species-wide
> 'phatic' ape cries—closed in the sense that each monolithic
> one of these cries can serve to display in the individual ape,
> and diffuse to the group, only one endocrine phatic state
> each—fear, anger, amorousness, and the like—into the
> more elaborated communications of merely group-wide
> articulate speech. Hominid hunters need language. But

> not only in the hunt. The adaptive necessity of intense
> group life among aggressive hunters also demands better
> communication and management of both aggressive and
> erotic drives in early man.[12]

La Barre underestimates the complexity of social life among the great apes. The same cries and gestures, in different circumstances, can mean different things. The multivocality of ape communication is close to the phatic expressions among people. Shouts, sobbing, plaintive whining, jumping up and down, foot-stamping, raising the fist—are all communications in a confused area between culturally specific modes of expression and universal human gesturing: the crying of a child, the sobbing and moaning of grief, the scream of pain, the gasp of terror—and the body action accompanying these sounds—are universally recognizable; yet each culture, each family, each person plays this repertory in its own way, significantly altering meaning and effect.

In Highlands New Guinea:

> When pigs are sacrificed to them, spirits are usually
> addressed in a peculiar screaming style. The message is
> delivered in staccato phrases, interrupted with increasing
> frequency by meaningless, loud, sharp yells until, just
> before the pig is struck on the head with the club, the
> staccato "Ah! Ah! Ah! Ah! has replaced words altogether.[13]

Here cognitive discourse—usually about how good the pig is, suitable for repaying an obligation—is transformed into phatic expression. Ordinary speech everywhere is immersed in a sea of ohs, ahs, uhs, stutterings, repetitions and variations in rhythm, pitch and volume that give to each utterance a unique and unrepeatable shape. In any situation of strong feeling this infrastructure becomes dominant: the cognitive value of words is submerged in a rising tide of phatic expression. The center of speaking actually shifts downward to diaphragmatic breathing and sound is released automatically. Not enough is known about this transformational process—about how cognitive speech gives over to vocal infralanguage.

In the high art of opera, Indian raga and jazz "meaningless" vocables temporarily replace cognates. The extension of sounds built on modulations of pitch, volume and duration that characterize the *aria*, the raga and the jazz riff is a formal way of giving over to the phatic quality of "pure music." In left-brain/right-brain terms (see Orenstein, 1972) an utterance that begins dominated by the left-brain stimulates the right-brain so strongly that the original cognitive function is overwhelmed—the singer, and the audience too, is "swept away," "overcome," "moved," "touched"—all images originating in the spatially oriented right-brain. A time of free play occurs which is kept aloft until a formal resolution restores the dominance of the left-brain. This structure, so clear in music, is implicit in many human encounters. The Greek tragedy with its fierce *agons* of pure, staccato speech bracketed by the longer rhythms of the choric odes is another formalization of the same pattern.

Andrei Serban and Elizabeth Swados in their *Greek Trilogy* have carried experiments in phatic language and sounds further than anyone else. Serban worked with Peter Brook and Ted Hughes in the creation of *Orghast* at Persepolis.[14] *Orghast* was a performance for which Hughes invented-constructed a "new language." Thus he could concentrate entirely on its sounds, inferring rather than being enslaved by predetermined meanings. For the *Trilogy (Medea, Electra, The Trojan Women)* Serban preferred to work with ancient Greek—a language neither the performers nor the audience understood.

> The reason we used ancient Greek was to really examine
> what is hidden in those sounds—in those particular
> sounds. What is there is the potential for a special energy
> to be acted, to be rediscovered again after being buried for
> 2000 years.[15]

I saw the performances. Language is pulled and screamed, chanted and pushed up against a wide array of percussive sounds composed and performed by Swados. Also the vocal range of the performers—especially Priscilla Smith's deep gutterals and shrieks—certainly displaces the ancient Greek transforming it into a medium for direct vocal communication between performer and spectator. The text may be the text of the plays; but the effect of the performance is to use the text concretely, as a way of finding sounds that embody the terror of the tragic themes. The text is used as a way of getting sound out of the performers; they do not "express" it, it extrudes sounds from them.

Eibl-Eibesfeldt points out the relationship between inborn releasing mechanisms and artistic expression, especially music. Breathing and heartbeat can be brought into harmony with metronomes or melodies; drumming raises body temperature. "By the artistic manipulation of the releasing stimuli the composer can create and dissolve tensions in the listener. The highs and lows of emotional experience are touched in an ever-changing pattern that cannot be experienced in everyday life."[16] Of course anyone who has ever wept at a performance of *Romeo and Juliet,* or a soap opera for that matter, knows how susceptible humans are to an artistic induction of feelings. It is even more so during performances where there is no obligation to intervene. Brecht struggled against these reactions, wishing to substitute thinking or sitting in judgement for tears. If even the tame shows of Western theatre are capable of inducing such strong reactions think how much more thorough are total theatre performances—dreamed of by Artaud but realized outside of the European context. Of countless examples two will be enough. I quote them because of the reliability of the sources, and the detail of the description of the spectator's reactions.

Shirokogoroff on Siberian shamanism: The rhythmic music and singing, and later the dancing of the shaman, gradually involve every participant more and more in a collective action. When the audience begins to repeat the refrains together with the assistants, only those who are defective fail to join the chorus. The tempo of the action increases, the shaman with a spirit is no more an ordinary man or relative, but is a "placing" (i.e. incarnation) of the spirit; the spirit acts together with the audience, and this is felt by everyone. The state of many participants is now near to that of the shaman himself, and only a strong belief that when the shaman is there the spirit may only enter him, restrains the participants from being possessed in mass by the spirit. [. . .] When the shaman feels that the audience is with him and follows him he becomes still more active and this effect is transmitted to his audience. After shamanizing, the audience recollects various moments of the performance, their great psychophysiological emotion and the hallucinations of sight and hearing which they have experienced. They then have a deep satisfaction—much greater than that from emotions produced by theatrical and musical performances, literature and general artistic phenomena of the European complex, because in shamanizing the audience at the same time acts and participates.[17]

Read on a New Guinea prenuptial ceremony: The extraordinary effect of the next half hour is difficult to describe. The house was packed to its capacity, but in the blackness I was unable to discover so much as a single feature of the man who sat beside me. Almost immediately, enveloped in disembodied voices, I felt the first stirrings of a curious panic, a fear that if I relaxed my objectivity for so much as a moment I would lose my identity. At the same time the possibility that this could happen seemed immensely attractive. The air was thick with pungent odors, with the smell of unwashed bodies and stranger aromatic overtones that pricked my nostrils and my eyes. But it was the singing, reverberating in the confined space and pounding incessantly against my ears that rose to cloud my mind with the fumes of a collective emotion almost too powerful for my independent will. [. . .] The songs followed one another without a perceptible break, a single shrill and keening voice lifting now and then to point the way to a new set. As the others joined in strongly, I felt close to the very things that eluded me in my day-to-day investigations, brought into physical confrontation with the intangible realm of hopes and shared ideas for which words and actions, though they are all we have, are quite inadequate expressions. In analytic language, the situation could be accommodated under the

> rubric of a rite of separation—an event by which a young
> girl in her father's house, surrounded by her kinsmen, was
> brought to the morning of the day on which she must
> assume a new status and be transferred to her husband's
> people, but its quality could not be conveyed in any
> professional terms. While the voices swelled inside the
> house, mounting to a climax, the barriers of my alien life
> dissolved. The sound engulfed me, bearing me with it
> beyond the house and into the empty spaces of the
> revolving universe. Thus sustained, I was one of the
> innumerable companies of men who, back to the shrouded
> entrance of the human race, have sat at night by fires and
> filled the forest clearings and the wilderness with recitals
> of their own uniqueness.[18]

For all the differences in style Shirokogoroff and Read report the same
pattern: a collective performance, rising to a climax, affording at that
climax an epiphany and subsiding into a calm, a meditation. It is the
same pattern that accompanies pentecostal church services, black and
white, in America, rock concerts, the whirling of sufi dancers and
maybe even the waltz or the tarantella in their heyday. All of these
events require a *congregation*: an assembly of believers, a social unit,
something more than a random audience of ticket buyers, though they
may also be just that. Listen to Abbie Hoffman describe the 1969
Woodstock festival:

> They were all piled up on People Hill and saw the spotlight
> eyes burn down on Creedence Clearwater, hypnotizing
> them, driving them into an orgiastic fury that shook the
> whole motherfuckin stage. It felt like the last scene from
> *Frankenstein* performed by the Living Theatre. [. . .] Every
> once in a while a straight dude from the Construction
> Company or the Safety Department or something like that
> would rush up to someone who looked like he was in charge
> and yell "We must stop this! The stage will collapse!
> Everybody must get off!" And always some shaggy-haired
> freak would hug him and say 'Swingin baby, we're gonna
> fly up here forever!' and the swingers and the faith healers
> and the astrology freaks were all right that Saturday night
> up there. That was one of the eerie things about
> WOODSTOCK NATION, every nut in it was right, even
> the Meher Baba buffs. [. . .] There is a way of integrating
> your own ego trip with a sense of community, with a
> concept of the 'we.' I feel a sense of this most strongly in
> these massive events, in what Artaud refers to as the
> 'festival of the streets.'[19]

The "concept of the 'we' " may not be limited to humans. V. and F.
Reynolds, while studying chimpanzees in the Budongo Forest, followed up on 19th-century reports of "carnivals." These are gatherings
of several bands of chimps accompanied by drumming and calling.

The Reynolds heard these "carnivals" six times, once when they were very close to the animals.

> The "carnivals" consisted of prolonged noise for periods of hours, whereas ordinary ooutbursts of calling and drumming lasted a few minutes only. Although it was not possible to know the reason for this unusual behavior, twice it seemed to be associated with the meeting at a common food source of bands that may have been relatively unfamiliar to each other. [. . .] Inside the forest we were attempting to locate the chimpanzees to observe, if possible, the behavior associated with the tremendous uproar. Unfortunately this proved impossible. Calls were coming from all directions at once and all groups concerned seemed to be moving about rapidly. As we oriented toward the source of one outburst, another came from another direction. Stamping and fast-running feet were heard sometimes behind, sometimes in front, and howling outbursts and prolonged rolls of drums (as many as 13 rapid beats) shaking the ground surprised us every few yards.[20]

The Reynolds have no firm opinion on what brings on the "carnivals." They seem associated with the meeting of bands, an abundance of fruit. This fits nicely with human celebrations: theatre so often occurs when divergent groups assemble to share food.

A great difference between human and non-human performers is the enhanced ability of humans to lie and pretend. Lévi-Strauss tells the story of Quesalid, a Kwakiutl who wished to expose the falseness of his people's shamans.

> Driven by curiosity about their tricks and by the desire to expose them, he began to associate with the shamans until one of them offered to make him a member of their group. Quesalid did not wait to be asked twice, and his narrative recounts the details of his first lessons, a curious mixture of pantomime, prestidigitation and empirical knowledge, including the art of simulating fainting and nervous fits, the learning of sacred songs, the technique for inducing vomiting, rather precise notions of auscultation and obstetrics and the use of 'dreamers,' that is, spies who listen to private conversations and secretly convey to the shaman bits of information concerning the origins and symptoms of the ills suffered by different people. Above all, he learned the ars magna of one of the shamanistic schools of the Northwest Coast: the shaman hides a little tuft of down in a corner of his mouth, and he throws it up, covered with blood, at the proper moment—after having bitten his tongue or made his gums bleed—and solemnly presents it to his patient and the onlookers as the pathological foreign body extracted as a result of his sucking and manipulations.[21]

Quesalid wanted to expose his teachers but before he had the chance he was called by the family of a sick person who had dreamt that Quesalid cured him. Using the techniques he learned, Quesalid was successful. He became known as a great shaman—but he credited his success to psychological factors. But, slowly, over the years, he came more and more to believe in his own methods, to discriminate against practices that were more false than his own.

> While visiting the neighboring Koskimo Indians, Quesalid attends a curing ceremony of his illustrious colleagues of the other tribe. To his great astonishment he observes a difference in their technique. Instead of spitting out the illness in the form of a 'bloody worm' (the concealed down), the Koskimo shamans merely spit a little saliva into their hands, and they dare to claim that this is 'the sickness.' What is the value of this method? What is the theory behind it? In order to find out the 'strength of the shamans, whether it was real or whether they only pretended to be shamans' like his fellow tribesmen, Quesalid requests and obtains permission to try his method in an instance where the Koskimo method has failed. The sick woman then declares herself cured.[22]

Thereafter Quesalid is invited to test his method against all others, and he invariably triumphs. Other shamans come to him and confess their tricks, but Quesalid no longer refers to the technique of the bloody down as a trick: he says nothing about it, but continues to use it, defending it against all other methods. "He seems to have completely lost sight of the fallaciousness of the technique which he had so disparaged at the beginning."[23]

How different is Quesalid's ultimate consciousness concerning his act than that of Peter Townshend of The Who?

> We did a thing at Detroit and we got to the end and I thought, Jesus, we've taken it completely the wrong route and we've already finished with what we normally finish with, we'd done that, we'd done the big ending, we've done the guitar spinning, we've leaped in the air, we're exhausted, we've gone thru every musical brain-wave we could possibly go thru and yet they, out there, don't think we're finished. So what do we do now? [. . .] So we play, like B sides of remote singles, and bit by bit we take the audience down and down and down and down and down until they're so desperate, right, we've got 'em, they're down where we are, they're desperate, where we are, then all we've got to do is jump three times in the air, spin a guitar and bang it on the ground, then kick a drum over and we're finished![24]

In both cases the performers are supremely confident of their techniques. This mastery is due to an objectification of the techniques.

A gap opens between the performer and his performances: the performer is not swept away by the performance, as the audience is; the performer is not taken in by the performance. Or if he is, it is as Quesalid was, by observing the effect the performance has on others and by measuring this effect against the less effective means of rivals. In fact, a double gap appears: (1) between the performer and his performances; (2) between the performance and the audience. Quesalid works on his patient, and his curing her works on his audience of supporters and rival shamans. Townshend works directly on his audience, manipulating his performance—changing plans—in order to work the audience into a place where the set can end. This double gap is inconceivable in any species other than the human; and once this gap is opened, in spills the drama.

Before considering the drama, which is the unique creation of our species, I want to examine more parallels between animal and human theatrical behavior. Up to now I've said that phatic behavior in humans is homologous/analagous to that of the great apes. This behavior includes drumming, dancing and shouting; threatening displays which sometimes include rehearsals or at least trial runs and preparations; and enthusiasm: contagious group moods, especially celebratory moods associated with the meeting of bands and the sharing of food. I think animal-human theatrical correlations occur at deeper levels too, in events ethologists call displacement activity, redirected activity and ritualization. These behaviors I connect to fantasy: daydreaming, nightdreaming, projections of the future, rembrances of the past, imaginary actions and staged imaginary actions. We do not know if animals other than humans have fantasy lives; my reasoning doesn't depend on assuming that they do. I say only that human fantasies are outgrowths and transformations of animal ritualizations and displays.

To ethologists a ritual is a behavior sequence which over the course of evolutionary selection is transformed both in shape and function. The transformations occur in the following way:

1. The behavior changes function.
2. The ritualized movement can become independent of its original motivation and develop its own motivating mechanisms.
3. Movements are exaggerated and at the same time simplified.
4. Movements frequently "freeze" into postures.
5. Movements become rhythmic, often repetitive.
6. Along with behavioral changes frequently there are the development of conspicuous body structures, such as a peacock's tail, a moose's horns, etc.[25]

In TOWARDS A POETICS OF PERFORMANCE I argue that ritualization in theatre is not a function of subject matter, or even of origins, but of the rehearsal-to-performance sequence, the periodicity of performance and, on the microsocial level, the prevalence of conventions designed to remove ambiguity from the communication. Here I want to discuss ritualization from the point of view of the performer's process and the spectator's response.

The debate concerning whether there is a "universal" body language is now running in favor of such a conclusion. A belly laugh, a howl of pain, a child's whining, the outstretched arms of a mother, the raised eyebrows of recognition are all understood everywhere. And there is a developmental continuity of behavior among primates. Also behavior sequences, mini-dramas, are universally the same: the child running for protection into the arms of its mother; the open-palm greeting; freezing in place when a suspicious or unknown threat is perceived; taking cover by means of hiding, crouching or flattening when an overwhelming force is encountered. There is a surprisingly large repertory of universally recognized situations. Theatre plays with these, often making out of misunderstandings and misinterpretations the nub of the drama; for with the ritualization of signals comes the possibility, among humans, of irony, deceit and intentional misinformation. And in an effort to outsmart each other double and triple misunderstandings occur—such is the trap Oedipus falls into when he tries to escape the Oracle after Jocasta before him tried to outsmart it; or Romeo's reading of Juliet's drugged sleep as death, even though she doesn't look dead: "Death, that hath sucked the honey of the breath/Hath had no power yet upon thy beauty." Theatrical costuming and gesturing are exaggerated, sometimes even outlandish, as in melodrama, Kabuki and Kathakali; but even in so-called naturalism the gestures are not natural but abstractions and exaggerations of natural ways of speaking and moving. The avant-garde in the West is in many ways approaching the stylization, masking and exaggeration of non-Western theatre.

There are two classes of body languages. The first are the natural languages studied by ethologists and the microsocial exchanges studied by Goffman and Birdwhistell. The second are the aesthetic, ritual or wholly artificial languages—different for each culture—at least as old as cave art and the Venus figures of Paleolithic times where the human body is exaggerated, distorted, transformed, masked and abstracted into unique shapes. The cave art is almost entirely an art depicting animals—but these animals occur in groupings that don't fit what goes on "in nature." Predators and prey are shown together but non-agonistically; other species are painted together that do not run together "in nature." And a few paintings are of imaginary animals such as the unicornlike figure at Lascaux. At least one figure suggests a person dressed in an animal skin and mask.[26] Thus from the earliest times—and continuing to the present—ironies, contradictions, transformations and imaginary beings and situations are part of art. People create what isn't there, make combinations from fantasies, actualize situations that occur only as art or performance. But these actualizations in the service of social organization, or rebellion, contain, transmit and (dare I say it?) create immense power. Are these two kinds of body language linked?

These displays can be fancy: threats, stamping, dances, etc., or plain ongoing social interaction. The fancy displays—those that qualify for the term ritualization—usually concern mating, fighting, territory: arenas of conflict where clear signaling is to the advantage of the individual and species. In people interaction also stimulates displays, but sometimes, I think often, the displays are blocked from full expression. Human societies are incredibly dense, multivocal and ambiguous; people learn early to hold back, to redirect their impulses inwardly. This is not just a "problem" of modern industrial societies but a characteristic of all human groupings. Art, custom, religion and social convention come from and cluster around these areas of blocked display. In animals "the damned-up excitation sparks over, so to speak, into another channel and there finds its discharge."[27] In people the excitation of an interaction is directed inward and happens as a fantasy.

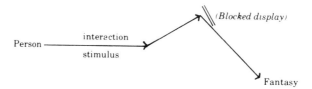

The fantasy is not necessarily—in fact rarely—a literal translation of the blocked display. The fantasy may pick up other materials associated with the blocked display and, like dreams, consist of clusters of apparently unrelated material. But actually the material is all connected. Ultimately, in some cases, where an acceptable channel exists, a socially sanctioned arena, the fantasy—plus its associated material from "other channels"—remerges in a new display. This display combines private matters and public ways of performing them.

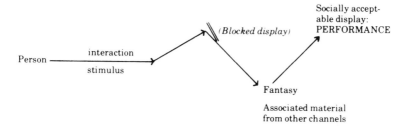

Thus performance has a restorative function analagous to its cathartic function. It is a way of getting at, and getting out, two sets of material simultaneously: (1) what was blocked and transformed into fantasy and (2) stuff from other channels." Seen this way performing is a public dreaming.[28] Just as dream work combines the day's events with the dreamer's interior life creating a symbolic drama with an audience/participator of one, so public performance re-presents the fantasies associated with blocked displays in gestures that are publicly acceptable. The display that can't happen ultimately happens, but in a traditional form. Even the avant-garde is traditional: there is a place for it in our society. Of course, performances sometimes deal with the taboo and are sometimes incomprehensible. This is so not only in the avant-garde but also in hermitic religious ceremonies, shamanistic performances where secrets are carefully guarded, initiation rites and so on. A balance is always struck between the public, the secret and the private. It isn't accidental that many cultures consider performances to originate in dreams: vision quests, hallucinations, trances, dreamtime, surrealistic automatic creation. Fantasy is interiorized display and performance is exteriorized fantasy.

But the interior and the exterior are open to each other; the borders between them are fluid. Human art deals in the imaginary—and these impossible worlds have had the greatest influence on social organization. The ritual process of animals is the basis for but not the end of human expression. The secondary languages of culture—verbal, mathematical, musical, pictorial, architectural, etc.—are continually interacting and transcending the primary ritual body language.

Drama is a recognizable script or scenario performed by people who are consciously enacting the script or scenario. Everyone knows some of the high points of drama: Athenian tragedy, Indian sanskrit dramas, Elizabethan theatre, Japanese Nō and so on. In fact, there is hardly a culture that has not, at one time or another, developed drama. But periods of drama come and go; it is not in the scope of this essay to discuss why. I want to deal with certain kinds of proto-dramas—what E. T. Kirby calls "ur-drama"[29]—that combine and transform social conflict into aesthetics. These proto-dramas are related to behaviors among different classes of animals where aggressive behavior is ritualized. I am speaking of trials (which are often more entertainments that judicial procedures), ritual combats, word-duels and "soundings," praise-singing, obscene farces and masquerades.

It is my view that much art is a human version of what, in animals, is called either "displacement activity" or "redirected activity." This latter is very simple:

> A redirected activity is just this: if I am furious with my
> boss, my fear may inhibit my aggression against him, so I
> release my aggression toward the underdog or toward
> anything else.[30]

On the personal level many examples in theatre could be found of redirected activities. The high incidence of sex and violence can partially be explained as redirected activities; performers frequently seek to work in the theatre as a way of "getting out" their feelings. Although examples are harder to find some exist where a whole theatrical tradition arose as a redirected activity. Among Highlands New Guinea tribes warfare was banned first by Australian colonial authorities and now by the native government of Papua-New Guinea. What has arisen in its place are trials and dramas. Among the Tsembaga:

> It is said that dancing is like fighting. The visitors'
> procession is led by men carrying fight-packages, and their
> entrance upon the dance ground of their hosts is martial.
> To join a group in dancing is the symbolic expression of
> willingness to join them in fighting.[31]

Of course many military displays around the world are dances; the aggressive potential of a "great power" is advertised in its parades. Among the Kogu, observed by Ronald M. Berndt in the 1950s, warfare and cannibalism were replaced by local courts.

Cannibalism was practiced by the Kogu as part of warfare and as the customary way of disposing of their own dead. "Dead human flesh, to these people, is food. [. . .] 'Cut my body,' a dying man or woman may say, 'so that the crops may increase. Eat my flesh so that the gardens may grow.' "[32] Enemies were eaten as a source of protein and as a way of acquiring their power. Cannibalism is the ultimate occupation of another's territory; it obliterates the other by transforming him into the eater. It is also a eucharistic feast. Among the Kogu were two kinds of cannibalism: the aggressive and celebratory in which an enemy was ingested with much shouting, dancing and feasting; the ordinary or simply murderous kind where a fellow villager was slaughtered because he or she was too old, sick or defenseless. One must guard against a romantic view of cannibalism—even thinking about it triggers (in me at least) a cathartic release of aggression/ triumph. Among the Kogu cannibalism was often murder followed by theft: the body was property, it was stolen from those who couldn't protect it, and used in the most obvious way as food.

The cruelty with which the Kogu dispatched of their enemies is reminiscent of Greek myths. In a battle a wounded enemy, Kricme, was taken prisoner.

> As they entered their district, they were greeted by all the
> women and children dancing and singing around them.
> They put Kricme in the center of the village clearing,
> where the people danced around him. It is said that he
> must have been in great pain, for the arrow with which he
> had been shot was still protruding. Nasecompa then came
> forward with a steel ax and began cutting at his knee;
> Kricme cried out, but Nasecompa severed the limb and
> threw it to one side. A woman danced forward singing,
> picked up the leg and danced away. Still Kricme cried as
> Nasecompa cut off the other leg and threw it to a man who
> danced forward, singing and carried it away. The same was
> done with one arm, then the other; still Kricme cried, until
> Nasecompa with a stroke of his ax severed the head, which
> was caught by a dancing man and carried away. Then the
> trunk was cut up and various parts distributed. When the
> feast was finished the bones were tied up in croton leaves
> and fastened to the Moiife stockade.[33]

Kricme's fate is uncannily like that of Pentheus of Euripides' *Bacchae*. In a case of adultery—also reminiscent of the Atrean myths—a Haita man, Auglimu, found his wife with a lover. He shot the man with several arrows, sliced his flesh while was still alive, severed both his arms and left him to bleed to death. Then he took his wife, and her lover's arms, back to her house; they roasted the arms, ate a meal of them and slept together. Berndt comments:

> Whether the cutting up of a victim while he is still alive is
> deliberate cruelty, as in the case of the husband who killed
> his wife's lover, is difficult to say. There is little doubt,
> however, that the people, who participated [. . .] appear to
> have enjoyed watching the man's suffering and hearing
> him cry as his limbs were hacked off. A number of men who
> took part in this particular feast [the killing of Kricme],
> including Nasecompa himself, thought it great fun and
> laughed uproariously in discussing it,with no sign of
> embarrassment.[34]

When warriors come home with a corpse often "many men and women indulge in uncontrolled behavior, assaulting the corpse and fighting over the best portions of meat."[35] If the victim is a young woman men will copulate with the corpse before cutting it up. The men act openly and their women:

> far from resenting it, apparently enjoyed watching them. It
> is said that they themselves often squat over dead men,
> pretending to have coitus with them or playing with the
> penes of corpses. Both men and women smear themselves
> with blood and hang from their head and shoulders various
> parts of the body in much the same way as is done with the
> meat of pigs during the pig festival.[36]

Is this sexual violence unique? Looting and raping are part of warfare, though the details are frequently glossed over. Even among the peaceful Arapesh (who live a few hundred miles from the Kogu) violence flares—but when it happens it is extraordinarily controlled.

> All clashes between hamlets start in angry conversation,
> the aggrieved party coming armed but not committed to
> fighting, into the village of the offenders. [. . .] If the
> aggrieved party is protesting more as a matter of form than
> from real anger, the meeting may end in a few harsh
> words. Alternatively, it may progress from reproach to
> insult, until the most volatile and easily angered person
> hurls a spear. This is not a signal for a general fracas;
> instead everyone notes carefully where the spear—which
> is never thrown to kill—hits, and the next most volatile
> person of the opposite party throws a spear back at the man
> who hurled the first one. This in turn is recorded during a
> moment of attention, and a return spear thrown. Each
> reprisal is phrased as a matter of definite choice. [. . .] This
> serial and carefully recorded exchange of spears in which
> the aim is to wound lightly, not to kill, goes on until
> someone is rather badly wounded, when the members of
> the attacking party immediately take to their heels. Later,
> peace is made by an interchange of rings,each man giving
> a ring to the man he has wounded. If, as occasionally
> happens, someone is killed, every attempt is made to
> disavow any intention to kill: the killer's hand slipped; it
> was because of the sorcery of the Plainsmen.[37]

It appears that our species is endowed with aggression, but this aggression can be trained in many different directions. And perhaps it is noteworthy that the gentle Arapesh have "no well-defined techniques; even the knots with which they tie the parts of a house together are varied and made in different styles. When they measure a length, they almost always get it wrong, and far from correcting it, they adjust the rest of the structure to the one mistake."[38] In Mead's words the people "lack belief in their own abilities" and depend "upon the artistic work of other peoples because they believe themselves incapable."[39] Arapesh ceremony is plain, while the Kogu are rich in mask-making, singing, dancing and farce. The one "art" the Arapesh have is their management of aggression which has been transformed into well-phrased dance. Maybe that's worth the sacrifice of the rest.

Once the Kogu were prevented from warring with and eating their neighbors (often kinsmen) "the official court was seen by these people as an alternative mode of settling differences, of righting wrongs and of obtaining compensation for injury.[40] This court is surely also a theatre.

> The informal court is held in the village clearing, or in front of the men's house. [. . .] The presiding authority takes the central position, flanked by other dignitaries. [. . .] In front of them on one side sits the complainant, on the other the accused (or defendant); each may be supported by patrikin [. . .] or others. The audience disposes itself as it pleases. It is all very informal; the complainant may be nursing a child, and children may play among the audience. Various witnesses are heard and sometimes cross-questioned. The complainant may give an impassioned speech or may leave the matter entirely in the hands of others (witnesses or kin). He may be interrupted at will by the court leaders, who will go over and over the matter. Repetition in discussion is the delight of such meetings, especially when the affair concerns sexual matters or when amounts of settlement are to be determined. Proceedings may continue for a couple of days or longer, usually depending on the entertainment value of the evidence.[41]

That the court is a theatrical redirected activity is very clear when we consider that the audience, the complainant and even the accused (when the punishment is not severe) look forward to the violent out-come of the trial.

> Many means of achieving excitement have been done away with through the banning of warfare and cannibalism; but some of the emotions expressed in these are diverted into the informal court, and in this respect there is great similarity between them. Prior to alien contact, physical violence was recognized as a necessary part of ordinary social life. Now, under the aegis of the informal court, it has been concentrated, as it were, and highlighted.[42]

Especially in sexual cases the court becomes a theatre, often resembling traditional farces (which coexisted with warfare and cannibalism, a strong fact that I'll discuss later). For example, Jowajaca committed adultery—was caught in the act by her husband. The court established that the adultery took place at least five times, but that Jowajaca had some cause because her husband didn't often copulate with her. Part of the judgment was that he copulate with her at once while the crowd watched. Throughout one night they were

made to copulate many times, always with witnesses. The next day
Jowajaca was punished this way:

> Her skirt was cut off and she was told to sit down naked
> before the people. A large tin was obtained and filled with
> stones and special ceremonial emblem was made. She was
> made to stand up and a man's fringed skirt was fastened
> around her, but not concealing her pubes. The wooden end
> of the emblem was then inserted into her vagina so that it
> protruded out and upward. Attached to the skirt behind
> her was a similar emblem. She was then told to place the
> tin of stones on her head and dance up and down. She
> began to dance to and fro across the village clearing, the
> emblems shaking as she did so. People crowded around to
> look at her, even coming from other villages and districts.
> They joked and laughed. Children rushed up and down
> with her, crying out and shouting obscenities. When she
> stopped dancing or showed signs of exhaustion she was
> threatened with a bow and arrow and urged on.
> Throughout the day she continued to dance, holding the tin
> of stones on her head; sweat poured from her body, and her
> head was swollen from the weight she carried. During the
> late afternoon she could hardly move and showed extreme
> exhaustion. Her mother and father began to wail, and the
> latter called out, 'Oh, my daughter what is this that you
> are doing? Give her back to us. Stop this punishment.' But
> they did not intervene because they were afraid of
> Ozazecna [the head of the court].[43]

At sunset Ozazecna stopped Jowajaca's dancing and summoned her
husband, Anaga. Ozazecna asked Jowajaca whether she wanted to go
back to her husband or with her lover, Aguvi. She chose Aguvi and
was beaten. The next morning Ozazecna ordered Aguvi to pay Anaga
five items of wealth; then Jowajaca was declared free to marry Aguvi.
The court was adjourned.

But Jowajaca didn't marry Aguvi. She went back to her house in
Anaga's village; she cooked for him but he always left her food un-
touched. But after a few weeks they resumed sexual relations. When
this went on for some time Jowajaca called all the men of the village
together and said: "Other men continually copulate with their wives
at night. Anaga always comes to me and copulates!" The men
laughed. They said: "He put his finger to his nose, yet he still copulates with her. You two continue copulating." Anaga was then considered to have remarried Jowajaca.[44]

This incident, taken as a whole, is both social and aesthetic drama.
The characters are real people, the events are actual and they are
consequential. At the same time the trial is an entertainment—the
story, the dancing, even the outcome suit farce. Not only this, which is
perhaps an outsider's analytic opinion, but the fact that the villagers

themselves regard the event as an entertainment. An even clearer coincidence between the court and the indigenous farces occurred when a prominent performer helped act out the punishment. The case involved Urolni who said she disliked her husband, Ameja, and refused to copulate with him. Ameja brought Urolni to trial and the headman decided that the punishment would be plural copulation with Urolni.

> Nomaja, a prominent performer in erotic farces and
> generally considered a great wit, squatted before Urolni
> and taking up her hands pretended to eat them. "Ah! This
> tastes good!" Then he pulled her labia majora and made as
> if to eat, remarking how good they were. The onlookers
> applauded. But at this juncture Urolni grabbed one of
> Nomaja's testes and pulled. Nomaja let out a cry. She
> tugged it again and Nomaja pretended to eat her face,
> making sucking sounds. "How good this tastes. Oh my
> vulva. Loose me now—it pains!" But Urolni pulled it again,
> and Nomaja fell over, pretending to die. "You have killed
> me now!" Urolni, becoming afraid, released his testicle.
> Nomaja jumped up and began to play with her vulva,
> passing remarks as the occasion demanded. Finally he
> picked her up in his arms and carred her to a nearby
> stream. Here he threw her into the shallow water and
> began to copulate. [. . .] Afterwards she said to him, "I have
> left my child behind. I will go and get it and come to you. I
> will leave my husband.[45]

Urolni went to Nomaja the next day; but she was beaten and returned to her husband with whom she remained. The action of this trial is almost identical to that of a well-known traditional farce.[46] Nomaja played a role with Urolni that he also played in the farce.

It is not only among New Guinea peoples that trials and dramas converge. Public punishment, in Europe and elsewhere, ostensibly a warning against crime, actually functions as entertainment. In medieval Europe disputes were frequently settled by duels or jousts waged by "champions," combatants who substituted themselves for those they represented.[47] Jousts and tournaments developed in two diverging directions: into athletics where individuals, guilds and cities have representative teams and into modern trials where the champion of the state is the prosecuter, that of the accused the defense attorney. The medieval champion performed the dispute of his master; the modern attorney also participates in a drama, or two dramas as Harbinger points out:

> When one observes an adversary trial, he sees a play; when
> he observes a while longer, he perceives a play within the
> play. [. . .] And from this form all else naturally proceeds:
> double plots, double casts, double settings, double
> audiences and double effects. [. . .] The "play without"

> stages the legal combat between the prosecuting attorney
> and the defense attorney. [. . .] The "play within" tells the
> story of the alleged killing [or whatever crime is in
> question] by the defendant.[48]

What Harbinger calls the "play without" is a ritual combat; the "play within" is a drama. Ritual combats can be direct contests between angry opponents (see my essay, ACTUALS, for an analysis of one such combat among the Tiwi) or, as in the jousts, champions may be employed.

Three other examples of ritual combats are interesting because they directly employ theatrical means. Among the Eskimos both in Alaska and Greenland

> all disputes except murder are settled by a song duel. In
> these areas an Eskimo male is often as acclaimed for his
> ability to sing insults as for his hunting prowess. The song
> duel consists of lampoons, insults and obscenities and the
> disputants sing to each other and, of course, to their
> delighted audience. (Incidentally, the West Indies calypso,
> now sung as an entertainment for tourists, similarly
> originated as a song of ridicule.) The verses are earthy and
> very much to the point; they are intended to humilate, and
> no physical deformity, personal shame or family trouble is
> sacred. As verse after verse is sung in turn by the
> opponents the audience begins to take sides; it applauds
> one singer a bit longer and laughs a bit louder at his
> lampoons. Finally, he is the only one to get applause, and
> he thereby becomes the winner of a bloodless contest. The
> loser suffers a great punishment, for disapproval of the
> community is very difficult to bear in a group as small as
> that of the Eskimo.[49]

Far from being improvised the Greenland singer prepares for the contest by singing his songs to his family until they all know them perfectly. "When the actual contest is in full swing, his householders reinforce his words in chorus."[50] The song duel is sometimes accompanied by punching and head-butting.

The Tiv of northern Nigeria employ a similar kind of theatricalized combat. Bohannan tells how early in the spring of 1950 Torgindi and Mtswen started feuding over the repayment of a debt.

> Torgindi went back to his compound [after the men
> exchanged angry words] and made up a song in which he
> said what a skunk Mtswen was. That night, when all was
> quiet, he drummed and sang the song as loud as he could,
> for the whole countryside to hear—including Mtswen, who
> lived a little over a quarter of a mile away.[51]

Torgindi repeated the song the next night—and everyone in his compound, and some from other compounds in his lineage joined in the chorus.

> The only thing for Mtswen to do was to make up a song of his own against Torgindi. But knowing he wasn't much of a songmaker, he hired the best songmaker in Shangev Ya to stay at his place and compose scurrilous songs about Torgindi and all his kinsmen and wives.[52]

Torgindi responded by hiring a songmaker. Soon the men were sponsoring songs and dances each night—"they each brewed beer and made food in order to attract dancers to come to dance and sing the songs directed at the other."[53] There are no fixed rules for composing the songs, except that incidents referred to must be true. If an accusation is false the slandered person calls a *jir* (foul) and the accusation is withdrawn. But if the event could not possibly be true then it can't be the basis of a *jir*. For example "one of the catchiest tuenes [. . .] told how Torgindi changed himself into a pig at night and made it unsafe for every sow in the countryside."[54] Everyone agreed that Torgindi couldn't transform himself therefore he wasn't entitled to call a *jir*. This rule encourages a combination of painful truths and the wildest fantasies.

The song duel between Torgindi and Mtswen went on nightly for more than three weeks before village elders decided that to continue would lead to violence. The elders summoned both men and their supporters to a central place where they were told to sing and drum: the elders would decide who was the winner. The elders went from one performing group to the other, listened to all the songs and then retired to consider the case. After two hours they ruled that Torgindi won the case, but Mtswen had the better songs.

A less elaborate, and possibly directly related word duel is common in American black ghettoes. "Soundings" are formal tradings of ritual insults—also called "the dozens," or "signifying." "The ways in which sounds are delivered, and the evaluation of them by the group, follow a well-established ritual pattern."[55] Sounds are "evaluated overtly and immediately by the audience."[56] The mark of winning is laughter. And when a traditional sound is rendered incorrectly the spectators will yell "mistake!" Among adolescent gangs the members know who the best sounders are and will rarely engage them in a duel. To be a good sounder is to be a leader in the group. The sounds, often rhymed couplets, are almost always sexual, and they usually involve insults concerning the performers' mothers or fathers—if these same insults were made outside the context of sounding, that is, "seriously," a fist-fight or worse would ensue. Some examples quoted by Labov:

> Iron is iron, and steel don't rust,
> But your momma got a pussy like a Greyhound bus.

> I hate to talk about your mother, she's a good old soul
> She got a ten-ton pussy and a rubber asshole.

These are "traditional" sounds, and the winner in this contest is the boy with the best memory. Other sounds are improvised. These are less elegant:

> Your mother got hair growin' out her dunkie hole.

> Your mother so old she got spider webs under her arms.
> Your mother so old she can stretch her head and lick out
> her ass.

All the traditional rhymed sounds are obscene, but the improvised ones often are not. They range across vast subjects suitable for insults: housing, work, physiognomy, eating habits, poverty, school—anything that is part of their communal life. The performance structure of sounding is exactly that of the Eskimo or Tiv duels. A boy sounds and the audience evaluates, his adversary sounds and the audience evaluates. Soon enough a winner is evident. Labov observes:

> The audience [. . .] is an essential ingredient here. It is true
> that one person *can* sound against another without a third
> person being present, but the pre-supposition that this is
> public behavior can easily be heard in the verbal style.
> Sounds are not uttered in a direct, face-to-face
> conversational mode. The voice is raised and projected, as
> if to reach an audience.[57]

Sounding is a contemporary version of the punning, wit and obscenity—however masked—of the duels between Shakespearean lovers, especially Beatrice and Benedict; it is also very like Aristophanes. Labov thinks the ritual nature of sounding, as ritual in general, offers a "sanctuary" wherein "we are freed from personal responsibility for the acts we are engaged in."[58] It is a neat definition of the performer's official function.

The Kogu court, the Eskimo and Tiv song duels and sounding are all examples of redirected activity. They may also be examples of "displacement activity," a process that operates on a deep level of behavior.

> Displacement activity happens if two mutually inhibiting
> motivations result in such a perfect equilibrium as to block
> each other completely. What happens then is that another
> movement, which is usually inhibited by both of them,
> becomes disinhibited because the other two neutralize each
> other. So, if a bird wants to attack and is afraid in more or
> less perfect equilibrium of these two motivations, he may
> start to preen or to scratch, or to perform other activities
> which are inhibited both by attack and escape, attack and
> escape being at the moment mutually inhibited.[59]

Slater applies this idea to human rituals:

> But what does it mean to "borrow" or "take from" an object
> of aggression an intangible attribute? Can an essentially
> magical act produce emotional changes of importance?
> Actually the process is not at all complicated. Let us
> suppose an individual is subject to two contradictory
> impulses which inhibit one another. If one impulse can
> somehow be discharged, the other will be free to express
> itself also. Or suppose an individual is conflicted about his
> sexual impulses. By attacking these impulses in another
> the ambivalent impasse is broken (the negative side
> having been expressed) and the impulses can be released.
> We can observe this phenomenon in the frequency with
> which aggression and sexuality are alternated in fertility
> rites, wherein the fertility symbolism is usually preceded
> by a bloody sacrifice, a beating, a free-for-all or a general
> orgy of vituperation. It is as if sexual expression (and hence
> fertility) were trapped by feelings of hostility, anxiety or
> inadequacy between the sexes and could only be released
> by some aggressive outburst. [. . .] It may be, then, that
> identification through aggression is simply a special form
> of this more general tendency to resolve ambivalence
> through alternation,and the notion of "taking from" the
> other a metaphorical account of the process of using
> another person as a vehicle for rearranging the elements in
> one's own internal economy.[60]

In the examples I've cited the themes—sexuality, violence, conflict,
obscenity—are transformations, redirections, of behavior prevented
their full expression. But the deep structures—social bonding, entertainment, laughing—are true "displacements" in the ethological
sense. What are the "mutually inhibiting motivations" behind the
Kogu, Eskimo, medieval, Tiv, ghetto—and by extension all other
proto-dramatic performances? In every case forbidden relationships—usually adulterous or incestuous—are blocked by law and
custom even as they are desired by individuals. Drama is about
the I-want-but-can't/shouldn't-have; or about the I-have-but-will-
pay-for, which amounts to the same thing. If forbidden relationships
are consummated in fact (as they are) the social order is threatened
(as it so often is). When the social order is threatened, even in wishes
and fantasies, a public performance is called for. This performance
sometimes uses "real people" as examples; sometimes the principles hire champions to substitute for them; often completely fictionalized transformations of the basic situations are performed.
But in every case what must be performed are the forbidden acts
which are thereby both released and contained. The formal nature of
these proto-dramas—the court, the trial, the duel, the song, the
rhymed couplet, the public sounding—insures some measure of con-

trol over the actions being enacted. Also the proto-dramas suggest their own development into full-fledged theatre. The fundamental opposition is between individual desire and social order; the resulting displaced activity—entertainment and laughter—is as different from its causes as a bird's preening is from its mutually blocked impulses to fight and flee. Instead of causing further anxiety the performance of forbidden actions relaxes tensions. Even among the violent Kogu the court and the farces it resembles so closely are less fearful than war and cannibalism. It is a fact of great importance that the first shape of performing taboo material is not tragedy but farce. What is liberated by performing forbidden actions is a celebratory, defiant laugh.

Laughter itself preserves this ambivalence.

> The rhythmic vocalizations [of laughter] remind one of
> similar sounds made by primate groups when they
> threaten in unison against an enemy. [. . .] In its original
> form laughing seems to unite *against* a third party.[61]

Laughter is aggressive, it is reassuring. The difference is between being "laughed at" and "laughing with." The model Freud proposed to explain "joke-work" (which he saw as analagous to dream-work) applies to farce. It also explains how farce accomplishes the complicated task of uniting an in-group, threatening an out-group and bringing repressed material not necessarily connected to the "story" of the farce to the surface.

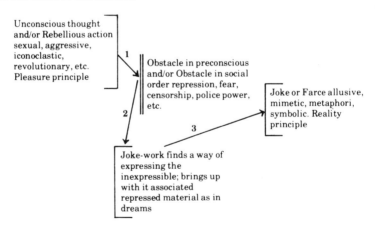

Joke-work is like dream-work. It condenses, inverts and displaces images, associations and actions. A successful joke—and a farce consists of a string of successful jokes encapsulated in an overall structure that is itself a joke—is a specially coded communication. In evoking laughter it liberates laughter's double purpose of threat and bond. Freud writes:

> And here at last we can understand what it is that jokes
> achieve in the service of their purpose. They make possible
> the satisfaction of an obstacle that stands in its way. They
> circumvent this obstacle and in that way draw pleasure
> from a source which the obstacle had made inaccessible.
> [. . .] The repressive activity of civilization brings it about
> that primary possibilities of enjoyment, which have now,
> however, been repudiated by the censorship in us, are lost
> to us. But to the human psyche all renunciation is
> exceedingly difficult, and so we find that tendentious jokes
> provide a means of undoing the renunciation and
> retrieving what was lost.[62]

Freud says that jokes have two purposes—hostility and obscenity. In
the first there is "criticism against persons in exalted positions who
claim to exercise authority. The joke, then, represents a rebellion
against that authority, a liberation from its pressures."[63] How can
this apply to the Kogu court presided over by the village head? The
court, like farce, is authorized rebellion: the adulterous acts committed *en masse* in public is behavior temporarily sanctioned, even displayed, but it is an entertainment-as-punishment that reproduces the
crime; so it is with all trials-as-entertainments, the "play within" (in
Harbinger's terms) is always an enactment of a forbidden event, and
its display is enjoyed vicariously even as it is formally deplored. In
farce—true drama rather than proto-dramas—there is no need even
to pretend to deplore the crimes, the outrages and reversals of social
order. Satire, parody, ridicule, caricature are all aspects of hostile
joking. These are at the heart of vulgar comedy (the opposite of the
comedy of manners which always maintain the facade of politeness)
which delights in excesses and reversals: the young take power from
the old, prodigality laughs away prudence, promiscuity replaces marriage, the ugly upstages beauty, the poor rule the rich. From Kogu to
Aristophanes, the Tiv to Harlem, Chaplin to the Marx Brothers there
is a strain of *sacer ludus* in farce—the coronation of the King of Mirth
and Fecundity and the disparagement of pride and hypocrisy.

Traditional farce actions can be used as political weapons. On
March 20, 1968, Colonel Paul Akst, director of New York City's selective service system was talking to Columbia University students
about the tough new draft law. "As Akst began fielding questions
from the floor, a group of students created a diversion at the rear of
the auditorium, and as everyone in the audience turned around, an
unidentified assailant walked up to the colonel and pushed a lemon
meringue pie squarely in his face."[64] The student uprisings of 1968
across Europe and America, sometimes joined by workers, combined
farce, eroticism and revolution. The first phase of a victorious
revolution—look at France, the USSR, Portugal—is often an orgy,
followed by a vituperative bloodbath. Ludwig Jekels, a follower of
Freud, interprets joking and farce in a unique way. If the Oedipus

complex is the basis of tragedy (argues Jekels) than its opposite underlies farce: "the feeling of guilt which, in tragedy, rests upon the son, appears in comedy displaced on the father; it is the father who is guilty."[65] Once the father—or the authority of the "old" state—is done away with "we find the ego, which has liberated itself from the tyrant, uninhibitedly venting its humor, wit and every sort of comic manifestation in a very ecstasy of freedom."[66] In revolution the liberation is actual, if temporary; in aesthetic drama, even the Kogu court and other proto-dramas, the liberation is monitored, controlled, overseen by the actual authorities who give permission for the temporary and occasional celebration of rebellion by the enactment of forbidden or taboo acts. In this way, the dynamics of revolution are enlisted in the service of maintaining the social order.

Although the devices are much more complicated than among animals—no animal other than human employs wit or humor: there is pleasure, perhaps laughter, but no metaphor, allusiveness or *mimesis*—the outcome and purpose is strikingly similar. Aggression is channelled, even strictly controlled; and a social order maintained. Changes in the social order—say Mike's replacing Goliath as Alpha—are accomplished through ceremony, and regulated ritual, rather than by life-and-death struggle. Among animals, in fact, two separate kinds of aggression appear, that directed against prey which is unemotional and deadly and that directed against conspecifics which is emotional but ritualized.

> An Oryz antelope will never use its horns to gore another
> oryz but fights according to strictly observed rules. It does,
> however, stab lions [with its horns]. A giraffe uses its short
> horns to fight rivals [giraffes], but uses its hoofs in defense
> against predators. A predator fights differently with a
> species member than with a prey and by electrical brain
> stimulation it could be shown in cats that these two types
> of behavior have different neural substrates in the brain.[67]

A similar separation between in-group and out-group violence is probably present in people. From this separation arises two conflict systems: (1) aggressive conflict against other peoples, or outsiders whoever they are or wherever they reside (prejudice, bigotry and even in-law hatred come from this); (2) aggressive solidarity where the conflict is played or organized into sports and other displays that stimulate group cohesion. Conflict resolution systems—such as mediation, courts and diplomacy—are attempts to convert the first kind of conflict into the second; and to achieve the goals of the first without the risk of out-and-out combat. Often the conflict-resolution process is a mirror or reduction-transformation of the conflict to be resolved; it is essentially theatrical. But, for reasons not really understood, the two conflict systems have lost their separate identities in human culture. Modern warfare especially, with its killing at a distance, anonymously, encourages a blurring between intraspecific and interspecific aggression. But this is not merely a modern problem, one exemplified by the "body count" of the "enemy." The wires have been crossed for a long time everywhere in human societies. Many societies think of themselves as humans and others as part of a different species.[68] For some the word for "people" is "us," and the word for "strangers" is the equivalent of barbarians, animals, non-humans. The deadly combat many other animals spend only on other species humans wreak on each other.

The problem is more complicated than wishing humans were peaceable. Lorenz notes:

> There is no nonaggressive animal able to form personal
> bonds. [. . .] Unless you get an animal in the physiological
> state of readiness to fight, and of a species which is ready to
> fight, you cannot get a personal bond. Or, putting it the
> other way round, as far as we know today there is no single
> case where a personal bond is formed either in a species
> which simply does not have the possiblity to fight or in
> animals which are in a physiologic state of non-fighting,
> even if they belong to a potentially fighting species. In
> other words, the nonfighting anonymous aggregation
> never shows any group formation, any personal
> interrelation between individuals.[69]

From an ethological viewpoint rituals evolve as a way of improving communications, removing ambiguities, making signals clear. This operation is biologically necessary in areas that are likely to cause trouble, questions of territory, hierarchy and mating. Rituals mediate interaction by creating a second reality as powerful as the direct combat rituals replace. In fact, rituals are a transformation of direct action into a second sphere of direct (performance) action. This second sphere is just as aggressive as the first but less deadly. In human theatre the subject matter, themes and actions include the most horrible deeds, conflicts between people, gods, demons and devils. But all this is also play: fun-and-games. This is because the fight-flight reaction—where an animal faced with a threat either fights or flees, but when it can do neither a third seemingly unrelated action arises—creates in people a complicated sequence of transformations, different in each culture, but cross-culturally recognizable as theatrical performances. An audience can enjoy watching/participating and performers enjoy playing what otherwise would be socially dangerous and personally forbidden or inhibited. The troubles of Oedipus, the murders of Macbeth, the adventures of Rama are sources of pleasure not terror. Even the struggle of a shaman against the demons yields enjoyment to its audience. In farce these pleasures which are an excess of energy overcoming obstacles and relieving tensions are even closer than in tragedy or serious drama.

All human performances—tragedies and serious dramas as well as farce; and all performances without clear themes such as some kinds of dances—are created by a process I identified with joke-work and dream-work: the conjunction of social action and individual fantasy. Joke-work and dream-work, in turn, are versions of displacement and redirected activities. Thus human performances arise precisely where animal rituals do, serve analagous functions, develop from the same processes and look very much alike. These performances are liminal events existing to mediate, explain or explore for pleasure those interactions that are potentially most disruptive. Where transitions/transformations are dangerous what van Gennep calls the "rites of passage" are invented. Where trouble is liable to break out, where communication/clarity and fun can help get through a difficult confrontation, there develops ritual, ceremony and theatre.

Alland says four tendencies underly art: (1) exploratory behavior and play, (2) rhythm and balance, (3) "fine grain perceptual discrimination of visual and auditory patterns as well as high memory capacity and long-term memory storage, (4) transformation-representation which includes such linguistic processes as metaphorization, metonymy, connotation and denotation in the general process of symbolization within the domain of semiology."[70] The first two qualities are present in many species, the third is found in the great apes and perhaps cetaceans, the fourth in humans only. But what about Mike's display with the kerosene cans? Is it not an example of the "general process of symbolization"? Recent experiments indicate that chimpanzees can think conceptually.[71] Scientists have long been prejudiced in favor of verbal and mathematical languages. But kinesics and semiotics reveal many levels of language, most of them nonverbal. Symbol-making can involve the transformation of the body, and the spaces around it, into full, unified fields of communication. And it is transformation, not conflict, that is the root of theatre.

Many animals employ disguises, prepare places for habitation, mating and ritual combat, drum, dance, sing and display spectacular manes, plumage, antlers, etc. Some even borrow other animals' bodies such as the fiddler crabs that live in abandoned sea shells. Humans of course imitate whatever they see: a shaman puts on a bear's skin, a woman wears a hat with feathers. But animals can't imitate freely—most of their performances are automatically released, fixed and stereotyped. There is no irony, no play back-and-forth between the role and the performer, no separation between character and actor. In animal performance to lose is to lose; but in human theatre to lose is often to win: theatrical careers are built by the skill with which a role is played not by the events of the story. No one shuns the actor who plays Oedipus. Even in the Kogu trials the guilty often gained status when they were "forced" to perform their punishment publicly.

In the gladitorial games the Romans tried to contain a life-action within the frame of a theatrical action: for the gladiators the games were matters of life-and-death; for the spectators the games were theatre.

The originality and force of ethological thought is its application of the processes of evolution to areas of behavior and culture. And on several levels human and animal performances converge and/or exist along a single continuum: (1) on the structural level where performances are displacement activities, redirected activities and/or improvements of signal functions; (2) on a processual level of dreamwork and joke-work; (3) on the level of techniques where drumming, rhythmic vocalizations, dances and visual displays are used to create, spread and share moods; (4) on a cultural level where performance is a means of social control providing avenues for the discharge of aggression, or where performance is a way of mobilizing people either to maintain or change a given social order; (5) on a mimetic level where animals imitate animals and people imitate animals—even appropriating their skins, feathers and faces—while projecting onto animals human social structures as in totemism. These similarities and convergences provide the basis for re-examining human theatre from the perspective of animal performances. A re-examination not of two opposed systems but a single bio-aesthetic web.

Notes

1. Schaller (1963), 227.
2. Schaller (1963), 233.
3. Lawick-Goodall (1972), 122-3.
4. Grotowski (1968), 142.
5. See Rainer (1974), Forti (1974) and TDR issues T-55 (1972) and T-65 (1975).
6. The unifying idea is the belief that visible behaviors, and what we can learn of deep behaviors through analysis of brain waves, skin temperature, glandular secretion and so on, correlate with what is happening socially, that is, between individuals and among groups. Their work is a holistic behaviorism that works also in depth analysis.
7. Lorenz (1967), 72-3.
8. Schaller (1964), 235.
9. TDR, T-62 (1974), 69. See also T-58 (1973), 33-57.
10. Barbeau (1958), 39ff., quoted in Rothenberg (1968), 51-2.
11. La Barre (1972), 343.
12. La Barre (1972), 77. Marshack (1972) shows how early mathematical systems developed as seasonal markers and accurate calendars. He finds these widely scattered over Eurasia and dates

them as early as the earliest cave paintings. If correct, Marshack establishes for humans a complicated notation system—writing—coexistent with the first artistic work.

13. Rappaport (1968), 128.
14. See Smith (1972).
15. Serban in the *Village Voice*, January 26, 1976, 107.
16. Eibl-Eibesfeldt (1970), 440.
17. Quoted in Lewis (1971), 53.
18. Read (1965), 251-2.
19. Hoffman (1969), 86, 5-6.
20. V. and F. Reynolds in Devore (1965), 409.
21. Lévi-Strauss (1963), 175.
22. Lévi-Strauss (1963), 176.
23. Lévi-Strauss (1963), 178.
24. Somma (1969), 134-5. Scott Powell, a member of the Sha-Na-Na who has observed The Who on tour writes the following description of their finale in the Spectrum in Philadelphia in 1975; this shows how consistent their performance is, and how it affects audiences: "The stage grows black. The synthesizer is playing through the dark hall. It continues for five minutes, and it seems as if the concert is over, with the expectation that the houselights will come up and the synthesizer will continue playing as exit music. But suddenly white spotlights simultaneously pick up Townshend in mid-air leaping from on top of his amplifiers, and Daltrey at the front of the stage, belting out a scream that fills the hall. The landing lights explode through the darkness; the lasers pierce to the ceiling once again. With the entire audience on its feet clapping, singing and dancing to the music, the band leads the audience through several choruses of the song, and hits a final chord. Townshend has his guitar by the neck and is beating it into the stage. Feedback and distortion ring through the hall. Daltrey flies feet first into a stack of amplifiers, toppling them back off the stage. Moon kicks through his drum-head and hurls his tom-tom at the rest of the kit. Townshend attacks his stack of amplifiers with a flying kick and they fall off the back of the stage. Entwhistle stands by the side of the stage and watches the destruction. Then, with a final kick at the guitar, clapping each other on the back, The Who disappear from the stage and the houselights come up." From an unpublished paper by Scott Powell, 1976.
25. From Eibl-Eibesfeldt (1970), 100-1.
26. This is the "sorcerer" or "shaman" of Les Trois Frères. The cave art, and the mobile art of the period too, suggests theatre: an art associated with physical action. The paintings in the caves must have been done by artificial light, some of the chambers are extremely difficult to get to: footprints frozen in clay suggest circular dancing in at least the caves of Niaux and the Grotte D'Aldène. And the "smaller-than-adult heel prints, as though in a ritual walk or dance,

surround a clay effigy of copulating bisons" at Tuc d'Audoubert (La Barre (1972), 162). The presence of imaginary animals, masked human dancers, venus figures which intentionally exaggerate the human female body all show a capacity not for representation but for distortion in order to make certain meanings clear: a kind of conceptualization-as-ritual. To be in the world is one thing, to represent it another, to transform it is the boundary of art; and to transform it as a way of representing its essence, its "as if," its potential, is the heart of the artistic process.

27. Eibl-Eibesfeldt (1970), 178.

28. Shands (1970), 300-4, discusses dreams as a form of drama.

29. Kirby (1975) sketches a new origin theory for theatre based on shamanistic performances across the world. In his introduction Kirby quotes Rappaport (1971): "Ethologists have also used the term ritual to refer to animal displays, some of which bear close formal resemblances to human rituals. Animal rituals are likely to involve stereo-typed, apparently non-instrumental postures and movements, and, as apparently useless paraphernalia are often manipulated in human rituals, so apparently useless biological structures are often waved, vibrated, suffused with color, or expanded in animal rituals. Like human rituals, animal rituals seem to occur under specified circumstances or at fixed times, and some animal rituals, like some human rituals, occur only in special places. [. . .] For a signal to be effective it must be distinguishable from ordinary instrumental activity. The more bizarre the ritual movement of structures the more easily may they be recognized as ritual" (63). Kirby comments: "This principle would run counter to imitation, since for the 'signal' of dramatic action to be effective 'it must be distinguishable from ordinary instrumental activity' " (xv-xvi). Thus theatre develops very early; it has its own language-system which may include mimesis but is not dependent on it. The key theatrical term is transformation, and transformation, culturally speaking is closely related to play—especially play in regard to crisis, or in regard to life situations that are problematical thereby demanding exploration, explanation, temporary or provisional solutions and, paradoxically, at the same time needing a great clarity in signals—like a boat trying to come into a rocky harbor on a windy night needs clear harbor lights.

30. Lorenz (1959), 187.

31. Rappaport (1968), 196. A "fight-package" is a bundle of sacred/ magic materials carried into battle designed to protect the fighter and bring him victory.

32. Berndt (1962), 271-2.

33. Berndt (1962), 279.

34. Berndt (1962), 281. Berndt warns against calling this behavior sadistic. But I don't know if the cultural-relativism argument can be carried over the edge. It is not justification to cite equal, or worse,

atrocities committed in the West. In *The Mountain People* (1972) Turnbull describes acts of neglect, murder and starvation; but the Ik were a doomed people, squeezed out of their niche, while the high-landers Berndt describes are relatively prosperous. There is even an economic reason given by the Kogu for their actions. "The sick or the aged person, it is assumed, will die soon anyway. Another factor is the virtual uselessness of anyone who is incapacitated and so un-able to contribute actively to the life of the community" (279). Such people are sometimes murdered and their meat eaten, not ceremoni-ously but as food.

35. Berndt (1962), 283.

36. Berndt (1962), 283-4. One incident Berndt describes, were it acted on a stage, might be farce. Groups of Aguara, Moiife and Kogu men and women gathered around corpses taken in battle to cut them up. Unapicna began on a woman named Pazucna—but instead of cut-ting her up he copulated with her. A Kogu woman, Aria, accused him of taking too long and as Unapicna ignored her she began to cut up Pazucna. "She cut further in and across, hacking away at the flesh; and since Unapicna's penis was in the woman's vagina, she cut most of it off." Aria blamed him: "You sit there copulating, not bothering to cut her up properly [...] Thus I cut off your penis!" Unapicna screamed at Aria, but then she removed the penis from the corpse, "popped it into her mouth, and ate it, and then continued with the cutting." Unapicna was helped back to his house; later when the meat was cooked he was given Pazucna's vulva to eat (283).

37. Mead (1968), 41-2.

38. Mead (1968), 63.

39. Mead (1968), 64.

40. Berndt (1962), 314.

41. Berndt (1962), 323.

42. Berndt (1962), 325.

43. Berndt (1962), 332-3

44. Berndt (1962), 334.

45. Berndt (1962), 362-3.

46. See Berndt (1962), 148-9

47. See Lea (1892, reprinted in Bohannan, 1967), 233-254.

48. Harbinger (1971), 122-3.

49. Farb (1969), 68-9.

50. Hoebel in Bohannan (1967), 259.

51. Bohannan (1967), 263.

52. Bohannan (1967), 263.

53. Bohannan (1967), 264.

54. Bohannan (1967), 264.

55. Labov (1972), 127.

56. Labov (1972), 144.

57. Labov (1972), 157. The amount of sounding that can go on in a

short time is astonishing. Labov reports that when 13 members of the Jets were crowded onto a microbus 138 sounds were deciphered from a tape made during the 35 minute ride (130). The structure of sounding is like that of classic farce, with the audience participating. "There are three participants in this speech event: antagonist A, antagonist B, and the audience. A sounds against B; the audience evaluates; B sounds against A; and his sound is evaluated" (146). Thus the participation of the audience as judge insured the formal progression of the combat which takes the shape of a duel. This is identical to the progression of dialogue in farce between comic, straight man and audience. Also, most clearly in sounding, the aggressive tendency of laughter is revealed. The laughing audience supports the sounder and is an attack on the person being sounded. If a sounder gets little or no laughter he is in trouble. But the laugh is only apparently "with" the sounder, it is really against the one being sounded. In this way the sounder enlists the audience in his attack. I think this is the basic structure of theatrical dialogue, even "serious" dialogue such as the agons in Greek tragedy. The audience's participation is not heard, but it judges nonetheless.

58. Labov (1972), 168.

59. Lorenz (1959), 188.

60. Slater (1966), 78-9.

61. Eibl-Eibesfeldt (1970), 132.

62. Freud (1963), 100-1. Interestingly Freud sees the pleasure in joking much the way Schaller sees the chest-beating sequence in gorillas; as a discharge of energy. In overcoming the obstacle a joke makes a short-circuit—a connection that is both surprising and true; surprising because inhibition prevents people from thinking of it. But once the short circuit is made the dammed up excitement, or energy, flows as if there were no obstacle. "This yield of pleasure corresponds to the psychical expenditure that is saved" (118).

63. Freud (1963), 105.

64. Avorn (1968), 32.

65. Jekels (1965), 264.

66. Jekels (1965), 269.

67. Eibl-Eibesfeldt (1970), 314.

68. A most striking example of this is provided by Ruesch and Bateson (1951). Just before Europeans landed in Java a large white monkey was washed upon the coast. It was taken to the Raja whose experts told him that the monkey was from the court of the god of the sea who had expelled him in anger and caused a great storm. The Raja ordered that the white monkey be chained to a stone. "Doctor Stutterheim [Dutch government archeologist in Java] told me that he had seen the stone and that, roughly scratched on it in Latin, Dutch, and English were the name of a man and a statement of his shipwreck. Apparently this trilingual sailor never established verbal communi-

cation with his captors. He was surely unaware of the premises in their minds which labeled him a white monkey and therefore not a potential recipient of verbal messages; it probably never occurred to him that they could doubt his humanity. He may have doubted theirs" (204-5).

69. Lorenz (1959), 182, 185.

70. Alland (1976), 5-6.

71. See Linden (1976). And an article in *The New York Times* (December 8, 1974, Section 4, p. 8) reported on the thinking of Lana, a chimpanzee. "Lana's conceptual breakthrough has been to grasp that language is abstract as well as functional; the abstraction for her so far is the name that represents an object she does not know how to identify. In a routine training session designed to teach her the name 'box,' Timothy V. Gill entered Lana's room with an empty bowl, and empty can, and, for her, an unknown object, a box with candy in it. This exchange took place:

> Lana: Tim give Lana this can?
>
> Tim: Yes.
>
> Lana: (putting aside the empty can): Tim give Lana this can?
>
> Tim: No can.
>
> Lana: Tim give Lana this bowl?
>
> Tim: Yes.
>
> Lana: (putting aside the empty bowl): Shelly?
>
> Tim: No Shelly. (Shelly, another technician, was absent.)
>
> Lana: Tim give Lana this bowl? (Before Tim can answer) Tim give Lana name of this?
>
> Tim: Box name of this.
>
> Lana: Yes. Tim give Lana this box?
>
> Tim: Yes. (Lana takes box and takes out candy.)

Tim and Lana converse by computer, one of several methods of communication developed because apes lack the anatomy for speech. Each punches symbol-coded buttons on a console and a computer prints out the message on a screen." Washoe, a female chimp discussed by Linden, communicates by means of Amesian, a language used by the deaf.

No animal in the wild has done what Lana or Washoe are doing, and there is some question whether these animals are talking or just learning complicated tricks. And no wild animal has ever been observed playing a role or drawing a picture of something. In the laboratory much work has been done to encourage chimpanzees to draw and paint—some will even choose a crayon over food. Their designs are patterned, showing a sense of symmetry and contrasting balance. In some ways their drawings are like the scribblings of a child of 12 to 18 months. But "there is no sign of imitative drawing, even in making single strokes," nothing of what Alland calls "transformation-representation." See Schiller, 3-19 in Otten (1971).

Recent research on the different functions of the human brain hemispheres reported by Richard M. Restak in *The New York Times* (January 25, 1976), Section 4, p.8 indicate a big break between ape conceptualization and vocalization and human speech: "Dr. Ronald E. Myers of the Laboratory of Perinatal Physiology of the National Institute of Neurological and Communicative Disorders and Strokes has studied the comparative neurology of vocalization and speech. His research indicates that human speech developed spontaneously at a certain level of hemisphere integration and is totally unrelated to the crude vocalization of the other primates. Efforts are now underway to continue this research and elucidate the contributions of both hemispheres to the development of the uniquely symbolic pattern of vocalization that comprises human speech."

Bibliography

Aldena, Guillermo E. 1971. "Mesa del Nayar's Strange Holy Week." *National Geographic,* 139:6, 780-94.

Alland, Alexander Jr. 1976. "The Roots of Art" in *Ritual, Play, and Performance,* ed. by Richard Schechner and Mady Schuman. New York: Seabury Press.

American Anthropologist, 1966. Special issue on *The Ethnography of Communication,* 66:6 part 2.

Arieti, Silvano. 1948. "Special Logic of Schizophrenic and Other Types of Autistic Thought." *Psychiatry,* 11 (November, 1948), 325-38.

Aristotle. 1961. *Poetics,* trans. S.H. Butcher, intro. Francis Fergusson. New York: Hill & Wang.

Arnott, Peter. 1969. *The Theatres of Japan.* New York: St. Martin's Press.

Artaud, Antonin. 1958. *The Theatre and Its Double,* trans. Mary Caroline Richards. New York: Grove Press.

Avorn, Jerry L. 1968. *Up Against the Ivy Wall.* New York: Atheneum.

Awasthi, Suresh. 1974. "The Scenography of the Traditional Theatre of India." *TDR,* 18:4.

Barbeau, Marius. 1958. "Medicine-Men on the North Pacific Coast." National Museum of Canada Bulletin No. 152, Ottawa.

Bateson, Gregory. 1958 (1936). *Naven.* Palo Alto: Stanford University Press.

Bateson, Gregory and Margaret Mead. 1942. *Balinese Character: A Photographic Analysis.* New York: Special Publications of the New York Academy of Sciences, Volume II.

Becker, George J., ed. 1963. *Documents of Modern Literary Realism.* Princeton: Princeton University Press.

Belo, J. 1960. *Trance in Bali.* New York: Columbia University Press.

Berndt, Ronald M. 1962. *Excess and Restraint.* Chicago: University of Chicago Press.

Berndt, Ronald and Catherine. 1964. *The World of the First Australians.* Chicago: University of Chicago Press.

Berne, Eric. 1961. *Transactional Analysis in Psychotherapy.* New York: Grove Press.

Bettelheim, Bruno. 1962 (1954). *Symbolic Wounds: Puberty Rites and the Envious Male.* New York: Collier Books.

————. 1967. *The Empty Fortress.* New York: The Free Press.

Birdwhistell, Ray L. 1952. *Introduction to Kinesics.* Louisville: University of Louisville Press. (Available only in microfilm from University Microfilms, Inc., 313 N. First St., Ann Arbor, Michigan.)

————. 1963. "The Kinesic Level in the Investigation of the Emotions" in *Expressions of the Emotions in Man,* P.H. Knapp, ed. New York: International Universities Press.

————. 1964. "Body Behavior and Communication" in *International Encyclopedia of the Social Sciences.* New York: The Free Press.

————. 1970. *Kinesics and Context.* Philadelphia: University of Pennsylvania Press. This book contains a bibliography of Birdwhistell's work to that date.

Boas, Franz. 1966 (1911, 1939). *The Mind of Primitive Man.* New York: The Free Press.

Bohannan, Paul. 1967. "Drumming the Scandal among the Tiv" in *Law and Warfare,* ed. by Paul Bohannan. Garden City: Natural History Press.

Bongartz, Roy. 1970. "It's Called Earth Art—And Boulderdash." *New York Times Magazine.* (February 1, 1970).

Brook, Peter. 1973. "On Africa." *TDR,* 17: September. 45-6.

Brustein, Robert. 1974. "News Theatre." *The New York Times Magazine.* June 16. 7ff.

Burke, Kenneth. 1961 (1941, 1957). *The Philosophy of Literary Form.* New York: Vintage Books.

————. 1962 (1945, 1950). *A Grammar of Motives* and *A Rhetoric of Motives*. Cleveland: World Publishing Co.

Burns, Elizabeth. 1972. *Theatricality*. New York: Harper and Row.

Campbell, Joseph. 1956. *The Hero With a Thousand Faces*. New York: Meridian Books.

————. 1959-68. *The Masks of God* (four volumes). New York: Viking Press.

Carpenter, C. R. 1964. *Naturalistic Behavior of Nonhuman Primates*. University Park: The Pennsylvania State University Press.

Cassirer, Ernst. 1946. *Language and Myth*. New York: Dover Publications. Written around 1920.

Castaneda, Carlos. 1968. *The Teachings of Don Juan: A Yaqui Way of Knowledge*. New York: Ballantine Books.

————. 1971. *A Separate Reality*. New York: Simon and Schuster.

————. 1972. *Journey to Ixtlan*. New York: Simon and Schuster.

Clarke, La Verne Harrell. 1966. *They Sang For Horses*. Tucson: Univeristy of Arizona Press.

Cooper, David. 1970. *The Death of the Family*. New York: Pantheon Books.

Darwin, Charles. 1965 (1872). *The Expression of the Emotions in Man and Animals*. Chicago: University of Chicago Press.

Devore, I., ed. 1965. *Primate Behavior*. New York: Holt, Rinehart and Winston.

Diamond. Stanley, ed. 1964. *Primitive Views of the World*. New York: Columbia University Press.

Dioszegi, Vilmos. 1968. *Tracing Shamans in Siberia*. New York: Humanities Press.

Dodds, E.R. 1951. *The Greeks and the Irrational*. Berkeley: University of California Press.

Ehrenzweig, Anton. 1970. *The Hidden Order of Art*. London: Granada Publishing.

Eibl-Eibesfeldt, Irenaus. 1970. *Ethology: The Biology of Behavior*. New York: Holt, Rinehart and Winston.

Eliade, Mircea. 1965. *Rites and Symbols of Initiation*. New York: Harper Torchbooks. Originally published under title *Birth and Rebirth*, 1958.

————. 1970 (1951). *Shamanism: Archaic Techniques of Ecstasy*. Princeton: Princeton University Press.

Elkin, A.P. and Catherine and Ronald Berndt. 1950. *Art in Arnhem Land*. Chicago: University of Chicago Press.

Erikson, Eric H. 1959. *Identity and the Life Cycle*. Psychological Issues, Monograph 1. New York: International Universities Press.

Evans-Pritchard, E.E. 1937. *Witchcraft, Oracles and Magic among the Azande*. London: Oxford University Press.

Fagan, J. and I.L. Shepherd. 1970. *Gestalt Therapy Now*. New York: Harper Colophon Books.

Farb, Peter. 1969. *Man's Rise to Civilization*. New York: Avon Books.

Feldenkrais, M. 1972. *Awareness through Movement*. New York: Harper & Row.

Fergusson, Francis. 1949. *The Idea of a Theater*. New York: Doubleday Anchor.

Firth, Raymond. 1967. *Tikopia Ritual and Belief*. London: George Allen and Unwin.

Forti, Simone. 1974. *Handbook in Motion*. New York: New York University Press.

Frankfort, Henri. 1948. *Kingship and the Gods*. Chicago: University of Chicago Press.

Freud, Sigmund. 1958 (1925). *On Creativity and the Unconscious*. New York: Harper Torchbooks.

———. 1961 (1900). *The Interpretation of Dreams*. New York: John Wiley & Sons.

———. 1962a (1913). *Totem and Taboo*. New York: W.W. Norton.

———. 1962b (1930). *Civilization and Its Discontents*. New York: W.W. Norton.

———. 1963 (1905). *Jokes and Their Relation to the Unconscious*. New York: W.W. Norton.

Gardner, R. and Heider, K.G. 1968. *Gardens of War*. New York: Random House.

Giddings, Ruth W. 1959. *Yaqui Myths and Legends*. Tucson: University of Arizona Press.

Giedion, S. 1962-4. *The Eternal Present* (two volumes). New York: The Bollingen Foundation.

Goffman, Erving. 1959. *The Presentation of Self in Everyday Life*. Garden City: Doubleday Anchor Books.

———. 1961. *Encounters*. Indianapolis: Bobbs-Merrill.

————. 1963a. *Stigma*. Englewood Cliffs: Prentice-Hall.

————. 1963b. *Behavior in Public Places*. Glencoe: The Free Press.

————. 1967. *Interaction Ritual*. Garden City: Doubleday Anchor Books.

————. 1969. *Strategic Interaction*. Philadelphia: University of Pennsylvania Press.

————. 1971. *Relations in Public*. New York: Basic Books.

Goodall, Jane van Lawick. 1971. *In the Shadow of Man*. New York: Dell Publishing Co.

Gordon, T. 1970. *Parent Effectiveness Training Active Listening*. New York: Wyden.

Gould, Richard A. 1969. *Yiwara: Foragers of the Australian Desert*. New York: Charles Scribner's Sons.

Grotowski, Jerzy. 1968. *Towards a Poor Theatre*. Holstebro: Odin Teatrets Forlag.

Haley, J. and L. Hoffman. 1967. *Techniques of Family Therapy*. New York: Basic Books.

Hall, Edward T. 1969. *The Hidden Dimension*. Garden City: Doubleday Anchor Books.

————. 1970 (1959). *The Silent Language*. Greenwich, CN: Fawcett Publications.

Halprin, Ann. 1965. "An Interview." *TDR*, 10:2, 142-67.

————. 1968. "Mutual Creation," *TDR*, 13:1, 163-75.

Halprin, L. 1970. *The RSVP Cycles: Creative Process in the Human Environment*. New York: George Braziller.

————. 1972. *Taking Part*. (Available through L. Halprin & Associates, 1620 Montgomery Street, San Francisco, CA.)

Hammel, E. and W. Simmons, eds. 1957. *Man Makes Sense*. Boston: Little, Brown and Company.

Harbinger, Richard. 1971. "Trial by Drama." *Judicature*, 55:3, 122-128.

Hardison, O.B. 1965. *Christian Rite and Christian Drama in the Middle Ages*. Baltimore: University of Maryland Press.

Hart, C.W.M. and Arnold R. Pilling. 1966. *The Tiwi of North Australia*. New York: Holt, Rinehart and Winston.

Hass, Hans. 1972. *The Human Animal*. New York: Delta.

Hoebel, E. Adamson. 1967. "Song Duels among the Eskimo" in *Law and Warfare*, ed. by Paul Bohannan. Garden City: Natural History Press.

Harbinger, Richard. 1971. "Trial by Drama" *Judicature*, Vol. 55, no. 3, 122-8.

Huizinga, Johan. 1955. (1938). *Homo Ludens*. Boston: Beacon Press.

Jekels, Ludwig. 1965. "On the Psychology of Comedy" in *Comedy: Meaning and Form*, ed. by Robert W. Corrigan. San Francisco: Chandler Publishing Co.

Kafka, Franz. 1954. *Wedding Preparations in the Country*. London: Secker and Warburg.

Kaplan, Donald M. 1968. "Theatre Architecture: A Derivation of the Primal Cavity." *TDR*, 12:3, 105-116.

———. 1969. "On Stage Fright." *TDR*, 14:1, 60-83.

———. 1971. "Gestures, Sensibilities, Scripts." *Performance*, 1:1, 31-46.

Kaprow, Allan. "Extensions in Time and Space," interview with Richard Schechner, *The Drama Review*, Vol. 12, no. 3, 153-9.

———. 1966. *Assemblages, Environments, and Happenings*. New York: Abrams.

———. Scenarios and announcements obtained directly from Kaprow.

Kirby, Ernest Theodore. 1972. "The Mask: Abstract Theatre Primitive and Modern." *TDR*, 16:3.

———. 1973. "The Origin of Nō Drama." *Educational Theatre Journal*. 25: October.

———. 1974. "The Shamanistic Origins of Popular Entertainments." *TDR*, 18: March.

———. 1975. *Ur-Drama: The Origins of Theatre*. New York: New York University Press.

Kirby, Michael. 1969. *The Art of Time*. New York: E.P. Dutton.

———. 1973. "Richard Foreman's Ontological-Hysteric Theatre." *TDR*, 17:2, 5-32.

Kris, Ernst. 1964 (1952). *Psychoanalytic Explorations in Art*. New York: Schocken Books.

La Barre, Weston. 1954. *The Human Animal*. Chicago: The University of Chicago Press.

———. 1972. *The Ghost Dance*. New York: Dell Publishing Company.

Labov, William. 1972, "Rules for Ritual Insults" in *Studies in Social Interaction,* ed. by David Sudnow. New York: The Free Press.

Laing, R.D. 1960. *The Divided Self.* Chicago: Quadrangle Books.

————. 1962, 1969. *The Self and Others.* New York: Pantheon.

————. 1967. *The Politics of Experience.* New York: Ballantine Books.

————. 1969, 1971. *The Politics of the Family.* New York: Pantheon.

Laing, R.D. and A. Esterson. 1964. *Sanity, Madness, and the Family.* New York: Basic Books.

Langer, Susanne K. 1953. *Feeling and Form.* New York: Charles Scribner's Sons.

Lea, Henry Charles. 1967. "The Wager of Battle," in *Law and Warfare,* ed. by Paul Bohannan. Garden City: Natural History Press.

Leach, Edmund, ed. 1967. *The Structural Study of Myth and Totemism.* London: Tavistock Publications.

Leslie, Charles, ed. 1960. *Anthropology of Folk Religion.* New York: Vintage Books.

Lévi-Strauss, Claude. 1963. *Structural Anthropology.* New York: Basic Books.

————. 1966. *The Savage Mind.* Chicago: The University of Chicago Press.

————. 1969a. *The Elementary Structures of Kinship.* Boston: Beacon Press.

————. 1969b. *The Raw and the Cooked.* New York: Harper and Row.

————. 1972. *From Honey To Ashes.* New York: Harper and Row.

Lewis, I.M. 1971. *Ecstatic Religion.* London: Penguin Books.

Linden, Eugene. 1976. *Apes, Men, and Language.* New York: Penguin Books.

Loizos, Caroline. 1969. "Play Behaviour in Higher Primates: A Review" in *Primate Ethology,* Desmond Morris, ed., 226-82. Garden City: Doubleday Anchor Books.

Lommel, Andreas. 1967. *Shamanism: The Beginnings of Art.* New York: McGraw-Hill.

Lorenz, Konrad. 1959. "The Role of Aggression in Group Formation" in *Transactions of the Conference on Group Processes of 1957,* ed. by B. Schaffner. New York: The Josiah Macy, Jr. Foundation.

————. 1961. *King Solomon's Ring.* New York: T.Y. Crowell.

————. 1965. *Evolution and Modification of Behavior,* Chicago: The University of Chicago Press.

———. 1967. *On Aggression*. New York: Bantam Books.

Lowen, A. 1967. *The Betrayal of the Body*. New York: Macmillan.

Lowie, R.H. 1936. *The Crow Indians*. New York: Holt Rinehart.

———. 1948. *Primitive Religion*. New York: Liveright Publishing Company.

Malina, Judith and Julian Beck. 1969. "Containment is the Enemen." *TDR*, T-43.

Malinowski, B. 1922. *Argonauts of the Western Pacific*. London: Routledge.

———. 1949. *Crime and Custom in Savage Society*. London: Routledge & Kegan Paul.

———. 1952. *Sexual Life of Savages*. London: Routledge.

———. 1954 (1916-25). *Magic, Science, and Religion*. Garden City: Doubleday Anchor Books.

Marshack, Alexander. 1972. *The Roots of Civilization*. New York: McGraw-Hill.

Matthews, Washington. 1902. *The Night Chant, a Navaho Ceremony*. New York: Memoirs of the American Museum of Natural History, Volume VI.

Mead, Margaret. 1968. *Sex and Temperment in Three Primitive Societies*. New York: Dell Publishing Company.

Mead, Margaret and Gregory Bateson. 1938. *Dance and Trance in Bali*. Available in the New York University Film Library.

Metraux, A. 1955. "Dramatic Elements in Ritual Possession" in *Diogenes* 11.

Morgan, Charles. 1961 (1933). "The Nature of Dramatic Illusion," *Reflections on Art*, ed. Susanne K. Langer. New York: Oxford University Press. 91-102.

Morris, Desmond. 1962. *The Biology of Art*. London: University Paperbacks.

———. 1967. *The Naked Ape*. New York: Dell Publishing Company.

———. 1969a. *The Human Zoo*. New York: McGraw-Hill.

———. ed. 1969b. *Primate Ethology*. Garden City: Doubleday Anchor Books.

Neill, A.S. 1960. *Summerhill: A Radical Approach to Child Rearing*. New York: Hart Publishing Company.

Opie, J. and P. 1969. *Children's Games in Street and Playground*. London: Oxford University Press.

Orenstein, Robert E. 1972. *The Psychology of Consciousness*. New York: The Viking Press.

Otten, Charlotte M., ed. 1971. *Anthropology and Art*. New York: The Natural History Press.

Painter, Muriel T. 1950. *A Yaqui Easter*. Tucson: University of Arizona Press.

Perls, F.S. 1971. *Gestalt Therapy Verbatim*. New York: Bantam Books.

Piaget, Jean. 1962. *Play, Dreams, and Imitation in Childhood*. New York: W.W. Norton.

———. 1967 (1948) *The Child's Conception of Space*. New York: W.W. Norton.

Plato. 1945. *The Republic*, trans. with intro. and notes by Francis M. Conford. New York: Oxford University Press.

Rajneesh, Yogacharya. 1971. *Yoga as a Spontaneous Happening*. Bombay: Jeevan Jagrati Kendra.

Ranier, Yvonne. 1974. *Work 1961-73*. New York: New York University Press.

Rappaport, Roy A. 1968. *Pigs for the Ancestors*. New Haven: Yale University Press.

Read, Kenneth E. 1965. *The High Valley*. New York: Charles Scribner's Sons.

Roheim, Geza. 1950. *Psychoanalysis and Anthropology*. New York: International Universities Press.

———. 1969 (1945). *The Eternal Ones of the Dream*. New York: International Universities Press.

———. 1971 (1943). *The Origin and Function of Culture*. Garden City: Doubleday Anchor Books.

Rojas-Bermudez, J.G. 1969. "The Intermediary Object." *Group Psychotherapy*, XXII, 149-155.

Rolf, I.P. 1963. *Structural Integration; Gravity and Unexplored Factor in a More Human Use of Human Being*. (Available through Guild for Structural Integration, P.O. Box 1868, Boulder, Colorado.)

Rothenberg, Jerome, ed. 1968. *Technicians of the Sacred*. Garden City: Doubleday.

Ruesch, J. and G. Bateson. 1951. *Communication*. New York: W. W. Norton.

Ruess, J. and W. Kees. 1972. *Nonverbal Communication*. Berkeley: University of California Press.

San Francisco Dancer's Workshop. 1973. *Selected Writings of the San Francisco Dancer's Workshop* (Available at 321 Divisadero Street, San Francisco, CA.)

Sayles, E.B. 1962. *Faith, Flowers, Fiestas: The Yaqui Indian Year, A Narrative of Ceremonial Events.* Tucson: University of Arizona Press.

Schaller, George B. 1963. *The Mountain Gorilla.* Chicago: University of Chicago Press.

Schechner, Richard. 1969. *Public Domain.* New York: Bobbs-Merrill.

————. ed. 1970. *Dionysus in 69.* New York: Farrar, Strauss, & Giroux.

————. 1971. "Incest and Culture: A Reflection on Claude Lévi-Strauss." *Psychoanalytic Review,* 58:4, 563-5.

————. 1972. "Surrounded—But Not Afraid." *The New York Times* (Sunday edition). Arts & Leisure Section. September 17. 5ff.

————. 1973a. "On Playwriting & Environmental Theatre." *Yale/Theatre,* 4:1, 28-36.

————. 1973b. "The Writer and The Performance Group." *Performance,* 1:5, 60-6.

————. 1973c. *Environmental Theater.* New York: Hawthorn Books.

Scheflen, Albert E. 1972. *Body Language and Social Control.* Englewood Cliffs: Prentice-Hall.

Schilder, Paul. 1950. *The Image and Appearance of the Human Body.* New York: International University Press.

Schiller, Paul H. 1971. "Figural Preferences in the Drawings of a Chimpanzee" in *Anthropology and Art,* ed. by Charlotte M. Otten. Garden City: Natural History Press.

Scientific American. 1972. Special Issue on Communication, September. 227:3.

Shands, Harley C. 1970. "Dreams as Drama" in *Semiotic Approaches to Psychiatry.* The Hague: Mouton.

Shirokogoroff, S.M. 1935. *Psychomental Complex of the Tungus.* London: Kegan, Paul, Trench, Trubner & Co.

Skinner, Elliott P., ed. 1973. *Peoples and Cultures of Africa.* New York: The Natural History Press.

Slater, Philip E. 1966. *Microcosm.* New York: John Wiley & Sons.

Smith, A.C.H. 1972. *Orghast at Persepolis.* New York: Viking Books.

Somma, Robert. 1969. "Rock Theatricality," *TDR,* T-45, 128-38.

Southern, Richard. 1961. *The Seven Ages of Theatre*. New York: Hill & Wang.

Spencer, B. and F.J. Gillen. 1968 (1899). *The Native Tribes of Central Australia*. New York: Dover Publications.

Spicer, Edward H. 1940. *Pascua: A Yaqui Village in Arizona*. Chicago: University of Chicago Press.

Stierlin, Helm. 1969. *Conflict and Reconciliation: A Study in Human Relations and Schizophrenia*. New York: Science House.

Stone, R. 1972. *The New Energy Concept of the Healing Act* (I), *The Wireless Anatomy of Man* (II), *Polarity Therapy* (III). (Available at 7557 S. Merrill Avenue, Chicago, Illinois.)

————. 1972. *Stepping to Better Health, Zone Therapy and Gland Reflexes Compression Massage*. (Available at P.O. Box 948, Rochester, New York.)

Tinbergen, N. 1965. *Social Behaviour in Animals*. London: Scientific Book Club.

Turnbull, Colin M. 1962. *The Forest People*. Garden City: Doubleday Anchor Books.

————. 1972. *The Mountain People*. New York: Simon & Schuster.

Turner, Victor W. 1969. *The Ritual Process*. Chicago: Aldine Publishing Company.

————. 1974. *Dramas, Fields, and Metaphors*. Ithaca: Cornell University Press.

Ucko, P.J. and A. Rosenfeld. 1967. *Paleolithic Cave Art*. New York: McGraw-Hill.

Van Gennep, Arnold. 1960 (1908). *The Rites of Passage*. Chicago: University of Chicago Press.

Von Uexkull, Jacob. 1957 (1934). "A Stroll through the Worlds of Animals and Man" in *Instinctive Behavior: The Development of a Modern Concept*, C. Schiller, ed. New York: International Universities Press.

Willett, John, ed. 1964. *Brecht on Theatre*. New York: Hill & Wang.

Williams, F.E. 1940. *The Drama of the Orokolo*. London: Oxford University Press.

Winnicott, D.W. 1971. *Playing & Reality*. London: Tavistock Publications.

Wissler, Clark, ed. 1921. *Sun Dance of the Plains Indians*. New York: American Museum of Natural History.